THE TIMEPIECE FROM
GOULDTOWN

THE TIMEPIECE FROM
GOULDTOWN

*An Initiation into
American Mysteries*

WILLIAM S. KING

WESTHOLME
Yardley

Facing title page: The timepiece containing John Brown's signature, inherited by Becky Lively from her grandmother, resident of Gouldtown, New Jersey. (*Photograph by Joe Eber*)

©2023 William S. King

All rights reserved under International and Pan-American Copyright Conventions. No part of this book may be reproduced in any form or by any electronic or mechanical means, including information storage and retrieval systems, without permission in writing from the publisher, except by a reviewer who may quote brief passages in a review.

Westholme Publishing, LLC
904 Edgewood Road
Yardley, Pennsylvania 19067
Visit our Web site at www.westholmepublishing.com

ISBN: 978-1-59416-408-8
Also available as an eBook.

Printed in the United States of America.

"There existed something of an organization to assist fugitives and of resistance to their masters. It was found all along the Lake borders from Syracuse, New York, to Detroit, Michigan. As none but colored men were admitted into direct and active membership with this *League of Freedom*, it is quite difficult to trace its workings or know how far its ramifications extended."
—Richard J. Hinton in *John Brown and His Men*

"[George J. Reynolds] has disclosed its objects [the eradication of slavery] to the members of a Secret Society (colored) calling itself the *American Mysteries*, or some other confounded humbug. I suppose it is likely that these people are good men enough but to make a sort of wholesale divulgement of matters at hazard is too steep even for me, who are not by any means over-cautious."
—Richard Realf, delegate at John Brown's Chatham, Ontario, convention, in a letter to his uncle in England

"The only free road, the Underground Railroad, is owned and managed by the *Vigilant Committee*. They have tunneled under the whole breadth of the land."
—Henry David Thoreau, *A Plea for Captain Brown*

CONTENTS

A TESTAMENT	IX
1. "O, That I Were Free"	1
2. "In Solemn and Secret Compact"	18
3. "I Want My Property, and I Will Have It!"	35
4. "We Need Arms More Than We Do Bread"	66
5. "'Give Them Jessie,' and Frémont Besides"	109
6. "There is the Most Abundant Material, and of the Right Quality, in this Quarter, Beyond All Doubt"	138
7. "I Consider it My Duty to Draw the Scene of Excitement to Some Other Part of the Country"	172
8. "Harper's Ferry is the Best News that America has Ever Heard"	197
EPILOGUE: MISCELLANIES OF A MOVEMENT	229
BIBLIOGRAPHICAL ESSAY: TIMEPIECES	239
NOTES	247
ACKNOWLEDGMENTS	259
INDEX	261

A TESTAMENT

When the British wrested control of New Netherland from the Dutch in 1664, Charles II, the restored British monarch, gave the entire lands between New England and Maryland to his brother, the Duke of York. The Duke retained New York for himself. The land between the Hudson and the Delaware Rivers he bestowed upon Sir George Carteret and Lord Berkeley.[1] The name New Jersey to designate the area was derived from the island of Jersey in the English Channel, commemorating a naval engagement fought near the island and a victory won in the war against the Dutch for commercial and territorial concessions.

Philip Carteret became the first governor of the colony, establishing the capital at Elizabethtown; Elizabeth being the name of his wife. In March 1673, to lessen his administrative burden, Berkeley sold his part of the colony to the Quakers, after which the lands were divided in two—East New Jersey flanked by the Hudson and West New Jersey abutting the Delaware, a division lasting until the two apportions became a unified Royal Colony in 1702.

The lands on the eastern bank of the Delaware River had been sold to John Fenwick, a member of the Society of Friends, and those on the western bank of the Delaware to William Penn and two others, also Quakers. Fenwick's ship, the *Griffin*, arrived from London in the early part of November 1675, carrying, along with stores and tools and scant household furnishings, passengers. Including Fenwick and his three daughters—his wife had declined the venture—there were one hundred and fifty emigrants all told.[2]

Allowed to occupy a settlement he called New Salem, located just off the river and at the mouth of Delaware Bay, after two years of wrangling with the governor and the Duke of York's representative at New York (that settlement lost the name New Amsterdam in 1664) and two imprisonments, Fenwick was given control of one tenth of West New Jersey and permitted to found his colony in the latter part of the year 1677. He negotiated with the local indigenous people for the lands that became Salem and Cumberland Counties.

The common cause of persons joining the Fenwick Colony was that all venturing to enlist with the colony from across the seas and establishing their homes within the limits of West New Jersey would enjoy "religious and political equality," with none of its propertied inhabitants entitled to "greater privileges, nor enlarged rights." Fenwick retained the title of Lord Proprietor of West New Jersey.

William Penn would arrive in 1682 to found his namesake colony and the city of Philadelphia, bringing with him the same political and religious orientation that already had been established across the river.

When John Fenwick died in 1683, the first form of representative government in the colony, "rude and ill-defined as it was," ended, only wanting further development.

By the time of his death Fenwick had built a considerable estate, said to resemble that of an aristocrat, including as it did residences at either end of his plantation near Salem, one called Fenwick's Grove, the other Ivy Point.

There is a tell-tale note in his will vital to the entire enterprise known as Gouldtown, with which this narrative begins. That passage read, "Item, I do except against Elizabeth Adams of having any ye leaste part of my estate, unless the Lord open her eyes to see her abominable transgression against him, me and her good father, by giving her true repentance, and forsaking yt Black yt hath been ye ruin of her, and becoming penitent for her sins; upon yt condition only I do will and required my executors to settle five hundred acres of land."[3]

This proviso was directed at Fenwick's granddaughter, Elizabeth Adams, the daughter of John Adams and Elizabeth Fenwick, Fenwick's daughter.

At the time of her arrival in West New Jersey in 1675, Elizabeth had been eleven years old. She was nineteen at the time that Fenwick made his will, stipulating that Elizabeth should have no share of his property unless she should repent of her sins and forsake "that Black that hath been the ruin of her."

That there would be an intermarriage such as this would have been exceptional but for the scarcity of population at the time, and, in any case, but for mutual affections that may arise. It also may be of account that the man Elizabeth married, called Gould—a coachman employed by Fenwick—was capable and energetic, encouraging Elizabeth to think that she stood to be provided for in their union and that her prospects would be good in regard to family life. The couple had two children, from which progeny have sprung the families of Goulds at the settlement called Gouldtown in Cumberland County, New Jersey. It is not known when Elizabeth died nor where she was buried, nor the first name of her husband. Thus, the originators of generations to come passed into obscurity.[4]

The son from this union was called Benjamin. He would take as wife a woman named Ann, who was a Finn. This Benjamin Gould became a dealer in cordwood and hoop poles, as well as owning a farm encompassing one hundred and thirty-six acres in Cumberland County. This husband and wife, as is seen in Benjamin Gould's will, had five children, four sons and a daughter.

To the daughter, Sarah, who remained unmarried, was bequeathed a featherbed. To his sons Anthony, the eldest, Samuel and Abijah, and the youngest, Elisha, Benjamin bequeathed his holdings in land and all his moveable property. From these four sons stemmed all the Goulds of Gouldtown, as from them the place derives its name.[5]

Down through the generations, through thrift and toil the Goulds considerably improved their lot as their progeny increased, their personal property coming to include the farm acreage, embracing cattle, sheep, oxen, horses, and the like. At the end of the eighteenth century the environs were still well forested with cedar, pine, and oak, and the Goulds, their neighbors, and company were "hardy woodsmen." The principal source of employment and commerce lay in felling and hauling logs, splitting rails for fencing, cutting cordwood, and supplying timber to sawmills, a "goodly" part of that lumber going up the Cohansey River to Philadelphia.[6]

In that time wood was also burned to make charcoal and taken to Philadelphia or New York to be sold, New York offering the favored price. The landing on the Cohansey became known as "The Bridge," and later "Cohansey Bridge," becoming the Bridgeton of today. "Hundreds and thousands of cords of wood were hauled from the country east of the Cohansey to those shipping-points and freighted to Philadelphia," write historians of Gouldtown. Gouldtown men took an active part in this work, as they, too, were, if not active on their own farms, employed as farm hands by Quaker farmers.

In 1777 Benjamin died; his eldest son Anthony Gould would leave a will dated June 23, 1803. That instrument directs all of Anthony's property be sold to his daughter Phebe Gould for six dollars, and divided between Phebe's daughters Christiana and Martha. [7]

This chronology, whose testament is given above, appears in an unusual book published in 1913 and written by a father and son in this lineage from Gouldtown. The authors were tracing events and facts of the settlement's existence, two centuries in the making, that in their time was beginning to reach into a third century. The book's title is *Gouldtown—A Very Remarkable Settlement of Ancient Date*; the authors, William Steward and his son, Rev. Theophilus Gould Steward. The wife of William was Rebecca Gould, the mother of Theophilus. Father and son, citing a history written in the nineteenth century, state that Gouldtown, ". . . a settlement of mulattoes, principally bearing the names of Gould and Pierce, scattered over a considerable territory, is of quite ancient date, the tradition is that they are descendants of Fenwick."[8] In this mixed-race community resided families who were White— principally Swedish, Finnish, and Dutch, and descendants of Quakers of English stock—together with free Blacks and "Indians." John Fenwick, who had seven Black servants, did not own slaves, nor did his neighbors, although William Penn did, as did other Quakers. The parts of the colony harboring the predominance of slaves in that time were in East New Jersey, in Middlesex County around the port town Perth Amboy, and in Bergen, Passaic, and Somerset Counties, all to the north. The term mulattoes generally indicates mixed blood, referring to people of African origin admixed with Europeans. But the term also refers to bloodlines contributed by the region's indigenous people, the Lenni Lenape. The original Lenape homeland had included all of today's New Jersey, encompassing three interrelated tribes of the Delaware Bay area and the Delmarva Peninsula. Locally in West New Jersey, the indigenes were known as "Cohansias," or "the Indians of Cohansey Bridge," and among other names were called "Alloways" or "Little Siconese." These people had never surrendered their tribal identity nor their inherent sovereignty and existed within Salem and Cumberland Counties in autonomous communities, mostly villages along creeks and rivers, as well as on the Atlantic coast.

In its earliest days Gouldtown's population went by either of two family names, Gould or Pierce, with separate sections known as Gouldtown and Piercetown, though collectively referred to as Gouldtown. That name still persists in the southern New Jersey district of Cumberland County, three miles southeast of Bridgeton, the county seat, while lying seven miles east is Millville. By the early decades of the eighteenth century, Gouldtown was noted for its thriving population and had the amenities of village and rural life, with two churches—a Methodist Episcopal parish and later an African Methodist Episcopal parish, their congregations dominated by the Pierce and the Gould families respectively. Three miles in breadth, Gouldtown eventually would have a store and a post office; adjoining farms extended for almost seven miles, settled contiguously.

The Stewards write in their monograph, "Several of the earlier Goulds and Pierces as well as Murrays intermarried with Whites, and members of their immediate offspring went away and lost their identity, and they and their descendants becoming White, while, from those who maintained their identity as people of color, there have come many who have reached distinction, and in whom their native Country shows merited pride."[9] Father and son also note that it was a "tradition among the inhabitants of Gouldtown" to maintain that Elizabeth Fenwick had married Gould, from whom they descended, "and that the five hundred acres of land was settled upon her and they inherited it." The area around which Elizabeth and her husband had lived and worked had been acquired, rather, through practical labor and had not been deeded to the couple's progeny, making this oral "tradition" seem a curious divergence. The tracts on which they lived had become largely exhausted of timber and the soil was relatively poor; even so, with attention and diligence, it often was possible to obtain fair yields. Gouldtown's inhabitants prizing education and reading, several of them "could be classed as well-read." The two churches doubled as schoolhouses, but neither church nor school, write the Stewards, taught anything that "had the slightest bearing upon their most burning question, How to wring a living out of a poor land?"—a query calling forth no sympathetic response from either institution.

Nevertheless, from generation to generation Gouldtowners reared their families, making the most of the decrement in their fortunes "through re-adjustment of both means and ends." Their hogs were well fattened and their horses tough, as they grew corn, wheat, and oats, along with potatoes, turnips, and cabbage, apples and pumpkin, a little clover hay with a fair sowing of buckwheat and rye. Most men coupled this near-subsistence farming with an annual harvest of salt hay, obtained from nearby marshes and used as fodder for cattle, oxen, and horses. To gather salt hay men left their farms and worked for a whole week living and toiling in the marshes, each man joining in the labor and loading the wagons.

Many of these men also took up trades, becoming mechanics and carpenters and teamsters, a few ascending from a minimally bare public education into clerical work, teaching, and even dentistry, some becoming traders or going to sea.

Theophilus Gould Steward (1843-1924), the superlative product of the Gouldtown environment and upbringing, in addition to being a minister to U.S. Colored Troops during the War of the Rebellion, was a noted historian, authoring *The Haitian Revolution, 1791 to 1804* and *The Colored Regulars in the United States Army* and becoming a professor at Wilberforce University in Ohio. His stance always was to offer a rebuff to discrimination, as he relentlessly refuted racist scholarship while promoting Black claims to political and social equality.[10]

Some of the farmers in the Gouldtown settlement would gather wool from scant flocks of sheep to be spun into yarn and woven into clothing, the women also spinning flax and repurposing rags and worn-out garments into floor coverings. The farms supplied well-cured hams, pork, and lard, with a fattened beef-cow annually slaughtered and its meat "corned," the few milk cows wandering "breachy" and "milkless." Yet, write the Stewards, the people of Gouldtown "have kept up from the earliest times those customs of social enjoyment, indoors in winter and outdoors in summer, which have made them famous for generous hospitality." It was said, too, of these folk that many of them did "not begin to grow old . . . until they came to three score years, and a number of whom have reached the century mark."

The Pierces of Gouldtown originated with two brothers, Richard and Anthony, both mulattoes, arriving in Greenwich, New Jersey, from the West Indies and bringing with them for wives two sisters, Marie and Hannah, who were Dutch. The couples came into the colony in the mid-eighteenth century. Also contributing to the racial amalgamation of Gouldtown, originating from Cape May, was Othniel Murray, a Siconesse Indian. He married a Swedish woman named Katharine, and they would have five children, three sons and two daughters.[11]

A fourth family in the genealogy of Gouldtown was the Cuff family of Salem, historically of slave origin. Cuff had been owned by a man named Padgett, who served in British forces during the French and Indian War and was killed. Cuff took care of Padgett's widow, and they eventually married. He was known around Salem as "Cuffee Padgett." In youth his three boys, taunted for being sons of "Old Cuffee Padgett;" pleaded with their father, who determined to call himself Cuffee Cuff. His sons were Mordecai, Reuben, and Seth,[12] who became farmers, Reuben later becoming a preacher; in 1816 he was one of the founders of the African Methodist Episcopal Church in America. The record shows Reuben left numerous descendants from several marriages. His first wife, Hannah Pierce, died in childbirth in 1804; Reuben took a second wife, Lydia Iler, who died in 1814. He was wedded a third time to Ann Gould. Mordecai married Margaret Thomas, sister to David Murray's wife. Seth married, but the record of that union has become so dulled that it cannot be deciphered.

The Gould, Pierce, Murray, and Cuff families, starting before the Revolution, intermarried, also making marriages with White partners, forming the stock of generations, each pairing having its own household. In the early years usually this was a rough cabin, while each family differed considerably in manners, in appearance, and in general habits. "Happily," write the Stewards, any antipathies among the family units, which existed in "no small degree . . . has passed away and the people are now much nearer unification."[13]

Anthony Gould married Phoebe Lummis, a White woman; Samuel Gould married Rhumah Pierce; Abijah Gould married Hannah Pierce; and Elisha Gould married Elizabeth Pierce. The son of Anthony and Mary Pierce, Wanaca Pierce, married Mary Murray, daughter of Othniel and Katharine Murray. And so it went.

The Goulds and Murrays were "light-skinned," with blue eyes and fair hair. The Pierces had darker complexions and black eyes—long lines of ancestry revealed in each coupling. "The young women," remarked the Stewards, "were noted for their good looks and regular features."

Like sparks rising from embers in the night air, the Stewards record this about the progeny of Gouldtown: Samuel Gould III, as a young man, went to Pittsburgh, which at the time was counted as being in the Far West, whereupon all trace of him was lost. Hannah Gould went to Philadelphia, where she married an East Indian sailor named Charles Gonzales Smith. Hannah's husband was lost at sea. Andrew Siro went to New Bedford and became a whaler, making many voyages to the North Sea. Another son, it was reported, was lost at sea. Samuel Gould, third son of the founder, sailed in 1780 aboard a privateer schooner, *Governor Livingston,* built at Cohansey. He retired to regular life after its second voyage. Benjamin Gould III went to Boston when a young man, and nothing was heard of him after the first year. Tamson Gould married William Cox, an Indian "halfbreed" who was the first dairyman to sell milk in Bridgeton. Upon coming of age his son, William, Jr., ran away and went to sea. The last ever heard from him was a letter from the Golden Gate, California. Isaac, another son, upon growing up, also "followed the water," ending up in Europe at the outbreak of the Civil War. He became a blockade runner, carrying English goods to the southern states. A third son, Levi, became a boatswain on a ship trading between Liverpool and China. He died on the deck of his ship in port at Liverpool.

Gouldtown residents' thriving existence—chopping logs, plowing grounds, digging for their own sustenance, living in peace and happiness—was "undisturbed by those things which, with education and culture, civilization and accomplishments . . . become so galling and unbearable." So wrote William and the Rev. Theophilus Gould Steward of the era preceding the War for Independence and the two decades after, before more starkly racialized views began to characterize and predominate in America with the rise of the Cotton Kingdom, as is implicit in the terms black and white.

"For people of the condition herein attempted to be described to amount to anything of recognized worth and escape the galling effects of this trait of the American character,—to escape humiliation and even insult and injury, unfair and even brutal treatment,—they must leave this country," wrote the Stewards. "It is only the clannish love of 'the old home' which keeps such people here."[14]

Henry and John Gould when young built an oyster schooner and carried oysters from Maurice River Cove to Philadelphia, as well as from the Chesapeake Bay to Baltimore. When oysters were out of season the brothers hauled produce and peaches to Baltimore and Philadelphia. "This was long before the War of the Rebellion," write the Stewards, "and was, of course, hazardous in those times, had their color been suspected."[15]

Returning from carrying oysters and peaches from the slaveholding territory, John and Henry Gould would regale friends, families, and neighbors with tales of the dire consequences for their freedom had it been known that they bore a trace "of colored peoples blood." During the war Isaac Cox would penetrate the heart of "Secessia"—Karl Marx's expression for the seceded states—going as far as Augusta, Georgia, as a blockade runner. Indeed, he had been taken, he said, "into the homes of those proud Georgians and feasted as an Englishman."

Chapter One

"O, THAT I WERE FREE"

D ECADES BEFORE THE DISENTANGLEMENT of the Union brought on by secession, the Cotton Belt began its triumphalist march across the American South, claiming lands in South Carolina and Georgia, Alabama and Mississippi, Louisiana and Arkansas, and finally Texas, in every dusty crossroads village and steamboat landing, from every hotel lounge and railroad depot, but especially along with the clink and libation offered in countless tavern bars and country estate drawing-rooms, the subject of exchange was ever cotton and slaves, slaves and cotton—or in that pithy epigrammatic expression telegraphing all the swagger of the age, "cotton and niggers; niggers and cotton."[1]

In the era beginning about 1820 Southerners confidently believed this pairing gave them one of the strongest suits held by any hand in the world economy, making them kingpins in a burgeoning international system that bound industry to finance with the mighty strand of a fibrous plant cultivated, harvested, and transported by black-skinned human labor.

But the foundation upon which "Southern civilization" reposed was problematic. A man's wealth and importance therein was reckoned by the number of slaves he owned—specimens of human chattel becoming, as it were, his calling card, and the basis from which accrued his social, his economic, and his political influence—all estimates of considerable consequence—having, as they did, their substance neither in things nor in capital. And while it looked to the planter as if his slaves by and large were docile and submissive to his will—when not influenced by extraneous circumstances—the ratio of *black* to *white* itself epitomized the Southerner's dilemma. At what point did it become dangerously problematic? Congregating in numbers, slaveholders observed, slaves often became insolent, with the planters always mindful of the experience of St. Domingo and, after 1831 in Southampton County, Virginia, with Nat Turner. Ever present in their calculations, these episodes represented a reckoning to be deferred at all cost; nothing could be allowed to get in the way of the alchemy of procuring wealth from cotton fiber and from black skins. That a slave could try to break his or her bondage by insurrection was a danger always to be mitigated. But the next most obvious path to freedom was by running away, as many bondsmen and bondswomen and their children, increasingly did from 1820 onward. These phenomena existed from the earliest days of American colonization and settlement, with the first importation of African-originated human chattels, and this from countless motives.

Throughout the Southern states many of the enslaved sought from the first to maintain themselves as maroons in swamps and in remote areas or else flee to Florida or along the border to the north into states that had begun manumitting their like held as chattels in the South, and where the system was not becoming entrenched with the introduction of the new conditions. This period saw constant intimations in letters and newspapers of incidents of insubordination and even outright insurrection.[2] For order in the "slave quarters" a thorough system of patrolling became the responsibility of every White man, particularly of those serving in the militia, with searches and ferreting for contraband and weapons a constant. But this system ineluctably depended on brute force and punishment—for a slave there was no deterrent in lengthening the term of service; they were already property for life, unless manumitted. The whip was an aggrieved owner's constant recourse.

Article IV, section 2, paragraph three of the United States Constitution read, "No Person held to Service of Labour in one State, under the Laws thereof, escaping into another shall, in Consequence of any Law or Regulation therein, be discharged from such Service or

Labour, but shall be delivered up on Claim of the Party to whom such Service or Labour many be due." The tendering of any aid, therefore, to any "person" absconding from their "service of labor" became a crime under this article. If the fugitive was not arrested or turned away—if a crust of bread be offered—the law was broken; if a shawl or cloak was given, the law was broken.

This, to Quakers and increasingly to many citizens of other denominations across what came to be called the Free States, was anti-Christian and against God's law. The founders, it was seen, had allowed this clause into the Constitution without arousing much rancor in the spirit of compromise, but also as a kind of blackmail endured in order to maintain the paramountcy of the "Union" without which that union would not have been formed. Yet hadn't the American republican slaveholders who amended article IV to the Constitution brought about therewith the complete wreckage of what the founders had intended? And was the article not in contravention of the very principle of religious liberty? In due time calls for disobedience of the law began to echo and re-echo across the Northern states. One sees in the growth of a Cotton Kingdom a new slavery corresponding to the modern factory system in its worst form,[3] with field hands compelled to labor in a mechanical task system, with its interposing layers of overseers and drivers. Slaves gestated in a society with a multiplicity of folkways and notions—songs and stories, sayings and tales of past times, superstitious beliefs and practices—all inflected with African origins; and having too their own code of behavior as a complement to the slave code. Antebellum Southern society was also distinctly regional: Upper and Lower South, Sea Islands, Tidewater, Deep South and Southwest; as was its produce: tobacco, cotton, sugarcane, indigo, rice, and hemp.

In the experience of many contemplating "stealing away," few could count examples of success, but many knew of failures and the price exacted for them. They knew that if apprehended they awaited cruel treatment and flogging and the near certainty of being sold into the Deep South.

With no knowledge of distance and direction, how could a bondsman know where one state ended and another began? Indeed, was there safety where they were going? Would they meet judicious friends whom they could trust, and could charge with their liberty, with their lives? And with escape also came thoughts of the human bloodhounds who would be set upon their track; of weariness and hunger on a course that often lay through thick and heavy woods and back lands, where one could venture forth only under cover of night. Solitary wanderers, away from home and friend, having for a guide only the North Star—melancholy travelers whose course northward had to be rapid, cheered only by the wild hope that someday they would be free. Yet with each advancing step came the prospect of utter destitution and thoughts of pursuers lurking, waiting to waylay "runaway niggers," eager to demand, by the law of slavery, who they "belonged to" and "where they had come from."[4]

Freedom seekers escaping into New Jersey came predominantly from Delaware and the Eastern Shore of Maryland; but also from Virginia and as far away as South Carolina. They did so by crossing the Delaware River or the upper Delaware Bay at night, plying the waters in boats with hushed oars. In the upper bay this involved crossing due west of Smyrna, up the road from Dover, by way of marshlands. Directly across the water is the mouth of the Cohansey River; the boatmen employed a system of signals, a yellow light on top of a blue light. When a similar configuration showed on shore, the escapees knew it was safe to land. A short transit through marshes brought them to Greenwich, with its Quaker meeting house accessible by water, where they could be met and conveyed to that municipality's northern extremity, Springtown, a well-known and oft-used sanctuary for those making the crossing into Cumberland County, with only a dozen more miles into Bridgeton and the nearby Gould settlement.[5]

Around 1800 land in Springtown had been sold in small tracts comprising the village to fugitives and manumitted Blacks. Samuel Ringgold Ward, someday to be a noted scholar and an important Black abolitionist and minister, lived in Springtown from 1820 to 1826, arriving in the New Jersey sanctuary wrapped in swaddling in the arms of his parents. They had absconded from Maryland's eastern shore; in 1826 the family moved to New York City, where Samuel was enrolled in the African Free School, a school for the children of slaves and free Blacks founded in 1787.

As he came of age, Ward quickly began to garner notice for his exceptional oratorical skills. This led him by 1840 at the age of twenty-three into the Liberty Party. Becoming an abolitionist, newspaper editor, and Congregational Church minister, Ward would tour Britain in 1853, authoring from speeches he gave there the volume *Autobiography of a Fugitive Negro: His Anti-slavery Labours in the United States, Canada and England.* Thus was a legacy unlocked, and as that legacy roused a response, a world comprised of absconding souls in a Republic supposedly founded on democratic principles by "free Men" began to take shape and be reflected in the literature and agitation of the time.

Among those soon to be joining Ward's brethren on the abolitionist and Liberty Party circuit would be Frederick Douglass, setting out from Baltimore in 1838 at age twenty-one. Garbed "sailor style" with a cravat tied loosely about his neck, Douglass hopped onto a train bound for Philadelphia with protection papers borrowed from a Black seaman attesting to his free status in his large sailor's pocket, under the head of the American eagle.

Reaching the Quaker City, Douglass enquired of the nearest friendly face, that of a Black man, how he could reach New York. Directed to the William Street Depot, he crossed by ferry to Camden where he awaited a train. Boarding at night, he reached his destination less than twenty-four hours after setting out.

Douglass would write about his bolt from slavery forty-three years later, in an article for *Century Magazine* in 1881. More than three decades after writing his first and ever popular autobiography detailing his experiences as a slave, *Narrative of the Life of Frederick Douglass*, published in 1845, he explained why he had withheld details of his escape for so long. The penalty was very severe for those implicated, and he did not want to give out information that could preclude others from using the means he had employed.[6]

Douglass would marry his betrothed, Anna Murray, a free woman from Baltimore who had provided the money for their escape, and who quickly followed him. Their wedding ceremony was performed by Rev. James W.C. Pennington, a Presbyterian minister and himself a fugitive from Maryland often referred to as "the blacksmith" because he'd trained as such when a slave. The ceremony took place at the home of David Ruggles, a Connecticut-born New Yorker and free man, abolitionist, and secretary of the Committee of Vigilance.

Pennington would receive a Ph.D. at the University of Heidelberg, and would, in 1841, write the first history of Blacks in America, *The Origin and History of the Colored People*. He published a memoir, *The Fugitive Blacksmith*, in London in 1849 at the end of a tour of Britain.

Overseeing the operations of the Underground Railroad in New York City, Ruggles maintained and ran a grocery store, the first such Black-owned establishment in New York, by his own testimony helping as many as 1,000 fugitive slaves. Ruggles adopted as his motto the slogan "who would be free, themselves must strike the first blow."

Since slave-catchers and bounty-hunters were rife in New York, particularly down by the wharfs and piers, a good part of Ruggles's and the Vigilance Committee's work was keeping watch over residents in these neighborhoods, free Blacks and fugitive slaves alike.[7] Afflicted by blindness, Ruggles went to Florence, Massachusetts, where hydrotherapy temporarily relieved his condition. Opening his own practice as a hydrotherapist, he gained many clients, among them Sojourner Truth, born Isabella Baumfree in 1797 in Ulster County, New York, and with her parents enslaved by Dutch settlers. The property since 1810 of John Dumont of West Park, New York, she had escaped to freedom in 1826; New York's legislature ended slavery in 1817, setting the date for the final manumission of all enslaved persons for July 4, 1827.

Another client of Ruggles was William Lloyd Garrison, born in Newburyport, Massachusetts, in 1805. At age thirteen Garrison had apprenticed to a printer and newspaper publisher, in time himself achieving these positions, becoming as well a prominent abolitionist, suffragist, and civil rights campaigner. Ruggles died at thirty-nine in December 1849, having gained prominence both as a radical abolitionist and as a therapist, while Garrison was just embarking on his era-spanning career.

Although exhilarated to be a free man and "dazzled with the wonders" on every hand, Douglass soon found New York less safe a refuge than he had supposed, particularly if he was to seek employment on its piers and in shipyards. The newlyweds determined in consultation with Ruggles and others to move to the port of New Bedford, Massachusetts, where as a "caulker" Frederick would be able to find employment in that sanctuary for fugitive slaves and center of whaling in the Northeast. Forty years later in *The Life and Times of Frederick Douglass*, his third autobiography—his second was titled *My Bondage and My Freedom*, published in 1855—Douglass wrote, "We arrived at Newport the next morning, and soon after an old-fashioned stagecoach with 'New Bedford' in large, yellow letters on its side, came down the wharf. I had not money enough to pay our fare and stood hesitating to know what to do. Fortunately for us, there were two Quaker gentlemen who were about to take passage on the stage—Friends William C. Taber and Joseph Ricketson—who at once discerned our true situation, and in a peculiarly quiet way, addressing me, Mr. Taber said, 'Thee get in.' I never obeyed an order with more alacrity, and we were soon on our way to our new home."[8]

As he was approaching his seventieth year, asked where he had gotten his education, Douglass replied unequivocally, "from Massachusetts abolition University: Mr. Garrison, president."[9] Douglass's first months in New Bedford were tough, but he had learned to grapple with difficulties and was quick to grasp new opportunities. Unable to hire on as a caulker in the shipyards because White men would not work alongside him, he found his first job loading casks of whale oil on a sloop bound for New York.

And so it is with these names—Samuel Ringgold Ward, Frederick Douglass, James W.C. Pennington, David Ruggles, Sojourner Truth, and William Lloyd Garrison, among others herein whose stories are to be recounted—we will see that without their "effective and self-sacrificing efforts . . . the abolition movement in the United States could not have been successful."[10]

The appellation Underground Railroad was not a term that could have gained currency much before 1840, but soon thereafter found its topical usage. From its beginnings in the colonial era through its heyday in the 1850s, that enterprise necessarily and understandably was shrouded in mystery—with those aiding the fugitive subject to heavy fines and jailing, and the condemnation of law and of neighbors.

The first "over-ground" railway in the U.S. chartered for commercial transport of passengers and freight, starting in 1827, was the Baltimore & Ohio Railroad. In 1831, the first track in operation in New Jersey, and the third in the nation, connected Perth Amboy and Camden, a total distance of sixty-two miles. A second railway in New Jersey, the Burlington & Mount Holly Railroad, began operating in 1836, as railroads were becoming ubiquitous in an emerging industrialized world. In 1838, at Morristown, New Jersey, Samuel Morse and Alfred Vail would make a public test of the telegraph, which became the most important tool for railroads and key to a burgeoning future for industrial capitalism. By the early 1840s, these technologies were becoming thoroughly embedded across the landscape, while an Underground Railroad too was "up and running."

Among other escapees to pass through Springtown in New Jersey were Levin Steel, his wife Charity, and their growing family, also from the Eastern Shore. Shortly after his arrival, Levin would change the family name to Still, and would subsequently move with his family to

Snow Hill in New Jersey. Later renamed Lawnside, that community resembled Springtown, being composed of fugitives and manumitted Blacks and having been established in the later eighteenth century. In 1840, land in Snow Hill had been subdivided and sold to Blacks by Ralph Smith, a Haddonfield abolitionist, who renamed the settlement Free Haven.[11] One of Levin's and Charity's sons, James Still, established a thriving practice of "folk medicine," using powders and tinctures, liniments, teas, and vegetable oils to treat patients. He became renowned as "The Black Doctor of the Pines." Another son, youngest of the Stills's fourteen children, also gained renown. In 1844 William Still moved to Philadelphia; in 1847 he was hired as clerk for the Pennsylvania Society for the Abolition of Slavery, and shortly afterwards became chairman of the Vigilance Committee. The famous chronicle of his activities and his interviews with as many as 800 absconding slaves was published in 1872 as *The Underground Railroad— A Record.*

The work of aiding fugitive slaves in New Jersey and Pennsylvania was for the most part in the early years in the hands of Quakers and Black refugees and free Blacks. In 1804 the New Jersey legislature had passed a law starting a gradual emancipation of its slaves, but the final curtain would not be drawn till the governor signed a bill abolishing slavery on January 23, 1866, making New Jersey the last of the northern states to do so. But over the years "The Garden State"—a term deriving from the produce New Jersey provided to Philadelphia and New York markets—began to exceed any other northern state in the number of its "colored" communities. The term "colored," rather than "African," came into usage after 1816 and the founding of the American Colonization Society. That imminently notorious organization had been founded in Washington, D.C., by Robert Finley, a Presbyterian minister, with the ardent support of the venerable politician and statesman-to-be Henry Clay, a Kentucky slaveholder and hemp grower, to ameliorate what he and Finley and others perceived as the problem of an increasing free Black presence in the United States. In 1790 the free Black population had been 60,000; by 1830 the tally was 300,000. But as of 1833, the American Colonization Society had transported only 2,769 individuals to Liberia, the society's favored destination for this out-migration, in a period during which census figures showed there to have been half a million births of Black infants in the United States, indicating how ineffective "colonization" was and would remain.

By 1832 the society was under attack by abolitionists, William Lloyd Garrison authoring *Thoughts on African Colonization,* in whose pages he pronounced the society a fraud, its point being that Blacks in America must remain slaves and, if manumitted, must leave the country. Garrison at first, along with the predominant anti-slavery opinion of the time, had espoused gradual emancipation reform, along with supporting colonization. But with the evangelism that had swept the country in the 1820s, the idea of immediatism based on repentance came to the fore, and in coming decades would become the central tenet of Garrison's abolitionism. On January 1, 1831, in Boston, Garrison began publication of the *Liberator,* espousing immediate emancipation without compensation to slaveholders, and without colonization of the freed Blacks. The New England Anti-Slavery Society would be formed at a meeting in Boston in November 1831 on a program of immediatism. Seventy-two names were affixed to the constitution of the new society, a few coming from the city's prominent lists, but most from more ordinary ranks, while nearly twenty were from among Boston's free Black and fugitive community.

Garrison, besides advocating immediatism, preached nonresistance, abstinence, anti-Sabbatarianism, Black equality, and women's rights. His signature slogan became "No Union with slaveholders!" Despairing of the efficacy of extending political action before consummating the moral struggle, he denounced the U.S. Constitution as "a covenant with death, and an agreement with Hell." Wearing steel-rimmed glasses and prematurely bald, he wore a black coat with a black cravat about his neck, giving him an austere, sectarian appearance; from the working class, he had an egalitarian ethos, admitting Black people and women, to the scandal of many, into the Massachusetts Anti-Slavery Society.[12]

Harriet Tubman was also known to use New Jersey on her many forays into Delaware and Maryland's Eastern Shore. But on her escape in 1849 she used the road on the west bank of the Delaware, through the "station" in Wilmington run by Thomas Garrett, also a Quaker. Thence, Tubman was "freighted" to Philadelphia. In her first years as a free woman—1849-1852—Harriet would work as a cook and kitchen hand in Cape May, New Jersey, at hotels and resorts, an indication of the importance New Jersey locales had to the thriving operations of the underground. Her jobs would underwrite her missions to the Eastern Shore, to which she reputedly made as many as 19 trips, bringing to freedom as many as 300 charges. She became so notorious that between 1858 and 1860, a $40,000 reward was offered by Eastern Shore slaveholders for her capture. It was said, W. E. B. Du Bois remarked in *John Brown*, "that 500 black messengers of this sort were passing backward and forward between the slave and the free states in this decade. . . ."[13]

At five feet in height, Tubman had a tough muscularity gained from the roughest fieldwork and driving oxen. With a religious disposition tinged with stories from the Old Testament, she became well-known for her recounted visionary experiences. Hit in the head and disabled in her early years by a two-pound metal object thrown at her, she suffered epileptic-like seizures and often seemed to fall into fitful unconscious states or semi-sleep. During these intervals, she was a recipient of potent dreams she regarded as divine premonitions.[14]

The "rails" on which "persons" were guided to their freedom by way of underground networks fell largely within four regions—in the Delaware Valley these routes ran on the eastern and western banks of the Delaware River into New Jersey, in its southern extremity, and in the west, up to Bucks County and into Philadelphia.

On the Atlantic coast, seaports were used, along with the section's coastal waterways and tributaries, swamps, and wetlands. Flight routes originating from Baltimore might use the Chesapeake Bay; sometimes more southerly ports were the starting points. Fugitives would begin at Wilmington, Georgetown, or Charlestown and travel north to Greenwich, New Jersey, or Philadelphia, New York, Providence, New Bedford, or Boston.

After reaching New York, fugitives used the Hudson Valley, a major branch of the Underground Railroad and a well-trodden pathway north on both sides of the Hudson River. Stations were predominantly operated by Quaker families and at meetinghouses along the way, or through Black settlements rife throughout the New York river valley counties. These routes then ran west across the northern tier of New York or else into Massachusetts and Vermont. Branches running through Connecticut often freighted passengers coming overland from New York. Arriving in Wilton, Connecticut, then up to Plymouth or Middletown, refugees were sent to Farmington or sometimes Torrington. Fugitives starting in the ports—at Stamford, New Haven, or Old Lyme—also passed over to Farmington, in later decades called the "Grand Central Station" of the Connecticut Underground Railroad, then north to Westfield or Springfield in Massachusetts.[15] Those beginning in New London or Westerly, Rhode

Island, traveled north through Norwich to Putman, then up to Worcester in Massachusetts.

A third important network in the system was active in the hill country west of Baltimore by way of Frederick and Hagerstown in Maryland and up into central Pennsylvania into Lancaster County and in the west beyond South Mountain into Mercersburg and up to Chambersburg, Bedford, and Pittsburgh. Fugitives in this region found haven in Columbia at the home of William Wright, another figure of the underground, who handled in his career as many as 1,000 passengers, who then might be moved on to Harrisburg, or to Philadelphia, or to New York and then Albany, crossing the northern tier to Utica, Syracuse, Auburn, Rochester, and Buffalo, thence into Canada, to Hamilton, St. Catharines, Chatham, and Toronto. Perhaps 9,000 freedom seekers were helped to freedom through this branch of the Underground Railroad prior to 1860.[16]

A fourth network, the most active, extended along the longest frontier between the free and the slave states: the Ohio River. The Ohio charts its course for nearly four hundred rolling miles, beginning at the confluence of the Allegheny and Monongahela Rivers between whose triangle the city of Pittsburgh was built; the great river ranging from western Virginia across the entire irregular northern frontier of Kentucky, terminating at the Mississippi River and the state of Missouri. Touching upon Ohio, Indiana, and Illinois, the Ohio presented a wide and brisk flowing stream known in slave folklore as the Jordan.[17] On its ice floes Eliza escaped with her baby in Harriet Beecher Stowe's novel *Uncle Tom's Cabin*, serialized in the *National Era* in 1852. Of her miraculous book and its reception, Stowe declared, "The Lord himself wrote it and I was but the humblest instrument." Priced at thirty-seven-and-a-half cents, the book would surpass one million copies in sales.

An important figure in the Underground passing through Ripley, Ohio, where his home overlooked the river, was Presbyterian minister John Rankin. The publisher in 1826 of *Letters on American Slavery*, Rankin was a founding member of Ohio's abolitionist society in 1834, and became the inspiration for Stowe's book, along with a fugitive slave from the national capital, Josiah Henson. Henson, said Stowe in the *Key to Uncle Tom's Cabin*, had been her model for the titular character Uncle Tom. In 1849, Henson published *The Life of Josiah Henson, Formerly a Slave, Now an Inhabitant of Canada, as Narrated by*

Himself. The fictionalization of his life, it could be said, had more weight than his actual person, co-opted as it was by an alter ego.

Another important branch of the "railroad" operated on the Mississippi, running through its riverside cities, towns, and villages, and utilizing riverboat and wagon traffic. This branch reached into Iowa and into Wisconsin or crossed over Illinois to Chicago and points north. One factor in opening the Mississippi to the Underground Railroad was the steam-powered riverboat, the first suitable design of which was in operation on the river by 1814. Now a vessel need not merely float downstream, but could go upstream and out of the "South" and into free states—a dynamic at play in *The Adventures of Huckleberry Finn*, a novel by Mark Twain, who as Samuel Clemens had been an early riverboat pilot, which experience Twain spun into a tale about the South of the 1830-to-1840 era, the fateful decade after the Missouri Compromise of 1820 opened that state to slavery while prohibiting the practice in adjacent states and territories.

The book's protagonist, Huckleberry Finn, was a boy of 13 or 14, living in a Missouri riverfront town; dressing in discarded overalls and sleeping in an empty hogshead barrel, he obtained his meals by scrounging—all the while eluding his drunken, abusive father, called Pap. Living free of any civilized care, Huck encounters a fugitive slave, Jim, and embarks with him by raft down the Mississippi, intending to float to Cairo, Illinois, then onto the Ohio, carrying Jim to freedom. In the pair's fictional adventures the author skewers the antebellum South, satirizing slavery for its absurdities in its treatment of Blacks and for its inhumanity—a book unequaled in American literature, before or since.

A last route on the Underground Railroad opened with the free state settlement of Kansas after 1854, running fugitives up from Missouri's northwest quadrant, where slavery predominated, into Kansas through Lawrence and Topeka and up into Nebraska and Iowa, between 1854 and 1861.

Cincinnati, Ohio, home to Levi Coffin—often called the "President of the Underground Railroad"—was the underground's active center in the West. Coffin was a Quaker, a farmer, and an abolitionist estimated to have "freighted" 3,000 fugitives to freedom. In his autobiography, *Reminiscences of Levi Coffin*, published in 1876, he avowed his anti-slavery convictions to have been an inheritance from his ancestry, also crediting the teaching of John Woolman, a Quaker from Mount Holly, New Jersey, who proselytized against slavery during the colonial era.

In the East, already noted, a prominent figure was Thomas Garrett of Wilmington, Delaware. An iron merchant and Quaker, he was as practical and effective a worker for emancipation as scores of others and was said to have aided more than 2,700 slaves to freedom. In Syracuse there was Samuel J. May, Unitarian minister and seminal radical abolitionist, who from his pulpit solicited aid for fugitives, and who in 1850 became one of the preeminent opponents of the Fugitive Slave Law. In Columbia, Pennsylvania, at the end of the bridge across the Susquehanna, resided another prominent station master, William Whipper. A lumber merchant, he had inherited his business from his White father, who had impregnated a servant. Apprenticing under his father, he attained the leading position at and ownership of the firm. Partnering in joint ventures with Stephen Smith, which extended to aiding fugitives, Whipper and his ally amassed holdings that included land in Pennsylvania and Canada with coal, lumberyards, railroad cars, and a steamship operating on Lake Erie. All these assets he used directly in assisting fugitive slaves, estimating that he spent $1,000 annually to help those escaping slavery. Regularly contributing, too, to the anti-slavery cause, he wrote articles that appeared in Garrison's *Liberator* and in Douglass's *North Star*, as well as in the *National Antislavery Standard*.

Active in Chicago was John Jones, a wealthy tailor and abolitionist; in Detroit, William Lambert worked in close association with George DeBaptiste; and in Boston's Beacon Hill, there was Lewis Hayden, a fugitive slave from Kentucky. Many other outstanding figures on the "railroad" were likewise fugitive slaves, such as Rev. Henry Highland Garnet, who escaped from New Market, Maryland, with his entire family. In Syracuse resided the Rev. Jermain Wesley Loguen, a fugitive from Tennessee who after 1850 dedicated himself full time to helping fugitives, becoming known as "the King of the Underground Railroad;" in Philadelphia, William Still would be known as "the President of the Underground Railroad."

In southeast Pennsylvania, systematic organizing for aiding fugitives began early, as has been noted, among the Quakers. Through here passed the largest number of fugitives for many years—1820 to 1840—as the region was a locus of strong sentiment against slavery. In subsequent years, this predominance would shift westward to Ohio, Illinois, Indiana, and Kentucky as these activities became regularized into the traffic and operations became systematized. By then, after the passage of the Compromise of 1850, with its stringent provisions for slave-catching, the roads carrying the bulk of absconding slaves began to terminate in Canada.

In New Jersey in the antebellum period, 1800 to 1860—some 50,000 to 70,000 fugitives passed through or came to reside within the state.[18] The routes through the state, starting in Cumberland and Salem Counties, ran through Camden and Burlington Counties, into Mercer and Middlesex and Essex Counties, terminating at Jersey City. It was from there, at the Morris Canal Basin, that fugitives were ferried to New York City to be dispatched north to New England or upstate New York, then on to Canada.

With networks of individuals and groups assisting the freedom seekers, refugees were provided with ready transport, lodging, food, and often money to offset expenses. These numerous philanthropic aiders and abettors scattered through the free states were predominantly clerics and abolitionists, often professionals such as doctors, innkeepers, and even escapees themselves, along with their sympathizers. To protect the identities of those involved and to guard the secrecy of routes, participants typically knew no more than the details associated with their particular locale, thereby having little understanding of the larger connecting links whose overall guidance was in the hands of the Vigilance Committees. If refugees were traveling by conveyance, the vehicle used might be a covered wagon, or a wagon over whose open bed a tarp was drawn, or with a false bottom constructed beneath; hay wagons were often resorted to. In many instances, actual rail lines, known as "lightning" railroads, were used to transport fugitives in the care of sympathetic trainmen; parts of the journey might be on water, in sea-going vessels, on river steamers, or canal boats, with fugitives posing as deckhands or bargemen.

In the early days of underground activity, most fugitives aided on these escape routes were males 15 to 30. Only later did whole families, even including elderly relatives, begin to hazard the secret roads. Harriet Tubman rescued her parents and brought them to live in Auburn, New York, making a home for them in a residence provided on generous terms by William H. Seward, the Republican politician and secretary of state in the Lincoln administration.

The typical distance traveled in a day between "stations" was in the range of ten to twenty miles, with fugitives upon arrival being succored, the horses rested or exchanged, or another contrivance held at the ready for the next leg. Messages would be sent to alert parties at locations ahead of the imminence of human "cargo." Often a "station" was merely a makeshift shelter— a haystack or a cave in a river bank.

At the starting point in Greenwich, New Jersey, the station had the use of a secret five-foot-square room beneath the altar at the Bethel African Methodist Episcopal Church. That chamber, built in 1838, received travelers bound for that leg's first safe house in nearby Springtown. After Springtown, the road passed through other Black or mixed-race communities such as Marshalltown, Gouldtown, Snow Hill, or Tumbuctoo in Burlington County, that would shelter fugitives.

In Salem, the Quaker sisters Abigail and Elizabeth Goodwin operated a station in their home. Joined by local Blacks, the sisters led efforts in their town to collect donations of food, clothing, and money to assist their charges. Becoming active in the 1830s, the Goodwins became widely known, Abigail from her correspondence with abolitionists across the Delaware River like William Still, Lucretia Mott, and James Miller McKim.

Another notable Salem resident, John S. Rock, was born there in 1825 of free parents. Rock attended New Jersey public schools, then worked as a teacher between 1844 and 1848. Pursuing medical studies with two local doctors, he was admitted to the American Medical College in Philadelphia. Practicing dentistry while continuing his studies, he also taught at a night school for Black Philadelphians and worked with the Vigilance Committee, treating fugitive slaves needing medical care.

Taking up the study of law in 1861, Rock moved to Boston, gaining admittance to the Massachusetts bar. Governor John Andrew appointed him Justice of the Peace for Boston and Suffolk County. Helping in 1863 with recruitment of Black troops into the 54th Massachusetts Infantry Regiment, Rock campaigned for these and other Black soldiers to receive equal pay. In 1865, with support from Senator Charles Sumner, Rock became the first African American lawyer to argue a case before the U.S. Supreme Court.

In Snow Hill, fugitives would stop at the residence of Peter Mott and his wife, Elizabeth. Mott, a free man from Delaware, had built a two-story home for himself and family in 1844. He would carry his charges to "friends" in Haddonfield or Mooretown. Richard Allen, founder of the African Methodist Episcopal Church, was pastor at Snow Hill's Mt. Pisgah Church, at which Mott also preached.

In Burlington, Wheatley's Pharmacy, a Quaker establishment, was used to harbor fugitives. The station in Cranbury was operated by

Quaker William S. Hall, owner of the Cranbury Inn, where Hall concealed fugitives in a trick chimney flue accessible by trap door. Known as "a body-hiding box," that contrivance had space sufficient to hold up to four people. In Jersey City, David Holden, a banker and amateur astronomer, maintained a safe house within a four-story building of single occupancy built in 1854 in the Paulus Hook section. Harboring fugitives in the basement, Holden would receive and send signals from the observatory he'd installed on the roof.

Wilbur H. Siebert in his 1898 study *The Underground Railroad from Slavery to Freedom* identifies five individuals engaged in the operations in Greenwich. They were Nathaniel Murry, brothers J. R. Sheppard and Thomas R. Sheppard, and a married couple, Alges and Julia Stamford. So, we see brothers working in conjunction with a husband and wife; and of Black working with White.

In Salem Siebert listed Abigail Goodwin and Rev. Thomas Clement Oliver, a Black also listed as a resident at Camden, indicating the breadth of his activity. In Burlington, Siebert identified as allies John Coleman and Robert Evans, Enoch Middleton, and Samuel Stevens. (Appendix E of Siebert's book enumerates over 140 Blacks in the lists of underground operatives).

Fugitives traveling north from Springtown could find refuge and work in Gouldtown among the ancient families there. Perhaps that was the point of sending them to Gouldtown, off the main northerly route, as some of the young men would be piloted by Lenape on trails through marshlands, an arduous trek of forty miles to Cape May, where absconders could find work.

These New Jersey operations were integrally adjoined with those issuing out of Philadelphia, affording fugitives three branches through New Jersey, two already delineated. This third branch, emanating from Philadelphia, crossed the Delaware by boat; fugitives were conveyed upriver to Burlington, a distance of twenty miles. This branch next passed through Bordentown, making a circuitous jump to Princeton, and continuing on to New Brunswick.

Stopping at the Raritan River, the most dangerous crossing in New Jersey, station master Cornelius Cornell would signal his counterpart on the opposite bank to ascertain if slave catchers were present. If he got an affirmative answer, the party would take the road to Perth Amboy, whence the passengers could be sent to New York City. If it was safe at the Raritan crossing, the road to Jersey City was open. Fugitives arriving in Jersey City were delivered into the care of the Quaker

John Everett or his servants, then conveyed to a railway station on the west side of New York City at which tickets would be provided for travel through to Syracuse.

The valley of the Delaware, along whose eastern branch the New Jersey routes ran, became vital to the Underground Railroad because it lay within and formed a crescent between two metropolitan centers, Philadelphia and New York. Many fugitives passing through the valley stopped and settled in the Black neighborhoods emerging in Camden or in Philadelphia's 7th Ward. By 1790 Burlington County had the largest free Black population in the Delaware Valley, as New Jersey's "gradual emancipation" policy in 1804 would accrue to that state the appellation the "cradle of emancipation."[19] Fugitives electing to reside in New Jersey eventually began referring to that state as "the Georgia of the North,"[20] because of its legislative tardiness in issuing an abolition edict and because the enactments of New Jersey lawmakers were among the most recalcitrant of the northern states on the so-called Black or Negro Question—not excepting Illinois, Indiana, or Ohio; and besides the Quakers, the majority of Whites in New Jersey were often uniformly imbued with the prejudice and the brutish racial animosity characteristic of the day, particularly in its great working centers like Newark.

Chapter Two

"IN SOLEMN AND SECRET COMPACT"

IN THE FEBRUARY 1952 issue of *Ebony* magazine, a feature article headlined "America's Oldest Negro Community" reported that Gouldtown, two hundred and fifty years old and with a population of 3,000, was named after a "black coachman" from whom the residents' lineage had sprung. Among the municipality's five principal families, the article stated, were over 800 Goulds, 1,000 persons bearing the name Pierce, with 300 Murrays, 200 Cuffs, and 100 Wrights. The settlement had been in existence without interruption since the eighteenth century, and "Old Gouldtowners" interviewed for the piece, who had delved into the issue and considered themselves "authorities of a kind on genealogy," insisted that most Goulds in the United States at that time were "related in some way to the line of Goulds started by the marriage of a White woman to a Black man named Gould."

Although the core of the community had remained unbroken, for generations preserving "their unique heritage and identity" and "quietly proud of their past," over the years and decades and centuries many Gouldtowners had made a "cultural exodus," departing the

Black world for the White world. A senior Gouldtown historian explained, "They realized that there were more opportunities for them in the white world than in ours and that the fight to live was not nearly as tough."

After the ending of the Civil War, Gouldtowners had gradually and largely left farming, retaining ownership of their land when they could, for jobs in local factories. Many went to work in Bridgeton and in nearby canneries, with scores of younger men and some women moving to Philadelphia for higher wages; still others hired on at textile plants within a ten to twenty-mile radius of Gouldtown. Many residents continued to be employed in the immediate vicinity as carpenters and electricians, as mechanics and firemen or policemen, or ran a shoe repair shop or a general store.

During the War of the Revolution, Gouldtown men overwhelmingly marched with Washington's army, which claimed the service of three quarters of them. During the War of the Slaveholder Rebellion, townsmen were thoroughly anti-Confederate, formally pledging in a letter to President Abraham Lincoln that they would raise a regiment of Gouldtown men to fight against slavery and for the Union. But, to their dismay, the government rebuffed their offer under its then-regnant policy of refusing to enlist Black men in the Union Army. Able to pass for White, many Gouldtown men slipped into state military units anyway.

Lincoln's Emancipation Proclamation on January 1, 1863, and the subsequent opening of recruitment to a Black soldiery brought Theophilius Gould Steward into uniform. Ordained a minister in the African Methodist Episcopal Church that year, he became a chaplain for United States Colored troops who by war's end numbered 180,000 men. Following the war, he helped organize the A.M.E. Church in South Carolina and Georgia. Moving to Macon, Georgia, during Reconstruction, Rev. Steward built and ministered to a church which recalcitrant White Southerners torched in 1872. Steward and the parishioners promptly rebuilt the church.

Those born and raised in Gouldtown and still conversant with its history held to the genesis tale, the *Ebony* article reported: that the settlement began with the marriage of Elizabeth Fenwick, granddaughter of John Fenwick, to "a black coachman" named Gould. But, *Ebony* averred, a basis for that presupposition "has not been accurately established."

Joseph S. Sickler, writing in 1937 of the founding of Gouldtown in his study *History of Salem*, also disputed the received history. "The writer does not believe this story to be founded upon fact," Sickler wrote. "Neither does Frank H. Stewart, one of the most painstaking and accurate historians of New Jersey. He . . . finds that Elizabeth Adams married a man by the name of Windsor within two weeks of the writing of her grandfather's will."

A century earlier, Robert Gibbon Johnson, not a historian but an area farmer and agriculturist, wrote in his *The First Settlement of Salem*, "Among the numerous troubles and vexations which assailed Fenwick, none appear to have distressed him more than the base and abandoned conduct of his granddaughter Elizabeth Adams, who attached herself to a citizen of color (as we say now-a-days.) . . . From that illicit connection hath sprung the families of the Goulds, at a little settlement called Gouldtown in Cumberland county."

There is no record of children from a marriage of Anne Adams to anyone named Windsor, and no one has been able to show such; Elizabeth's reputed marriage, said to have occurred two weeks after the drafting of Fenwick's will and before his unexpected death, may have been an attempt to salvage her portion of his estate and to mitigate the wrath between them. Was that match an "arranged marriage" made for the sake of propriety? At the time of the birth of a son named Benjamin Gould, his mother Anne would have been thirty-six, and this was years after Fenwick's will was written. Evidently, she remained for many years with Gould. There was no public record beyond the designation "a coachman" for the father; but like his progeny, perhaps he, too, was a Benjamin. Acknowledging, as we do today, the long historical record of illicit or recognized progeny conceived, whether in violence or in affection, in instances of Black and White sexual congress—a notable example being Thomas Jefferson and Sally Hemmings, his slave—and the oral tradition expressing the Hemming descendants' acceptance of the fact of that matter, we similarly may defer to residents of the "Gouldtown settlement" and to their tradition.

This author has come to know some of these proud descendants. One day, knowing of my study of many years' duration regarding the antebellum period of our history, and my long-maintained interest in all things John Brown, a friend wed to a Gouldtown woman mentioned that a cousin of his wife's living in town had John Brown's pocket watch. The timepiece had been discovered in a chest long unattended in an attic, he said.

"I've got to see it," I said immediately. "Please set up a meeting."

The holder of said watch, Becky Lively, had been born and raised in Gouldtown and after college had gone to live in Virginia. She taught in Prince George County, had an award-winning pedagogic career in art education with the public school system, and had married a musician, a bassist. The couple had retired to Ocala, Florida, as had I.

The day of our meeting in the community center, she brought out a small broach box that contained two watches, one the Brown pocket watch on a chain, the other a smaller watch, which she said was of the kind train engineers once used.

Holding the larger watch to dangle from its chain, I thought the tarnished case to be silver or perhaps nickel. No etching on the cover or the back of the watch identified an owner.

I asked how she had concluded that the timepiece had been John Brown's. With a small hatpin she pried open the back. Inside was a slip of old paper bearing John Brown's signature. The paper bore faint but regular horizontal lines—faded notebook paper, I surmised—but of a heavier stock than we might encounter today. The signature was in pencil, and likewise faded but still legible. I had seen that signature many times; it was unmistakably his—here appearing at the center of a circular piece of paper. At regular intervals around the edge, the paper had been scissored, evidently so that it would fit inside the rim of the watch case without tearing or curling the paper.

"There is another paper underneath," Becky said. Removing the first circle carefully, I could see another, also scissored at intervals. On it was plainly handwritten "1839."

The first of those four numerals seemed to have been elaborated upon, evidently by an untrained calligrapher, almost as if to change the numeral "1" to resemble a column. A design meant to hint at a special significance? In relation to what? To the year 1859, I surmised: a twenty-year span.

But if they were dates, what might those two dates mean? How did the years 1839 and 1859 relate to the life of John Brown, and to the momentous and fiery culmination to which he brought those antebellum decades? Beneath these two relics were two more pieces of paper. The first had printed on it three images of roses, perhaps an auspicious talisman. But further scrutiny revealed this to be an industrial product, cut by machine, and not, as appeared to be the case with the two former inserts, with scissors. Perhaps the manufacturer had inserted it. Beneath this, completely dried out and crumbling, was the manufacturer's tag, reading "J.B. Oliver Clocks, Watches and Jewelry Conetantey Harrisburg, Penn. No. 26 North Second St."

These items had come from a chest that had been in the attic of Becky Lively's family home for many years in Gouldtown. Only gradually had she dared examine its contents, because as a girl she had not wanted to be in that attic alone. There were a dozen books from the 1880s or before; some appeared to be rudimentary manuals, used to teach children, adolescents, or illiterate adults. Others were for more advanced, even collegiate tutelage. There were two modified hymnals, she said, whose interiors had been hollowed out to make hiding places. These had been used, family lore went, to conceal the papers of fugitive slaves who had sought refuge in Gouldtown.

Asking about the chest's other contents, I was assured that they were, likewise, all very old, but, like the hymnals, long since distributed as mementoes to different families, and no longer available— garments, perhaps a shawl or quilt, and other articles, she recalled.

How did John Brown's watch get in the chest, I asked. Becky said the watch had come from a man who lived in Harrisburg at the time of Brown's foray at Harper's Ferry, Virginia, where the fellow had worked as a banker or clerk. Later he'd come to Gouldtown, bringing the watch and marrying the sister of Becky's great-aunt. The man's name was Clifton Mosely. That is all that was known, or that now could be recalled.

Becky also related a story of a time years back when she had traveled to the Smithsonian Institution in Washington, D.C., thinking that that august museum would be interested in having such a significant memento. But the Smithsonian already had John Brown's pocket watch, she was informed by a curator who, not even deigning to look at the signature, said the institution felt no need for another. "Well, I guess it belongs to me now," she said to herself.

Looking over the items, my mind began to conjecture: The papers on which the signature and the numerals had been written were hand cut. The hands had not been those of Brown or of the men with him at the Kennedy Farm, I presumed, as they gathered just outside Harper's Ferry in preparation for their historic strike. Perhaps these had been fashioned or induced by the two young women also residing at the house, as they sat at the kitchen table with the "old man." These were Brown's daughter Anne, sixteen, and her sister-in-law, Martha Thompson, a year or two older, who had been brought down to the farm from the Brown family domicile at North Elba in the Adirondack Mountains of New York. They were to provide the farmhouse outside Harper's Ferry with a modicum of normality and to assist as recruits to the "raid" slowly began "reporting for duty," Martha preparing food and Anne largely acting as her father's "watch-dog," sitting on the porch much of the time in order to intercept prying neighbors, alerting the men as anyone approached so that they might take cover in the attic. The women must have both often sat with Brown when he was on the premises as he discussed what concerned him most, relating his thoughts on the action about to be undertaken and recounting how that action had emerged gradually out of the tumultuous history of the previous twenty years.

And what of the numerals: did they represent a particular year? What significance did they have to this story, and to John Brown's life? And how did the watch get into the hands of Clifton Mosely in Harrisburg?

If Brown already had a pocket watch, and evidently, he did, and he passed though Harrisburg on his way south, perhaps he felt in need of another, or in need of several additional watches? Knowing that Brown intended to introduce a force into the Blue Ridge Mountains, and that these men were to operate in sub-groups, sometimes independently of one another, at other times in conjunction—one wonders, wouldn't these, too, need timepieces to coordinate their movements and actions? How else to keep track of timetables such as railroad schedules; along with the compendium of maps, tables and charts, spyglasses, compasses, and the mirrors for signaling, and other instruments, such as boatswain's whistles, which we know they also acquired and carried among their stores. There were seven such whistles.

And regarding the watch's evident return to Harrisburg, and the place of its manufacture? Osborne Anderson, a Black Canada-based recruit to Brown's campaign, after the failure of the "raid," escaped into the north via York and then Philadelphia. In Philadelphia, Anderson would have been put on a train and speedily transported to Rochester, New York, going promptly to the Frederick Douglass domicile. Thereupon Anderson and Douglass, equally implicated in the "insurrection at Harper's Ferry," fled to safety in Canada just ahead of pursuing federal marshals. Had this Mosely been associated with the underground in Harrisburg and its environs?[1] Or had he known people who were? Maybe the watch was a token given Mosely for his solicitude? Harrisburg was a major station on the Underground Railroad, with ready connections east to west, as into the north and from the south into central Pennsylvania, and assuredly, based upon his procedure elsewhere, Brown knew of persons there and likely consulted with them.

Local historians today estimate there were eighteen to twenty Underground Railroad "stations" in the immediate Harrisburg area, that town being by 1850 home to nine hundred free Blacks and fugitives. Most of these resided in a single section behind the state capitol, along a narrow road called Tanner's Alley, incidentally not far from the watchmaker's address, surely a locale traversed by and known to Brown.

One station operator in Tanner's Alley was Joseph Bustill, who had been associated with underground operations since age seventeen. He was of African, English, and Lenape aboriginal American extraction, very like the people of Gouldtown. Of a family of "ancient" origin, Bustill was from Philadelphia; his brother Charles was an important member of the Philadelphia Vigilance Committee, and so was in contact with William Still. A few of Joseph's letters were published in Still's book, showing among other details their use of code as regards their charges, Joseph Bustill mentioning in one letter "four large and two small hams" being sent to a correspondent in Reading, referring to the transport of four adults and two children. These epistles, a reader will discern, are also noteworthy for the evident care the men took, their concern for their charges, and the scrupulousness they evinced.

And what of the year 1839? I thought first of the murder of Elijah Lovejoy in Alton, Illinois, and of the Lovejoy memorial meeting near Hudson, Ohio, at which Brown was said to have risen publicly to pledge himself and his family in a war against slavery in America. No doubt 1839 was a significant year to Brown, as he gathered his forces to commence such a war. But Lovejoy's martyrdom had been in 1837. Clearly 1839 was of special significance to Brown; and the twenty-year interval to 1859 might indicate a weighty parallel between two events. Then, I realized, the year invoked must and could only be a reference to the trial of the *Amistad* "mutineers" in New Haven, Connecticut, a saga that began in August 1839.

La Amistad was a Cuban schooner, and hence Spanish owned, whose cargo included a Mende warrior from a chief's family. Sengbe Pieh, better known as Cinque, along with fifty-three fellow tribal members had been kidnapped from the British colony of Sierra Leone and, along with five hundred other Africans transported to Cuba to be sold into slavery. At the Havana slave market, the Mende were bought as a single lot by a Spanish planter who intended to put them to work cutting sugarcane on his plantation on the northern coast of Cuba. Four days into the voyage from Havana, while the ship was at sea, Cinque managed to free himself from his shackles, also freeing others. Seizing cane knives from the ship's stores, the men slew the vessel's cook and captain. Two sailors escaped in a boat; the two slave owners aboard the insurgents let live, thinking they could compel the pair to pilot *La Amistad* back to Sierra Leone.

Instead, after sixty-three days on a circuitous twisted route during which no port could be sought, *La Amistad* terminated its journey off the eastern end of Long Island, New York, on August 26, 1839. Intercepted by the United States Navy, the Africans were arrested and the Spanish slaveholders freed, while the vessel was seized and towed to the prize court in New London, Connecticut, for adjudication. Two kidnapped Africans had died in the uprising and eight had died of starvation on the journey up the coast. The forty-three surviving Africans—thirty-nine men, one boy, and three girls—were lodged in the jail at New Haven. None of the Africans spoke English, and the slaveholders had lurid tales of murder and mutiny that they began to relate.

The charges lodged against the Africans would be murder and piracy. The case drew inordinate attention, not only from curiosity seekers but abolitionists, and the Africans' jailer soon began charging a fee to admit a long line of onlookers queuing to walk through the jail to gawk at the captives. Let out on the green to get fresh air and exercise and to regain their strength, the Africans attracted even more attention, which further increased when word got around of the Mende warriors' acrobatic athleticism as gymnasts.

A Yale linguist, Professor Josiah Gibbs, soon determined that Cinque and the majority of the men were Mende, and a search was raised in eastern ports for a sailor from the tribe who could serve as an interpreter. An Amistad Committee was formed by Lewis Tappan, a wealthy merchant, abolitionist, and founder in 1833 of the American Anti-Slavery Society. Tappan was joined by Joshua Leavitt and Simeon Jocelyn to raise money and secure legal representation for the defendants, and to provide the Africans with a tutor to teach them English.

Abolitionists saw in the case an opportunity to challenge the laws institutionalizing slavery in federal court. The whole of the Eastern Seaboard, and soon the nation, was following the case in the newspapers; the Africans of *La Amistad* and their chief, Cinque, offering the drama of a quest for freedom playing out in a federal venue, implicitly focusing readers on political ramifications for the "peculiar institution." Word spread that the Africans had not been slaves, and that they had been kidnapped in a country under the British dominion where the slave trade was outlawed; the men had rightly taken the first opportunity, it was seen, to resist, even to slay, their captors. Wouldn't any other free man do the same, and be justified?

James Covey, a Mende speaker, was found aboard a British vessel in New York harbor, and the trial was able to proceed. Having interviewed Cinque, John W. Barber, author of *History of the Amistad Captives, etc.*, wrote of the man's "uncommon decision and coolness, with a composure characteristic of true courage," describing Cinque as "a negro who would command in New Orleans, under the hammer, at least $1500" on the auction block. John Greenleaf Whittier wrote of the prisoner, "What a master spirit is his. What a soul for the tyrant to crush down in bondage."

Portraits of Cinque were soon being circulated, as were prints of a painting of *La Amistad* in anchorage off Long Island and of a drawing depicting the vessel during the revolt. Sketches of others among the *Amistad* captives were as well published, and the New York *Sun*, one of the new penny newspapers whose bargain price reflected the application of steam to the printing process, had an artist produce a full portrait of Cinque standing proudly on the deck of a ship dressed in sailor's pants and jersey, his hand gripping the cane knife he had used in the bid to secure freedom.

The administration of President Martin Van Buren, mindful of the impending 1840 election and of the need to maintain the support of slaveholders, pressed to see the case through to a conviction for murder and piracy. Spanish Queen Isabella II and her government had taken an interest too, although the case, in the U.S. government's view, was fraught with uncertainties. The British, as had the Americans and the Spanish, had outlawed the Atlantic slave trade decades before—Spain in 1820, the other two nations in 1807 and 1808—and the Africans being tried had manifestly been brought against their will to Cuba and sold into slavery. In Washington, Secretary of State John Forsyth consulted with cabinet colleagues, and all held that treaty obligations with Spain took precedence, requiring that the United States deliver the confiscated *Amistad* property, including the slaves, to Spanish authorities in Cuba. Forsyth directed the U.S. attorney in Connecticut to keep the captives in federal custody whatever the verdict and to be ready to transport the Africans.

At trial, speaking through interpreter James Covey but using powerful gesticulations, Cinque described his abduction in Africa, the frightful passage across the Atlantic, and the sale of the kidnapped Mende in a Havana slave market. On January 13, 1840, the judge found that the Cuban planters had no claim to the Africans, who were not property under Spanish law, the Atlantic slave trade having been abolished in Spanish territory. "If, by their own laws, they cannot enslave them, then it follows, of necessity, they cannot be demanded," he ruled. The Mende were free as far as Spain was concerned, but that status had not freed them from federal custody.

The ruling was appealed to the U.S. Supreme Court, where former president John Quincy Adams, now a congressman, represented the defense. On March 9, 1841, after an eight-and-a-half-hour argument, the Supreme Court ordered Cinque and the Mende freed. The Africans returned to Sierra Leone in 1842 on a chartered vessel paid for with funds raised by the Amistad Committee. In the interim between their acquittal and their return to Africa, the Mende were housed in Farmington, Connecticut, making fast friends among the inhabitants and turning many into staunch abolitionists. In subsequent years Farmington was to garner laurels as the central routing station on the Underground Railroad in Connecticut.

On the return trip with the Mende were two missionaries of the American Missionary Association, a body formed out of the Amistad Committee to combat "the sins of caste, polygamy and slave-holding." The Rev. James Pennington, then a resident of Hartford, presided over the missionary group.

So accustomed had the North become to the standing reality of slavery that the region had become numb to the malign institution's influence, John Brown had observed, even as slavery-related issues were becoming more and more entangled in the politics of the country. John Brown's wife was to remark to Franklin Sanborn that her husband never took an active part in nor cared about politics or parties after the presidency of Andrew Jackson (1829-1837), seeing as he did that the essential component on the national scene was in the actual collisions between slavery and freedom. In 1837 Lovejoy's murder had shocked Brown's sensibility, and the issue begun to turn in new ways in his mind. Then in 1838 Pennsylvania Hall in Philadelphia was burned, days after the wedding in that city of abolitionists Theodore Weld and Angelina Grimke, and soon after Marlborough Chapel in Boston was sacked, a scene at which W. E. B. Du Bois imputes John Brown may have been present and if so took part in battling the mob. That there could be peaceful emancipation in the United States was plainly being shown to be a fallacy; slaveholders would need to be compelled to emancipate, or abolition would not happen in the lifetime of those currently engaged in the project. John Brown had reached the point where he would become the bane of slavery.

Du Bois noted in his *John Brown*, published in 1909, "It was in 1839, when a Negro preacher named Fayette was visiting Brown, and bringing his story of persecution and injustice, that this great promise was made. Solemnly John Brown arose; he was then a man of nearly forty years, tall, dark and clean-shaven; by him sat his young wife of twenty-two and his oldest boys of eighteen, sixteen and fifteen. Six other children slept in the room back of the preacher. John Brown told them of his purpose to make active war on slavery, and bound his family in solemn and secret compact to labor for emancipation. And then, instead of remaining standing to pray, as was his wont, he fell upon his knees and implored God's blessing on his enterprise."[2]

Other Abolitionists too had come to see far-reaching sequelae for the *Amistad* case, the first ever held in a federal court to adjudicate issues arising from slavery. The case had offered a national exhibition in effect that would contribute to the radicalization of many, even outlasting the two decades yet to come before the Civil War; and the promise of offering assistance to the slave in attaining freedom—having been solemnly made—it was the duty and obligation of all embracing the proposition to see "the thing through." The forcible and complete emancipation of the bondsman was, in Brown's view, a matter of signature. In 1839, to him, *La Amistad* was heralding the beginning of the end for American slavery!

This promise had clearly arisen upon the contours of the then existing Underground Railroad, of which Brown would say he "never let an opportunity slip," and out of which had blossomed, as recorded in fugitive slave narratives, America's most characteristic claim to a "romance." As would be seen too in the following decade in America's most affecting works: Herman Melville's *Moby Dick*, published in

1852, and in *Uncle Tom's Cabin* by Harriet Beecher Stowe, published that same year, and in Walt Whitman's *Leaves of Grass*, first prepared for publication in 1855.

In 1858 in an essay titled *The Liberty Bell*, Thomas Wentworth Higginson would remark, "The romance of American history will of course be found by posterity in the lives of fugitive slaves." The ongoing flight of these fugitives from perpetual bondage in the South was bringing them to the attentions of a wider world, and their heroism had won them important allies, galvanizing the debate on the future of slavery in the republic. John Brown's eldest daughter Ruth is quoted in James Redpath's *The Public Life of Captain John Brown*, published in 1860, as saying of her father, "How often have I heard him speak in admiration of Cinques' [*sic*] character and management in carrying his points with so little bloodshed."[3] The escaping bondsmen's self-liberation too was introducing Blacks into free communities, and into their churches, organizations, and educational opportunities, raising up from among these new human arrivals a vitalized *Black* leadership whose presence effectively was redoubling the abolition cause.

It was not merely economic loss that the slaveholder feared, but the will of a people, however dire their present circumstances, to obtain free agency. John Brown saw that their education and organization would act like a "firing powder" against the rock of slavery;[4] it was only a matter of time before that rock would shatter. But Brown saw beyond this inevitability, recognizing above all that innate American inclination, as shown by the response to the *Amistad* case, and as we still see today, toward a national admiration for resistance to oppression. Thinking about what an effective campaign against slavery would be led him naturally to give his cherished scheme a thoroughly military grounding.

Countless observers have asked when John Brown began to take the first steps that would lead him onto the path culminating at Harper's Ferry. In 1858, in Kansas, a year before that event, in an extended talk with Richard J. Hinton, a future biographer, Brown said that for twenty years he had never made any business arrangement which would prevent him "at any time answering the call of the Lord. I have kept my affairs in such a condition that in two weeks I would wind them up and obey that call, permitting nothing to stand in the way of that call, neither wife, children or worldly goods."[5] This is the origin and significance of the years 1839 and 1859 for John Brown;

the cryptic reference, invoking as it did no other connection, indicates, it would seem, the continuing nature of that commitment.

In *Life and Times of Frederick Douglass*, Douglass begins his chapter entitled "John Brown and Mrs. Stowe" this way: "About the time I began my enterprise in Rochester I chanced to spend a night and a day under the roof of a man whose character and conversation, and whose objects and aims in life, made a very deep impression upon my mind and heart. His name had been mentioned to me by several prominent colored men, among whom were the Rev. Henry Highland Garnet and J.W. Loguen. In speaking of him their voices would drop to a whisper and what they said of him made me very eager to see and to know him. Fortunately, I was invited to see him in his own house."

Douglass indicates that he first met John Brown in 1847, without stating the exact date. In fact, it was only weeks after Douglass's return from his first tour of Great Britain, in 1845-47. Garnet and Loguen informed Douglass about an unusual White man they'd met among their brethren in Springfield, Massachusetts. Whether one or both personally conveyed an invitation from Brown to Douglass probably cannot now be known, but Douglass received such and lost no time in traveling to Springfield, arriving on May 15. Brown wrote to his eldest son on that date saying he was "in hourly expectation of a visit from [Douglass]."

Arriving at Perkins & Brown, where Brown conducted business, Douglass found and entered a substantial brick building on a prominent and busy street, giving him the impression that the man he'd come to see must be wealthy. After extending a cordial welcome, as the hours of business were ending, Brown conveyed his guest to his home.

Now Douglass confronted an entirely new set of perceptions—the house in which his host resided with his family was a small wooden structure on a back street, in a neighborhood chiefly occupied by laboring men and mechanics. Plain as the outside was, the inside, Douglass observed, was even plainer; "its furniture would have satisfied a Spartan." Still, his "welcome was all that I could have asked," he wrote. "Every member of the family, young and old, seemed glad to see me, and I was made much at home in a very little while." The meal prepared for him was a hearty beef soup with cabbage and potatoes, served by all the members of Brown's large family on a table of the plainest workmanship, a repast which "passed," Douglass remarked, "under the misnomer of tea." After the meal, the two men withdrew into the parlor where they engaged in discussion from eight that evening till three the next morning.

Apprehending opposition to his views, and knowledgeable of Douglass's rising importance and position as a notable "Garrisonian" abolitionist, Brown began cautiously. Holding the contrary view—namely that the liberty of the slave could not be accomplished by "moral suasion" alone, nor even by political action, as opponents of Garrison within the abolitionist movement were contending, Brown, Douglass wrote, "said that he had long had a plan which could accomplish this end, and he had invited me to his house to lay that plan before me." Brown remarked significantly that he had been for some time looking for colored men to whom he could safely confide, and at times he had almost despaired of finding such men, but that now he was encouraged, "for he saw heads of such rising up in all directions."

"He had observed my course at home and abroad, and he wanted my cooperation," Douglass wrote. "He was not averse to the shedding of blood," and "thought the practice of carrying arms would be a good one for the colored people to adopt." It would give them a sense of their manhood, for "no people," said Brown, "could have self-respect, or be respected, who would not fight for their freedom."

Du Bois wrote that this earlier scheme probably looked toward the use of Negro allies almost exclusively outside his own family. This was eminently fitting but impractical, as Douglass and his fellows must have urged. White men could move where they would in the United States, but to introduce an armed band exclusively or mainly of Negroes from the North into the South was difficult if not impossible. Nevertheless, some Negroes of the right type were needed and to John Brown's mind the Underground Railroad was bringing north the very material he required.[6]

Brown now drew Douglass's attention to a map of the United States, pointing out the far-flung Allegheny range, stretching from the border of New York into the remotest fastnesses of the Southern states; the Alleghenies' powerful ridges holding in turn New York, Pennsylvania, and Maryland, then sweeping into Virginia, North and South Carolina, and Georgia, and thrusting into Tennessee. "These mountains are the basis of my plan," said Brown. "God has given the strength of the hills to freedom; they were placed here for the emancipation of the Negro race; they are full of natural forts, where one man for defense will be equal to a hundred for attack; they are full also of good hiding-places, where large numbers of brave men could be concealed, and baffle and elude pursuit for a long time."

By that year Brown's proposal was to establish an armed force to act in the very heart of the South, and because of his plan's two components—the strategic thrust of the mountains and the manner in which the Black bonded population was distributed through these states—Brown felt they had the sanction of God.

The "plan" as Brown proposed it was "to take at first about twenty-five picked men, beginning on a small scale"—and supply them with arms and ammunition, posting them in squads of five on a line of twenty-five miles. The most persuasive and judicious of these were to go down to the fields from time to time "as opportunity offered, and induce the slaves to join them, seeking and selecting the most restless and daring."[7] These mountains, Brown said, afforded an excellent "pathway for a grand stampede from the Slave States, a grand exodus into the Free States, and through the latter, into Canada."[8]

"But," countered Douglass, "suppose you succeed in running off a few slaves, and thus impress the Virginia slaveholders with a sense of insecurity in their slaves, the effect will be only to make them sell their slaves further south." "That will be what I want first to do; then I would follow them up," Brown countered. "If we could drive slavery out of *one county*, it would be a great gain—it would weaken the system throughout the state."

"But they would employ bloodhounds to hunt you out of the mountains," Douglass suggested. "That they might attempt," Brown agreed, "but chances are, we should whip them, and when we should have whipped one squad, they would be careful how they pursued."

"But you might be surrounded and cut off from your provisions or means of subsistence." That could not be done, Brown maintained, so that they could not cut their way out.

"He often said to me though life was sweet to him, he would willingly lay it down for the freedom of my people," Douglass informed his audience in a speech he delivered at Harper's Ferry, West Virginia, on May 30, 1881, at the founding of Storer College. "And on one occasion he added, that he had already lived about as long as most men, since he had slept less, and if he should now lay down his life the loss would not be great, for in fact he knew no better use for it."[9]

In a similar vein, in *Life and Times*, Douglass cites Brown, saying, "I might have noticed the simple manner in which he lived," observing "that he had adopted this method in order to save money to carry out his purposes.... Had some men made such display of rigid virtue, I should have rejected it, as affected, false, and hypocritical, but in John Brown," Douglass wrote, "I felt it to be real as iron or granite."

"From this night, while I continued to write and speak against slavery," Douglass remarked significantly, "I became all the same less hopeful of its peaceful abolition. My utterances became more and more tinged by the color of this man's strong impressions."[10] "Speaking at an antislavery convention in Salem, Ohio," Douglass continues, "I expressed this apprehension that slavery could only be destroyed by bloodshed, when I was suddenly and sharply interrupted by my good old friend Sojourner Truth with the question, "Frederick, is God dead?" "No," I answered, "and because God is not dead slavery can only end in blood."

In 1851, while in Springfield, Massachusetts, among his new Black associates and amid the tribulations wrought by the newly enacted Fugitive Slave Law, Brown had formed an organization for the self-defense of fugitives, the so-called League of Gileadites. The name was drawn from the biblical injunction, "Whosoever is fearful or afraid, let him return and depart early from Mount Gilead"—a remote section of the ancient lands of the tribes of Israel, described in the Bible as pasturage set within a mountainous terrain whose people sought to preserve their ancient prophetic traditions against incursions by their enemies. The League's agreement and resolutions in John Brown's iteration of the injunction, with a letter of instructions on what to do in consequence of a fugitive slave's arrest, was signed by forty-four persons, all of them Black excepting Brown.

In "Words of Advice" to members, Brown wrote, "Nothing so charms the American people as personal bravery. Witness the case of Cinque, of everlasting memory, on board the 'Amistad.' The trial for life of one bold and to some extent successful man, for defending his rights in good earnest, would arouse more sympathy throughout the nation than the accumulated wrongs and suffering of more than three millions of our submissive colored population.... No jury can be found in the Northern States that would convict a man for defending his rights to the last extremity."[11]

Brown began his comprehensive study of the literature on insurrectionary and irregular warfare no later than 1840 if not before, but he assuredly would have had more time to devote himself to that effort from the middle of the decade on. His residence in Springfield brought him into extensive contact with the people for whom his vision of emancipation was intended; at the time about three hundred Blacks, most of them fugitive slaves, were living in the western Massachusetts town. Brown became immersed in their affairs during his several years of residence (1846-1851), visiting and confiding with them, hiring them in his business, and worshiping with them at the Sanford Street Church, where the Rev. John Mars was pastor. Situated at the top of the valley of the Connecticut River, Springfield was a regional center of the Underground Railroad, and Brown appeared in a well-known photograph taken during this time standing next to a flag decorated with the initials S.P.W., for "Subterranean Passage Way," the name of the route to which he was connected. With his right arm and hand raised and extended, he is shown in the gesture of a man solemnly taking an oath.

In summer 1859, as he sat in the kitchen at the Kennedy farm with his daughter and daughter-in-law at his elbows, Brown, and perhaps they in conversation with him, decided it appropriate to commemorate the twenty years he'd given in preparation, before engaging militarily in that struggle again. And in a gesture of consecration, someone inscribed the year that a beginning had been made twenty years before on a piece of paper inserted into the case of a newly bought timepiece. Discovered in a chest in Gouldtown, New Jersey, a century later by Becky Lively, and interpreted decades later by this author—that timepiece is testament to an historic avowal.

Chapter Three

"I WANT MY PROPERTY, AND I WILL HAVE IT!"

R EFLECTING ON WHAT WAR with Mexico would mean to the United States and to its citizens, Ralph Waldo Emerson wrote, "The United States will conquer Mexico, but it will be as the man swallows the arsenic, which brings him down in turn. Mexico will poison us all."[1]

When the treaty between the warring nations was signed at Guadalupe Hidalgo on September 14, 1847, concluding sixteen months of fighting, the nation at the north enlarged its territory by nearly one quarter, while the nation to the south shrank by nearly half. During the debate in Congress the previous year on an appropriations bill for the war, Pennsylvania representative David Wilmot had proposed an amendment "that, as an express and fundamental condition to the acquisition of any territory from the Republic of Mexico . . . neither slavery nor involuntary servitude shall ever exist in any part of said territory."

The words "Wilmot Proviso" would ripple like a banner over the presidential contest in 1848, as that phrase found voice on lips throughout the North and in the West. It was as if David Wilmot had struck Goliath as surely as did David of old. The House of Representatives twice passed his bill, which twice failed in the Senate. The tempest the proviso raised in the electoral competition the following year became a watershed for Frederick Douglass, just as his meeting with John Brown had the year before. Douglass underwent an evolution away from Garrisonian orthodoxy toward advocacy of "the ballot," instead orienting himself to stand in favor of forcible resistance as "the way to hem in, head-off and dam up the desolating tide of slavery." On June 10, 1848, he hailed the watershed moment in a column under the headline "Great Uprising of the North" in his *North Star*. "We look upon the Wilmot Proviso and its supporters as indications of the presence of a great principle in the national heart, which by patient cultivation will one day abolish forever our system of human bondage."

Out of this fervor came the Free-Soil Party, as the old Democrat and Whig parties split in nearly every Northern state. The Democratic National Convention that May had nominated the lusterless Lewis Cass of Michigan for president on a platform framed to appease the South, while Zachary Taylor, freshly laureled for service in the Mexican War, was nominated in June on the Whig ticket, without a platform, but, like the Democrats, repudiating the "Proviso."

Now Liberty Party adherents, "conscience" Whigs, "free-soil" Democrats, and New York "barnburners"—named for a Dutch farmer who burnt his barn to rid it of rats—landed together at Buffalo to form the Free-Soil Party, nominating Martin Van Buren on a rousing platform: "We declare that Congress has no more power to make a slave than to make a king.... We inscribe on our banner: 'FREE SOIL, FREE SPEECH, FREE LABOR, AND FREE MEN,' and under it will fight on, and fight ever, until a triumphant victory shall reward our exertions."

Douglass would avow that, in the political evolution of the North witnessed that year, anti-slavery agitation theretofore "had only been sheet-lightning" but "the Buffalo convention sought to make it a thunderbolt."[2] The presidential contest embroiled all politicians and parties in slavery issues, bringing Zachary Taylor into office. Born into a Virginia slaveholding family, he joined the early immigration to Kentucky and by the time of his presidency made his home in Baton Rouge, Louisiana, where he owned a Mississippi River plantation along with a hundred slaves. In the war with Mexico, Taylor won the heralded Battle of Buena Vista, opening "the road to the city of Mexico and the halls of Montezuma...."

As president, however, Taylor—whose preferred topic of conversation, it is said, was cotton—would not be a defender of Southern sectional interests. "Old Rough and Ready" was by then thoroughly an American nationalist. With controversy raging over the Wilmot Proviso, Taylor invited settlers in New Mexico and California to draft state constitutions, bypassing the territorial stage. Southern congressional leaders were furious, accusing the president of usurping their policy-making prerogative; the president's plan, said Jefferson Davis, was one "of concealing the Wilmot Proviso under a so-called state constitution."[3] While opponents on each side clamored to end slavery and the slave trade in Washington, D.C., or, alternately, on behalf of a more effective fugitive slave law, Southern leaders met in conference with the president in February 1850, threatening to secede. The president responded by declaring that if they did so he would personally lead the army against them, hanging persons in rebellion against the United States with less reluctance than he had hung deserters and spies in Mexico.

John Calhoun of South Carolina, Henry Clay of Kentucky, and Daniel Webster of Massachusetts for as much as four decades had dominated the U.S. political scene, and by the late 1840s constituted a powerful triumvirate in the U.S. Senate. Now they would meet in what would prove to be the last episode in each titan's storied career.

Clay had played a determining role in 1812 in the war with Britain, as he did in the formation of the American Colonization Society in 1816 and in the Missouri Compromise of 1820. Renowned under the moniker "Great Pacificator," he was regarded as the preeminent statesman of the West.

Calhoun had been the leading exponent of the Southern sectional position in general, and given his conviction that slavery was a "positive good" and as an upholder of "state's rights," he has been aptly described as having "cast iron rigidity." He was high-strung, with a severe countenance, not noted for possessing charisma. He had been a secretary of war, twice secretary of state, and is portrayed as stately and reserved. His theory of a "concurrent majority," whereby through the doctrine of nullification a state had a right "to interpose, in the last resort, in order to arrest an unconstitutional act of the General Government within its limits," was the last line in his defense of the South.

Daniel Webster too would appear in the role of secretary of state and was equally admired and an important member of this trio. A gifted orator, he was a lawyer, originally from New Hampshire, who had relocated to Boston, where he became closely identified with families having cotton-spinning interests in Lowell and Lawrence that had produced the wealth and ostentation with which Webster was enamored.

In the debate on the famous Compromise of 1850, each of the three would be delivering his final national performance in the Senate chamber, intended to resolve the issues raised by the Mexican cessions. Among these was seen to hang the fate of the nation—whether freedom or slavery was to be national. On January 29, 1850, Clay stepped before an expectant Senate to present a series of eight resolutions intended to "adjust amicably all existing questions of controversy . . . arising out of the institution of slavery." Paired to appeal to majorities on both sides of the issues, Clay's resolutions would be merely a prelude in a seven-month drama that sought ostensibly to safeguard the national union but would prove only a temporary adjustment, before the final debacle debuted with the election in 1860 of a Republican presidential candidate named Lincoln.

The first set of resolutions admitted California as a free state, with the remainder of the Mexican cession to enter the territorial stage without "any restriction or condition on the subject of slavery." The next settled a boundary dispute between Texas and New Mexico in favor of New Mexico, the federal government compensating Texas by assuming debts incurred during that state's interregnum as an independent republic. A third would abolish the slave trade in Washington, D.C., while guaranteeing the legitimacy of slavery in the capital. The final pairing resolved that Congress had no power over the interstate slave trade, while providing slaveholders with a more stringent fugitive slave law.

At the end of the first act, Calhoun was to set forth the South's position on Clay's resolutions. Too ill to deliver the speech himself, he remained seated silently by as his text was read by Virginia senator James Mason. Wracked by tuberculosis, emaciated and spectral, the gaunt Carolinian sat wrapped in black flannel, his piercing eyes staring from deep sockets as from within a shroud. Douglass later wrote, "The mighty man of slavery, [had been] found to be mightier in his silence than in his eloquence."[4]

Calhoun's speech asserted that equilibrium between the sections was destroyed. The admission of California as a free state and the abolition of the slave trade in the District of Columbia were not negotiable. The speech rehearsed a long litany of northern "aggressions";

the sovereignty of states was at issue. Three days later Calhoun was again in the Senate, a brooding presence as Daniel Webster delivered his famous March 7, 1850, speech. Enduring for three and a half hours, as the orator reached the final words of his text, Calhoun, wrote one of his biographers, "sat motionless . . . sweeping the chamber now and again with his deeply luminous eyes."[5] Webster, having opposed the Mexican War and supported the Wilmot Proviso, dealt at length in his speech with the premise that the northern states needed to break with the past and deliver up the fugitive slaves to the South. By the end of the speech everyone knew Webster's star had fallen; he could not now be re-elected.

On March 11, New York senator William Seward delivered his "Higher Law" speech. The crisis being addressed, Seward said, "embraces the fearful issue whether the Union shall stand, and slavery, under the steady, peaceful action of moral, social, and political causes, be removed by gradual voluntary effort, and with compensation; or whether the Union shall be dissolved and civil war ensue, bringing on violent but complete and immediate emancipation."

With the matter of Clay's resolutions in abeyance, on April 19 a committee of thirteen was selected with Clay as chairman and each senator, Whig and Democrat, chosen as representative of sectional interests, or because he sought to bridge that divide.

On March 31 Calhoun died. Zachary Taylor died unexpectedly on July 9, succeeded by Millard Fillmore. Webster resigned his Senate seat to become the new president's secretary of state. At the end of July, Henry Clay, ill with consumption, would withdraw for the sake of his health to Newport, Rhode Island.

The new president, sympathetic to the Compromise, bent toward the South as much as his predecessor had tipped toward the North. With Clay's "omnibus bill" defeated, for the final act Stephen A. Douglas occupied center stage as the Compromise of 1850 was reached. With the passing of the triumvirate, Douglas became the dominant figure in the Senate of the 1850s. Nicknamed the "Little Giant" because of his short stature, he was a tireless worker known as an adroit tactician.

As debate began in the previous January, on the floor of the Senate Virginia's James Mason had given notice he would introduce legislation to facilitate a "more effectual execution" of the Fugitive Slave Law enacted in 1793. The following day the bill was read, printed, and referred to the Judiciary Committee.

The bill had four sections. The first provided that the owner or his agent, after seizing a fugitive slave, could take the fugitive "before any judge of the circuit or district courts, or marshal thereof, or any postmaster . . . or collector of customs" within the state where the arrest was made. If satisfied as to the claim on the proof of the claimant, the officials were required to issue a certificate which would be "sufficient warrant for taking and removing such fugitive . . . to the State or Territory from which he or she had fled." The second section stipulated that upon proper application, a warrant would be issued to a federal marshal for the arrest of the fugitive slave. A third section mandated that anyone attempting to harbor, conceal, or rescue a fugitive would be liable to a fine of $1,000. The final section required that the officials enumerated in the first section would proceed as if the slave had been arrested by the owner or his agent in the same manner.

Frederick Douglass gave two years of intensive study and discussion to the issue of whether the U.S. Constitution was pro-slavery, a cardinal trope in the Garrisonian anti-slavery stock to which Douglass adhered. The first indication of this reevaluation appeared in the *North Star* on February 9, 1849, when he wrote, "On close examination of the Constitution, I am satisfied that if strictly construed according to its reading, it is not a pro-slavery instrument." Six weeks later he noted that if he could be convinced the Constitution was anti-slavery in its origins and purpose, he would be quick to use the ballot box, but he still harbored doubt. In a careful and systematic way Douglass arrived at the view espoused by Gerrit Smith and William Goodell, to wit, that in its preamble the Constitution was anti-slavery, its object being to establish "a more perfect union," "promote the general welfare, and secure the blessings of liberty." He now repudiated Garrison's notion of dissolution of the Union on the grounds that a northern secession would deny slaves their most important allies and isolate them, leaving them at the mercy of their masters. Instead of "No Union with Slaveholders," Douglass would say, "No Union with Slaveholding."

This change of creed did not become public until 1851. Informing Stephen S. Foster and Samuel J. May of his new stance, Douglass then informed Gerrit Smith in a letter dated May 21, 1851. Douglass began his journey of conversion to a radical abolitionist as a result of his own identifiable and significant outreaching of thought and activity, but under extraneous guidance. In the *North Star* of February 11,

1848, he noted his "private interview" with John Brown of Springfield, Massachusetts. "Though a white gentleman," he wrote, Brown was "in sympathy a black man, and as deeply interested in our cause, as though his own soul had been pierced with the iron of slavery." Douglass would never deviate from this view throughout his twelve-year alliance with Brown and reported significantly of his first meeting with him that Brown had expressed joy at the appearance of Black men "possessing the energy of head and heart to demand freedom for their whole people." The result "must be the downfall of slavery."[6]

Another of those having a marked influence on Douglass's evolution was the Englishwoman, Julia Griffiths. Douglass, the *North Star* failing, had been compelled to mortgage his home. In March 1850, Griffiths took charge of the finances of Douglass's paper, devoting almost all her time for nearly eight years to its interests. A skilled editor with a flair for journalism and promotion, she was Douglass's closest associate and intimate during these years, as he was in every sense her eager apprentice and ready confidant.

Five hundred persons filed into City Hall in Syracuse, New York, on October 4, 1850, to protest the just enacted Fugitive Slave Law. The mayor presiding, the Rev. Samuel Ringgold Ward led off on the rostrum; up next was the Rev. J.W. Loguen to propose that Syracuse be made an "open city" for fugitive slaves. Thundering defiance, Loguen declared, "Your decision tonight in favor of resistance will give vent to the spirit of liberty, and it will break the bands of party, and shout for joy all over the north. . . . Heaven knows that this act of noble daring will break out somewhere—and may God grant that Syracuse be the honored spot."[7]

On October 14 a similar meeting drew hundreds to assemble in protest at Boston's Faneuil Hall. Charles Francis Adams presided over the gathering, at which, among others, Wendell Phillips and Theodore Parker spoke, as did Frederick Douglass. Parker vowed to do all in his power "to rescue any fugitive from the hands of any officer who attempts to return him to bondage. . . . What is a fine of a thousand dollars and gaoling for six months to the liberty of a man?"[8]

Meetings of indignation and protest also convened in Worcester, Massachusetts, and in Ohio's Western Reserve. In Chicago, the Common Council voted 10-3 to condemn the law as "revolting to our moral sense, and an outrage upon our feeling of justice and humanity," and pledged not "to aid or assist in the arrest of Fugitives from oppression." Illinois senator Stephen Douglas took the immediate action of persuading the council to rescind its vote; but this did nothing to allay sentiment against the law.[9]

In a letter to his wife dated November 28, 1850, John Brown wrote from Springfield regarding the measure's passage: "It now seems that the Fugitive Slave Law was to be the means of making more Abolitionists than all the lectures we have had for years. It really looks as if God had His hand on this wickedness also. I of course keep encouraging my colored friends to 'trust in God and Keep their powder dry.' I did so to-day at Thanksgiving meeting publicly."

Writing to his wife on December 22, 1851, from Boston, Brown alluded to the international context in which his keen eye was discerning events then playing out. In that correspondence, he appraised the European revolutions of 1848-49 and their reverberations in the United States. Brown's commentary indicates the breadth and tenor of husband and wife in their private consultation and solicitousness, indicative of his view on the equality of the sexes: "There is an unusual amount of very interesting things happening in this and other countries at present, and no one can foresee what is yet to follow. The great excitement produced by the coming of Kossuth, and the last news of a new revolution in France, with the prospect that all Europe will soon again be in blaze seem to have taken all by surprise. I have only to say in regard to these things that I rejoice in them from the full belief that God is carrying out his eternal purpose in them all. . . ."

The Hungarian Revolution of 1848 had been one of numerous uprisings closely linked throughout Europe during a year that saw France, Italy, the various states of Germany, and the Hapsburg Empire caught in the throes of the fight for liberty and for parliamentary government. When news of the February Revolution in France reached Hungary, a province of the Habsburg Empire, Louis Kossuth in a stirring speech given in German demanded parliamentary government for his nation. The speech became an item in the agitation of students in Vienna, helping precipitate the fall of Austrian interior minister Klemens von Metternich. Establishing a government, Kossuth was defeated in the following year and fled into exile; reaching Turkey, he was imprisoned. In a March 1850 resolution Congress asked President Taylor to intercede and bring Kossuth to the United States. The intercession succeeded. Disembarking from the U.S. Navy frigate *Mississippi* at Gibraltar, Kossuth would tour England before arriving in New York on December 4, 1851. He was to receive a tremendous reception, particularly among newly emigrating Germans, as

"Magyar-mania"—Hungarians are also known as Magyars—spread like a contagion across the country in the winter of 1851-52. Here was a liberator and worker in the cause of universal emancipation! On December 6, Kossuth was given a monster reception in New York City; President Fillmore received him at the executive mansion on January 5, and he would address a joint session of Congress. Feted at banquets and receptions in Philadelphia and Baltimore, Kossuth toured New England, the South, and the Midwest, giving six hundred speeches—a tour which was, Edmund Quincy Adams wrote, "one continual Festival." In his honor, many in his audiences were donning "Kossuth hats," a display of public enthusiasm paralleling that accorded the Marquis de Lafayette decades earlier.

Kossuth, however, took great care to demur on the issue of slavery, saying he wished to escape "entanglements." Five days after his arrival he had met with a reception committee on behalf of the "Negro people," and was addressed by George T. Downing. "May you, when you leave our shores," the address declared, "in furtherance of your heaven-high mission, carry with you the sympathy of *all*, the active countenance of *all*."[10] Garrison and the American Anti-Slavery Society produced a stirring *Letter to Louis Kossuth* published as a 112-page pamphlet. Douglass urged in a column that Kossuth not be blind to "the lineaments of our national face."[11] But Kossuth could not be dissuaded from his professed "neutrality."

The tidings reported by Brown of a "new revolution in France" had proved to be the *coup d'etat* of Louis Bonaparte, or the "little Napoleon," not yet fully appreciated in its implications. But the deleterious effect of the Fugitive Slave Law's enactment was soon to be evident in the United States, as a fugitive named James Hamlet was arrested in New York City in December 1850, and ordered remanded to slavery at government expense. Days later at Harrisburg, Pennsylvania, two more fugitives were taken and remanded to slavery, while to the west in Bedford, Pennsylvania, eight fugitives were seized and returned without due process. In the following days Blacks were seized in Detroit and in Philadelphia but released. Then three fugitives were seized to be remanded in Quincy, Illinois, followed by three more in New Albany, Indiana. Before another week was out another fugitive would be arrested in Marion, Illinois.[12]

With these inauspicious tidings as a backdrop, in early January 1851 in New York City Henry Long was arrested and taken to a federal commissioner for a hearing. With Long's identity quickly ascertained, he was remanded to the custody of a federal marshal who delivered the "slave" to Alexandria, Virginia. Long was subsequently sold in a Richmond slave market to a trader from Atlanta, Georgia, who posted a $3,000 bond stipulating that he would sell the slave farther south.

Then on February 15, Boston papers reported that a fugitive had been arrested and was being held at the jail for arraignment. The case of Frederick Minkins, or "Shadrach," was the first in a series of challenges to the Fugitive Slave Law that "brought odium upon" that measure and all those who attempted to enforce it, in effect rendering the Fugitive Slave Law, as Douglass put it, "a dead letter."

Shadrach had escaped in May 1850 from the "service" of John Debree of Norfolk, Virginia, a purser in the U.S. Navy. Arriving in Boston Shadrach found employment as a waiter at the Cornhill Coffee House. Hearing of his whereabouts, his "owner" made out an affidavit in a Virginia court and sent an agent to secure the rendition of his slave. A warrant was issued and the fugitive arrested.

At the fugitive's appearance in court, his defense appealed for a delay to prepare his case. The delay was granted. Seated between two constables, the constables waited with their prisoner, as the court was cleared. Thomas Wentworth Higginson recalled the scene in his memoir *Cheerful Yesterdays*, published in 1898. "The fact was noted in a newspaper by a colored man of great energy and character," Higginson wrote. Asking leave from his employer, the fellow hurried to the courthouse at whose doors many Blacks were seen milling. Known to those working in the court, the man in question assumed an air of frivolity, strolling into the courtroom where Shadrach was seated unshackled, with others spontaneously falling in behind him. "There were but constables on duty," Higginson wrote, "and it suddenly struck him, as he and his followers passed near the man under arrest, that they might as well continue on and pass out of the courtroom by way of the opposite door, taking among them the man under arrest but unfettered." After a moment's beckoning, the prisoner saw his opportunity, fell in with the jubilant procession, and amid continued uproar was gotten outside the courthouse whereupon the crowd scattered in all directions.[13] Richard H. Dana, the attorney for Minkins, had just returned to his office across from the court, from whose window he witnessed the episode. "[W]e heard a shout from the Court House, continued into a yell of triumph, & in an instant after, down the steps came two huge negroes, bearing the prisoner between them, with his clothes half torn off, & so stupefied by the sudden rescue and the violence of his dragging off, that he sat almost down, & I thought had fainted," Dana wrote in his diary. "... they went off toward Cambridge, like a black squall, the crowd driving along with them & cheering as they went."[14]

No one had been injured in the rescue, which apparently had momentarily shaken Shadrach, but the "sword of justice" that the commissioner displayed on his desk was carried off by one among the rescuers, said to be an elderly man.[15] There were to be no arrests; a hundred or so Black men were said to have scattered thereafter, and were not to be seen around Boston for a period of time. This hurried, even slapdash display was treated in Washington as if it were a political earthquake. President Fillmore issued a proclamation calling upon all citizens and officials "in the vicinity of this outrage, to aid and assist in quelling this and other such combinations."[16] Professing consternation because the rescue had been carried out by a "band who are not of our people," Henry Clay introduced a resolution in the Senate requesting that the president disclose full information about the affair. Secretary of State Daniel Webster, in a letter to business leaders in New York forming the Union Safety Committee, said the incident constituted "strictly speaking a case of treason."

Eight persons were indicted in the Shadrach case; there were no convictions due to hung juries.

Commenting many years later in *Life and Times* on the effect of the Fugitive Slave Law on people exposed by its enforcement, Douglass wrote, "Fugitive slaves who had lived for many years safely and securely in western New York and elsewhere, some of whom had by industry and economy saved money and bought little homes for themselves and their children, were suddenly alarmed and compelled to flee to Canada for safety as from an enemy's land—a doomed city."[17] Douglass noted that even his "old friend" Samuel Ringgold Ward "found it necessary to make off to Canada, and thousands were following his example."

Now there began a "refugee march," particularly among fugitive slaves residing on routes along which they had been deposited for years by the Underground Railroad. Many escaping Blacks now were purchasing tickets on actual railroads, in many places helped by abolition societies and vigilance committees contributing toward their fare. Whole families, determined not to be taken, bundled their meager belongings as large groups armed with pistols and bowie knives trekked through the country northward. It has been estimated that nearly 3,000 fugitives relocated to Canada within three months of the law's enactment. Nearly all the Black waiters employed in Pittsburgh hotels fled to Canada, an estimated three hundred taking flight from that city only ten days after the president signed the bill.[18] Black church congregations in Rochester and Buffalo and other border towns saw the preponderance of their members flee, reducing occupancy in pews in some instances from hundreds to a handful.

The next case to attract public interest concerned Thomas Sims. "A spruce-looking" seventeen-year-old, Sims had absconded from Chatham County, Georgia. Arriving in Boston in March 1851, he found work as a waiter but was closely followed by his master, who had heard his slave had stowed away on a Boston-bound vessel. On April 4 Sims was arrested, and his hearing scheduled for April 11 in a courthouse now cordoned in heavy chain and rope. The *Boston Courier* reported the additional presence within of "a large posse of police officers," as a detachment of soldiers stood without.

Summoned from his home in Newburyport to join in the consultations of the Vigilance Committee at the *Liberator*'s office, Higginson wrote later in *Cheerful Yesterdays*, "It is impossible to conceive of a set of men, personably admirable, yet less fitted on the whole than this committee to undertake any positive action in the direction of forcible resistance to authorities." In the first place, half of them were non-resistants. Others on the committee, being political abolitionists or "free-soilers," had insuperable reasons not to wish to appear unfit as citizens. Remarking on the state of indecision at the meeting, Higginson observed that at least the Blacks had proved their mettle, and doubtless would do so again. To which the former Kentuckian Lewis Hayden nodded cordially, "Of course they will."[19]

Without having settled on a plan, the meeting had adjourned when Hayden drew Higginson aside, startling him. "I said that for bluff, you know," said Hayden. "We do not wish anyone to know how really weak we are. Practically there are no colored men in Boston; the Shadrach prosecutions have scattered them all. What is to be done must be done without them."

Given all the precautions and preparations at the courthouse, and the overwhelming force in favor of the authorities, resistance was futile. Escorted by three hundred deputized police and United States Army soldiers to the wharf before dawn, Sims boarded the navy brig *Acorn* for Savannah, Georgia. Soon he was standing on an auction block in Charleston's Slave Mart and being sold to a New Orleans trader, then to an owner in Vicksburg, Mississippi. Sims survived, and was free again by summer 1863, when General Ulysses Grant wrote out a pass authorizing his use of government transportation back to Boston.

On April 16 President Fillmore wrote his Secretary of State, "I congratulate you and the country upon a triumph of law in Boston. She has done nobly. She has wiped out the stain of the former rescue and freed herself from the reproach of nullification."[20]

That spring, Daniel Webster, accompanied by the president, embarked on a campaign across the North to carry the message of the administration. In a swing through the northern tier of New York starting at Albany, Webster said that resolutions recently passed by conventions in Ohio, New York, and Massachusetts excoriating the law were "distinctly treasonable" and the rescue of Minkins "was an act of clear treason . . . [it was] levying war against the Union." In Syracuse, standing on a balcony across from City Hall, in a signal toward events and showing the administration's desire for high level prosecutions, Webster vowed that the Fugitive Slave Law would be enforced "here in Syracuse in the midst of the next anti-slavery convention, if the occasion shall arise."[21]

Enforcement of the Fugitive Slave Law continued unabated. On May 21, from Harrisburg, Pennsylvania, three fugitives were remanded by federal tribunal at government expense. They were Daniel, Ally, and Carolina Franklin by name. Then Elizabeth Williams was taken in West Chester, Pennsylvania, and remanded by a federal tribunal, followed in July by eighteen fugitives taken in one sweep in New Athens, Ohio, and returned without due process.

On July 26 at Lancaster, Pennsylvania, Daniel Hawkins was taken to be remanded at government expense, followed by William Smith at Harrisburg and Daniel Davis at Buffalo, and on August 26, by John Bolding at Poughkeepsie, New York. [22]

On September 11, 1851, in the pre-dawn hours a slaveholding farmer from Maryland, Edward Gorsuch, arrived outside the home of William Parker near Christiana, Pennsylvania, together with a U.S. marshal and his deputy and a posse of six other men, two of them his sons, and one a neighbor of his, a doctor. They carried warrants for the arrest of four of Gorsuch's fugitive "servants."

A fugitive from Maryland himself, Parker had come to the central Pennsylvania district with his brother in 1839 to make a life and raise a family. William Parker had risen into leadership of Blacks in the area, forming an "organization for mutual protection." Forewarned of the posse by a messenger sent by William Still, Parker reported in an article, "The Freedman's Story," published in the February 1866 *Atlantic Monthly*, that the warning "spread through the vicinity like a fire in the prairies." Inside the home were his wife Eliza, his brother-in-law and his wife, another man, and two of Gorsuch's fugitives—all anxiously apprehensive, but determined to resist arrest.

With the marshal, Gorsuch—whose family dated from the colonial era in Maryland and who was well-known among his class—invaded the house. Insisting the fugitives give up, Gorsuch called on "his men" in the upper rooms to surrender peacefully.

Standing on the stairs, with the sound of guns being loaded behind him, Parker demanded, "Who are you?"

"I am the United States Marshal."

"Take another step, and I'll break your neck," Parker warned.

"Yes," the marshal said. "I have heard a negro talk as big as you, and then have taken him; and I'll take you."

"You have not taken me yet, and if you undertake it you will have your name recorded in history for this day's work."[23]

So that there might be no misunderstanding, the marshal read the warrant aloud, but to no effect. With the marshal threatening to burn the house down unless there was compliance, Eliza Parker blew a horn from the garret window. "It was a custom with us, when a horn was blown at an unusual hour," Parker wrote, "to proceed to the spot promptly to see what was the matter."[24] Sounding the horn again, Eliza was fired upon from multiple pistols, none of the shots hitting her as she withdrew from the well of the window where she stood.

Now beside himself, Gorsuch declared, "I want my property, and I will have it." The marshal, who had gone outside, fired a shot at Parker through a window, shattering the glass. Parker returned fire, grazing Gorsuch's shoulder.

In a momentary lull, an exasperated Gorsuch again called out, "I want my property and I will have it." The marshal, pretending to be writing a note to the sheriff in Lancaster, bluffed in a loud voice to one of his men that there would soon be one hundred reinforcements on hand.

With the sun now well up, news that kidnappers had surrounded Parker's house was spreading through adjacent fields. Men, many of them Quakers, dropped their tools and hastened to the site. Leavening the spirits of those in the house, an even more salutary influence began showing up, as Blacks summoned by Eliza's horn were seen coming out of the woods and across the fields—among them two of the Gorsuch fugitives—and those not carrying firearms were carrying any weapon at hand: stones, scythes, corn-cutters, rails, pitchforks.

With Gorsuch threatening Parker, who now stood in his doorway with the others crowded behind him, and with the armed Black men arriving, the marshal saw the wisdom of discretion. As he "hallooed" his men to move off, the fighting resumed. Gorsuch, struck with a club, fell to his hands and knees. Raising a pistol, one of Gorsuch's sons was clubbed and shot in the side. As Gorsuch rose to his feet, he declared with a "calm and stern" look, "My property is here, and I will have it or perish in the attempt."[25]

Gorsuch was knocked down by one of his own slaves, and as he got to his feet was felled again; the antagonists clubbing opponents with their weapons as soon as they were discharged. Holding his pistols to the last, Gorsuch was beaten down by his own man, who "bent his gun" in subduing him. Edward Gorsuch lay in his own blood, flies buzzing around his corpse, as the marshal and his posse retreated.

Parker and three Christiana Resisters soon fled on foot. Author R.C. Smedley, drawing on the records, conveyed a sense of the underground in action in his *History of the Underground Railroad in Chester and Neighboring Counties of Pennsylvania*, published in 1883, setting out the routes and the individuals aiding in the escape of the *Christiana Resisters*.

Two White women, Elizabeth Coates and Ann Preston, drove up in broad daylight in a "well-covered" dearborn carriage and conveyed the fugitives to the home of James H. Taylor in West Marlborough. Taylor then drove them in his own conveyance to the home of Isaac and Dinah Mendenhall in Kennett township.

There, the four men slept in a barn, and the next day husked corn as if they were regular hands. They continued in this manner until word arrived that they were no longer safe, when Dr. Bartholomew Fussel, a resident of nearby Hammonton, came to retrieve them. Fussel transported the fugitives to the residence of his niece, Graceanna Lewis, and her two sisters near Kimberton in Chester County, a home "always open to fugitives," where they arrived about midnight.

Secreted in a third-floor room whose door locked from the inside, the men were told not to unlock it unless hearing a specified signal. Meanwhile, fearing a girl staying in the house would become suspicious if alerted by the preparation of inordinate amounts of food at a late hour, the sisters obtained food from a neighbor.

The following day J. Pierce West drove the refugees to the house of a friend a mile or more outside Phoenixville. After dark Pierce and his brother drove the fugitive men six miles past Downingtown. It was by then September 13, two days after the men had set out.

With Philadelphia in uproar over the affair, it was decided they must continue by way of Norristown, which they accomplished on foot.

After a day's rest at the home of Dr. Jacob L Paxson, a faith healer, they took shelter in a carpentry mill under wood shavings piled three feet deep; food was passed to the men using an oven peel held across a four-foot alley from the adjacent home of a Black man. During this time U.S. marshals were watching every part of town, and so a plan of escape was devised that involved hiring five wagons, each to leave that evening, four to be sent out from the mill as decoys.

After the decoy wagons rolled out, occupying the marshals' attention, the four fugitives came out of hiding. Shaving and arranging their clothes so as to be as presentable as possible, they walked to the home of William Lewis, a Black man, where the fifth wagon waited, and were driven down the road to Quakertown. On September 16, they arrived at the home of Richard Moore. After a brief rest, all set out again on an overnight journey, bedding down late under hay mows.

On September 17, all took breakfast in a country inn on the road to Wind Gap. Continuing in a hired transport—the driver, when asked his charge, readily answered, "One dollar and fifty cents." Their destination was the home of John Thomas.

Arriving in Wind Gap but not having the address of or directions for Thomas's home, Parker went to the post office and asked for a letter for John Thomas. There was no letter, said the clerk, but Parker obtained directions to the house from the postmaster.

On September 18, the men again stopped at a country inn, had their supper "politely served," and got a night's rest. Reaching Tannersville, they caught a train to Homerville and afterward rode a stagecoach to Big Eddy.

There they would have recourse to the "lightning" cars, and tickets were purchased through to Rochester.[26] Arriving at 9 a.m. September 20, they walked some three blocks from the station, encountering a "colored man" who readily guided them to the domicile of Frederick Douglass on the outskirts of town.

Douglass described the occasion in *Life and Times*: "The hours they spent at my house were . . . hours of anxiety as well as activity. I dispatched my friend Miss Julia Griffiths to the landing three miles away on the Genesee River to ascertain if a steamer would leave that night for any port in Canada, and remained at home myself to guard my tired, dust-covered, and sleeping guests, for they had been harassed and traveling for two days and nights, and needed rest. Happily for us the suspense was not long, for it turned out that that night a steamer was to leave for Toronto, Canada."

When the hour came, Douglass put the men in his carriage and started for the landing. Arriving fifteen minutes before departure, Douglass remained on board until the order to haul in the gangplank was given. Shaking hands with Parker and the others, Douglass "received from Parker the revolver that fell from the hand of Gorsuch when he died, presented now as a token of gratitude and a memento of the battle for liberty at Christiana."[27]

On September 15, deputy marshal William Kline went before the Christiana justice of the peace to begin proceedings against the resisters. Thirty-seven Blacks were charged, along with four Whites, with "aiding and abetting in the murder of Edward Gorsuch." Warrants were written out, with two of the accused, Castner Hanway and Elijah Lewis, both Quakers, turning themselves in upon hearing they were to be arrested.

On October 13 the Lancaster district attorney was in Christiana with a "strong party of armed men"; Kline too was there with a detachment of Philadelphia police. The U.S. District Attorney from Philadelphia had also arrived with U.S. fugitive slave commissioner Edward Ingraham and forty-five U.S. Marines from the Philadelphia Navy Yard, as had a lawyer representing the Gorsuch family with a posse of armed volunteers from Maryland. Once assembled, parties of men soon began to "scour the country" for participants in the resistance.[28] Pennsylvania's governor issued a proclamation offering a $1,000 reward for the capture and conviction of the guilty parties, while Maryland's governor wrote an open letter to President Fillmore calling for action in the case, with "the fullest retribution upon the criminals."

An eyewitness, the abolitionist C.M. Burleigh, stated he saw Black people "hunted like partridges upon the mountains" by a "relentless horde" of Whites.[29] Another witness, schoolmaster Francis Lennox, met a number of marines billeted at the Red Lion Hotel and asked what they were doing. "We are going to arrest every nigger and damned abolitionist," was the reply. And sure enough, this witness stated, the marines arrested "every colored man, boy and girl that they could find."[30]

In the days following Gorsuch's slaying the press in North and South carried conflicting editorial statements. The moderate view in both sections still professed that the controversy around the Fugitive Slave Law and the "Compromise" could be adjusted within the Union, with many on both sides holding that the resisters should be promptly tried and severely punished. But many also advocated for punishment reaching beyond the mere actors in the crime to reach the "pestilent agitators," as the Washington, D.C., *Republic* asked September 15, "who had caused the resistance." If these perpetrators were not punished, papers from Louisiana to Florida warned, disunion would be the only remedy. On September 18, the Jacksonville *Floridian and Journal* opined, "Are such assassinations to be repeated? If so, the sword of Civil War is already unsheathed."

Meanwhile on September 20 in Boston the *Christian Register* declared, "All the natural rights and claims and apologies are on the fugitive's side." As the New York *Tribune* had remarked September 15 that while its editors were "deeply shocked at the blood shed . . . we cannot hold the negroes guilty of the crime of murder." They had defended "an inalienable right . . . to their own persons." The *National Anti-Slavery Standard* was even more outspoken on September 25: "That Gorsuch should have been shot down like a dog seems to us the most natural thing in the world. . . ."

Many of the Blacks arrested and found fit to be held for trial were shipped to Philadelphia "in a cattle car" and incarcerated in the Moyamensing jail, a badly heated and airless facility, just as winter was approaching, one of the inmates consequently dying from a lung condition.

In Baltimore on September 15 an indignation meeting drew 6,000 persons to Monument Square, where speakers called the Christiana "riot" an abuse against the "constitutional rights of every Southern man." Philadelphia's Independence Hall drew a strident mass meeting outside that building two days later on a promise "to ferret out and punish the murders."[31] Philadelphia had the largest amount of southern trade of any northern city, and its merchant class was incensed, as "interwoven with it were large business interests throughout the entire Commonwealth." Some speakers argued that Blacks henceforth should be prevented from settling in Pennsylvania and that "Utopian Philanthropists and insane fanatics" had just seen their doctrines exemplified "in treason and blood" at Christiana."[32]

As news of the incident flashed across the wires to Washington, the U.S. Attorney for Philadelphia was summoned to a meeting with President Fillmore, Secretary of State Webster, and Attorney General John Crittenden at which it was decided defendants prosecuted in the case would be charged with treason and murder. Maryland's authorities had been clamoring for "the most complete vindication of the laws and the fullest retribution upon the criminals." If this was not done, the state's governor had avowed, the sooner the Union was dissolved the better. The president and his top advisors were unanimous; although they conceded it was quite possible the defendants would win acquittal, the cost to defendants of fighting the prosecutions would have the beneficial effect of deterring others from taking a similar course.

On November 13 indictments were brought against forty-one men, thirty-six Black and five White. The case against Castner Hanway, whom Kline alleged counseled the resisters to fire on Gorsuch, was the only one to be brought to trial, with an able defense conducted by abolitionist Thaddeus Stevens, congressional representative for Lancaster County. Upon Hanway's acquittal, charges against all other defendants were dropped.

When Secretary of State Webster stood in the spring on the balcony at City Hall in Syracuse, he had vowed to enforce the Fugitive Slave Law even as an anti-slavery convention was taking place. At noon on October 1, months after Webster had made his vow, the Liberty Party staged its statewide convention at the First Congregational Church on East Genesee Street in Syracuse; the same day in that city police led by federal marshal Henry Allen entered Morrell's cooperage to arrest one of the firm's employees, a Black man named William Henry known locally as "Jerry." He was told his arrest was for theft; Daniel Webster had now obtained the precedent he sought.

Jerry had absconded from the service of John McReynolds of Marion County, Missouri, and had settled about a year previous in Syracuse. Brought before commissioner Joseph Sabine, he now learned he'd not been arrested for theft but as a fugitive slave. On hearing this, Jerry began to put up a considerable fight and was subdued and heavily manacled.

As the inquiry began, a large and indignant crowd gathered outside the commissioner's office, while church bells tolled, summoning Liberty Party conventioneers. Several lawyers soon offered themselves as Jerry's counsel, objecting to his appearing before the court in irons.

The commissioner ordered the restraints removed. As the court was about to adjourn for lunch, a group of men, led by a thick-set Black man who worked as an iron-maker, impatient of further delay, rushed the commissioner's office. These interlopers seized the fugitive and hustled him onto the street, then across a bridge over the Erie Canal to a waiting conveyance. Overtaken there by police, Jerry was again heavily manacled, then driven in a wagon to the city jail under heavy escort to await the resumption of the hearing that afternoon.

With the Liberty Party meeting temporarily adjourned, participants met at the office of Dr. Hiram Hoyt to devise a plan of rescue. While no plan other than a forcible seizure of the detained was determined, all were resolved to secure Jerry's freedom at all costs. The leading figures in this meeting were Gerrit Smith, Samuel May, C.A. Wheaton, and the Rev. Jermain W. Loguen.

As evening set in, the crowd outside the commissioner's office was becoming more agitated as it grew larger with each passing hour, while Marshal Henry Allen, assisted by the marshals of Auburn, Canandaigua, and Rochester, maintained custody of the fugitive. The crowd in the streets was now overflowing; in addition to the Liberty Party meeting, the county fair was taking place; soon there were many people both for and against the process standing outside. Would-be rescuers were intent on forcing the door of the commissioner's office, and the tools for doing so, and even for removing brick if needed, had been placed outside Wheaton's nearby hardware store. But without recourse to these implements, many had determined the moment for action had come. The doors were now forced open by strong arms and Jerry was forthwith removed from the custody of those attending him. Spirited away in a wagon, he would remain in hiding for several days in Syracuse, before being driven to a landing on Lake Ontario to sail to Kingston, Ontario.

As tempers momentarily cooled, a well-earned triumphalism settled upon those responsible for Jerry's deliverance. In a speech two weeks later, Samuel May said there had really been no plan other than seizing the fugitive and would only say "indignation flashed from every eye." Notables in the crowd that freed William Henry included the Reverends Loguen, Samuel Ringgold Ward, and Samuel May, as well as Gerrit Smith and Charles Wheaton, among others.

When the Liberty Party reconvened the day after the successful rescue, Gerrit Smith introduced a resolution which passed and which read, "Whereas, Daniel Webster, that base and infamous enemy of the human race, did in a speech of which he delivered himself in Syracuse last Spring, exultingly and insultingly predict that fugitive slaves would yet be taken away from Syracuse and even from anti-slavery conventions in Syracuse, and whereas the attempt to fulfill this prediction was delayed until the first day of October, 1851, when the Liberty party of the State of New York were holding their annual convention in Syracuse; and whereas the attempt was defeated by the mighty uprising of 2,500 brave men, before whom the half-dozen kidnappers were 'as tow,' therefore, RESOLVED, that we rejoice that the city of Syracuse—the anti-slavery city of Syracuse—the city of anti-slavery conventions, our beloved and glorious city of Syracuse—still remains undisgraced by the fulfillment of the satanic Daniel Webster."[33]

Another notable present at the "Jerry rescue" but rarely credited with having been there—a presence occasioned by the Liberty Party meeting and his wish to be on hand when Webster attempted to fulfill his promise—was John Brown. Hearing of Loguen's avowal to make Syracuse a "free city," Brown had come to the convention determined, he said, that when he saw Loguen he would clasp his hand so tightly he'd nearly make it snap.[34]

The district attorney attempted to make a case of constructive treason against Smith, May, Wheaton, and five other defendants, and hoped to add sixteen others to the list for aiding and abetting the escape of a fugitive slave. But, for lack of evidence because the alleged offense occurred amid such hubbub and confusion, the district court refused to indict. A federal grand jury in Buffalo did bring charges against twenty-six individuals, not for treason but for being "engaged in the Syracuse riots." All these ended in acquittals after an ordeal of two years, except for one man whose appeal could not be heard because he had died. Loguen fled for a time to Canada; Samuel Ringgold Ward and his wife, too, became refugees, choosing to live thereafter in the Queen's Dominion.

That previous September, Ward had been on an anti-slavery tour of the Midwest and North speaking at abolitionist meetings about the Fugitive Slave Law. He and his wife, while in Ohio, read an account in the papers of the "Gorsuch case in Christiana." Alarmed and outraged by the wholesale arrest of Blacks in the area and the prosecutions brought by the government, Ward wrote, "Upon reading this, I handed the paper containing the account to my wife; and we concluded that resistance was fruitless, that the country was hopelessly given to the execution of this barbarous enactment, and that it were vain to hope for the reformation of such a country."[35] They jointly resolved "to wind up our affairs, and go to Canada."

Douglass elaborated on the feeling among his colleagues vis-à-vis the Fugitive Slave law in *Life and Times*: "Bishop Daniel A. Payne of the African Methodist Episcopal Church came to me about this time to consult me as to whether it was best to stand our ground or flee to Canada. When I told him I could not desert my post until I saw I could not hold it, adding that I did not wish to leave while Garnet and Ward remained, 'Why,' said he, 'Ward? Ward, is already gone. I saw him crossing from Detroit to Windsor.' I asked him if he were going to stay, and he answered. 'Yes; we are whipped, we are whipped, and we might as well retreat in order.'"[36]

Henry Clay, having retired from the Senate in September 1851, died of tuberculosis on June 29, 1852, joining John C. Calhoun, deceased on March 31, 1850. In September 1852, the last of the senate's mighty trio, Webster, returned to his Marshfield estate. He died that October 24 of cirrhosis of the liver and subdural hematoma, prompting John Greenleaf Whittier to write, "When faith is lost, when honor dies, the man is dead!"

Writing on January 23, 1852, from Troy, New York, John Brown had addressed a letter to his "Dear Children," in Akron, Ohio—"If you find it difficult for you to pay for Douglass' paper, I wish you would let me know, as I know I took liberty in ordering it continued." This remark seems to make clear that Brown valued his relationship with Frederick Douglass. The longest letter extant between these two was dated January 9, 1854, sent from Akron to Rochester. Brown began by confiding that he had "thought much of late of the extreme wickedness of persons who use their influence to bring law and order and good government, and courts of justice into disrespect and contempt of mankind." His only reassurance for sending the letter was as a suggestion, he wrote, and that Douglass might "take it up and clothe it in the suitable language to be noticed and felt."

Drawing this colloquy to a close, Brown added, "There is one other set of the same throngers of the 'broad way' which I have not mentioned.... I mean Editors of, and writers in the pro-slavery newspapers and periodicals. These seem to vie with each other in urging men on to greater and still greater lengths in stifling conscience, and insulting God. . . . But I have done. I am too destitute of words to express the tithe of what I feel, and utterly incapable of doing the subject any possible degree of justice, in my own estimation. . . . I want to have the enquiry everywhere raised—Who are the men that are undermining our truly republican and democratic institutions at their very foundation."[37] The answers to Brown's interrogatories came from two directions.

The presidential contest in 1852, in which Millard Fillmore had won the support of southern Whigs while northern members of the party threw their support behind Winfield Scott, had been the last for that party. On the fifty-third ballot Scott became the Whig nominee. Pledging fidelity to the Compromise of 1850, Franklin Pierce became the Democratic nominee. With the Free-Soil Party moribund, Pierce and the Democrats won in a landslide.

On January 4, 1854, a bill to repeal the Missouri Compromise by dividing the Nebraska Territory in two was reported in the Senate. The idea of a transcontinental railroad had been gaining purchase, and as many would-be settlers and land speculators began casting covetous eyes toward the Nebraska Territory, Illinois senator Stephen Douglas, a hard-edged political infighter, invested the balance of his rising presidential aspirations in a bill designed to garner southern congressional support for opening the territories to settlement. But this would propel an entirely new political alignment and organization into existence, soon to be called the Republican Party.

Following the precedent of the Mexican cession as regarded New Mexico and Arizona, the "Kansas-Nebraska" bill stipulated that slavery was to be allowed in the territories based on the votes of eligible voters settling in those territories. Joining the Illinois senator in driving through the enactment—with the expectation that the Kansas Territory would fall prey to Missouri—was David Rice Atchison of Missouri, president pro tempore of the Senate. Ostensibly proposed to strengthen the compromise already framed, yet derisively called the "Squatter Sovereign" bill, the legislation passed in the Senate on March 4, 1854, and the House on May 22.

Less than a week after a fugitive slave was arrested in Boston, President Pierce signed the legislation, which became law May 30. As the fugitive was standing before a judge in Massachusetts, Charles Sumner stood in the Senate to announce that the Kansas-Nebraska bill "annuls all past compromises with slavery, and makes all future compromises impossible. Thus it puts Freedom and Slavery face to face, and bids them grapple."[38]

Fugitive Anthony Burns, 24, had arrived in Boston on March 24, 1854, aboard a vessel arriving from Richmond, Virginia. He was the slave of Colonel Charles Suttle, a merchant living in Alexandria, Virginia. His owner had hired Burns out to work on ships docked at Richmond's wharves for William Brent, who had employed Burns's brother for five or six years. Arriving in Boston, Burns obtained employment at a clothing store on Brattle Street owned by Coffin Pitts. He wrote to his brother of his new circumstances, using the subterfuge of mailing the letter from Canada but inadvertently dating it from Boston. Intercepting the letter, Brent notified Suttle of the whereabouts of "his property." Obtaining an affidavit from a Virginia court, Suttle sailed for Boston.

In Boston the Virginian presented his document to U.S. Marshal Watson Freeman, who issued a warrant and assigned his deputy the task of finding and seizing Burns and detaining him at the courthouse. Knowing that an out-and-out arrest of a fugitive slave was sure to raise a strong protest and resistance, and to justify Burns's apprehension by city officials, the deputy decided to take Burns into custody by charging him with theft. (The next year when Anthony Burns was again a free man due to the intercession of the Rev. Leonard Grimes—pastor of the Twelfth Baptist Church, known as "The Fugitives Church"—who arranged to purchase him, he recounted his story.)

One night on his way home, Burns related, he heard footsteps rapidly coming up behind him. As a hand gripped his shoulder, a man called out, "Stop, stop; you are the fellow who broke into a silversmith's shop the other night." Burns replied that he was being mistaken for someone else, but before he could utter another word, he was lifted up and restrained "by six or seven others." Once at the courthouse Burns would wait for some time without the supposed silversmith appearing, and, not having eaten, stated that he wanted to go home to his supper. A man then appeared at the door, Burns later wrote. "[H]e didn't open it like an honest man would, but kind of slowly opened it, and looked in. He said, 'How do you do, Mr. Burns?' and I called him, as we do in Virginia, 'Master!'"

Asked by Suttle why he had run away, Burns replied, "I fell asleep on board the vessel where I worked and, before I woke up, she set sail and carried me off."[39]

"Haven't I always treated you well, Tony?" Suttle asked. "Haven't I always given you money when you needed?"

Burns replied, "You have always given me twelve and one-half cents once a year."

At this, the court had all the evidence needed under law that Burns recognized Suttle as his master and was his chattel in Virginia.

A little before nine o'clock the next morning, May 25, appearing before U.S. commissioner Edward Loring, Burns was confused and frightened. He had not had a bite to eat since being picked up and carried off, and was not liable to contest Suttle's claim to him. With the fugitive slave inquest in progress, Richard H. Dana, Jr. and Charles Mayo Ellis proffered their counsel to the defendant. Likewise, passing on the street and hearing of the arrest, Theodore Parker came into the court, convincing a reluctant Burns that he might challenge the proceedings. Dana asked that the hearing be rescheduled, which request Loring granted, setting a new date of May 27—a Saturday.

Boston's Vigilance Committee immediately swung into action, distributing handbills calling for a public meeting in Faneuil Hall that evening. To assure a sizable attendance, abolitionists in towns and villages in the vicinity were also notified. So that Thomas Wentworth Higginson might be there and bring a contingent, Samuel J. May wrote him in Worcester the same day. "Give all the notice you can," May urged Higginson. "The friends here are wide awake and unanimous.... The country must back the city, and, if necessary lead it. We shall summon all the country friends."

Higginson alerted several persons, especially Martin Stowell, who had taken part in the rescue of Jerry at Syracuse, urging that all act promptly. As news of Burns's arrest reached Troy, New York, by telegraph, John Brown was sitting in his lawyer's office going over testimony from a suit involving his bankrupt wool dealership in Springfield. He suddenly rose from his chair, rapidly pacing the room several times in long strides. Abruptly turning to his counsel, he said, "I'm going to Boston!"

"Going to Boston?" the lawyer queried. "Why do you want to go to Boston?"

"Anthony Burns must be released," Brown said, still pacing, "or I will die in the attempt."

Dropping his pen in consternation, Brown's counsel was a long time dissuading his client from departing for Boston.[40]

Arriving on the morning train from Worcester that same day, Higginson found himself, he wrote, "presently in a meeting with the Vigilance Committee not essentially different from those which had proved so disappointing three years before." Not only had the meeting failed to devise any plan, those participating had "no set purpose of united action" at all. As the committee adjourned, Higginson remained behind with Lewis Hayden and others willing to take part in forcible resistance. The members of the committee reduced from sixty to thirty, Higginson was chosen chairman, and after spirited advice from Dr. Samuel Gridley Howe—a veteran in the cause of liberty in Greece and advocate of Polish national determination—a committee of six was chosen to give definite leadership to an emerging plan. This body included Wendell Phillips, Parker, Howe, Higginson, and an energetic Irishman named Kemp, a former sea captain from Newburyport, a roster to which was added, at Higginson's insistence, Stowell. Their deliberations ended, however, without having produced a cogent plan.

Decades later in *Cheerful Yesterdays*, Higginson wrote that all hopes rested on Stowell, who was to arrive from Worcester at 6 p.m. Meeting him at the train, Higginson went over the state of affairs, with Stowell at once suggesting "a new plan as the only thing feasible."

The fugitive had to be freed forcefully from the courthouse, but the rescue could not be done in "cold blood." Success required the momentum of a public meeting, such as that which was to occur at Faneuil Hall that evening. An attack at the conclusion of the gathering would be hopeless, that would be just what the marshal was expecting, Stowell declared; they must act before the meeting adjourned. Could an attack at the very height of the meeting not be brought about in this way? Let all be in readiness; let a picked body be distributed near the Courthouse and Square; then let some loud-voiced speaker, previously alerted—Phillips, if possible—seize the opportunity and send the whole meeting pell-mell to Court Square, ready to fall in behind the leaders and bring out the prisoner. "The project struck me as an inspiration," Higginson wrote. He accepted the plan heartily, later remarking, "it was one of the very best plots that ever—failed."[41]

At seven that evening, an immense throng massed at Faneuil Hall, the largest ever seen in that historic meeting place. With the din of animated conversation filling the air, Higginson tried to convey the plan to the other members of the Vigilance Committee. Howe and

Parker were reached, but not, in the pandemonium, Phillips. Those filling the hall were roused to a pitch of excitement as Wendell Phillips rose to his feet.

"Mr. Chairman and Fellow Citizens—You have called me to this platform—for what?" Phillips asked. "Do you wish to know what I want? I want that man set free in the streets of Boston. . . . When law ceases, the sovereignty of the people begins. I am against squatter sovereignty in Nebraska, and I am against kidnapping sovereignty in the streets of Boston. . . . The question tomorrow is fellow citizens whether Virginia conquers Massachusetts. If that man leaves the city of Boston, Massachusetts is a conquered State. . . . Will you adhere to the precedent of Thomas Sims? Will you adhere to the case of Sims and see this man carried down State Street between two hundred men? . . . Nebraska, I call knocking a man down, and this spitting in his face after he is down."[42]

Consulting with Lewis Hayden, Higginson said he had five men with whom to begin the rescue of Burns, to which Hayden said he could bring ten. All were to go singly and without hurry to the courthouse so as not to attract attention. Fortuitously, the building would be open thanks to a night meeting of the Supreme Court, and thus entry by way of the doors would not be impeded.

Higginson positioned himself at the entrance as he awaited the others. Suddenly one of the many deputies inside ran up from the basement and, looking directly into his face, barred the door. Now Stowell was coming up the courthouse steps, axes in hand. He said to Higginson, "Some of our men are bringing a beam up to the west door, the one that gives entrance to the upper stairway." As the makeshift battering ram was being brought up, Higginson gripped the front end with one of Hayden's stout men, as Hayden and Stowell and others grabbed hold behind. Under battering the door began to splinter; however, it was reinforced from the inside. A new blow knocked the door off one of its hinges, making space enough for a man to squeeze through. As a pistol shot was fired, Higginson and his companion pushed through. A half-dozen officers began pummeling the pair with their nightsticks, as the interlopers lustily countered with their fists. In the melee Higginson was cut on the chin by a saber that left a life-long scar, and a twenty-four-year-old deputy marshal, a Boston truckman named Batchelder, was mortally wounded in the groin by a blade thrust.

From the gallery in Faneuil Hall a youth with a stentorian voice announced the commencement of the attempt to free Burns. The crowd, however, misunderstood, many supposing that declaration to be an attempt to break up the meeting. With Phillips and other leaders still on the platform, the first of the audience began exiting, but only in a dilatory movement, toward the courthouse. As several hundred persons milled outside the well-lighted building, the only further disturbance was excoriation from the crowd and stone throwing. With Higginson assessing whether another attempt could be made, a man quietly came out of the crowd and began ascending the steps alone. Reaching the spot where Higginson stood, he asked, "Why are we not within?" "Because these people will not stand by us," was Higginson's disparaging reply. His inquisitor was the transcendental philosopher A. Bronson Alcott. "He said not a word, but calmly walked up the steps—he and his familiar cane," Higginson later wrote. "He paused again at the top, the centre of all eyes, within and without; a revolver sounded from within, but hit nobody; and finding himself wholly unsupported, he turned and retreated, but without hastening a step. It seemed to me that, under the circumstances, neither Plato nor Pythagoras could have done the thing better."[43]

Hearing of the attack on the courthouse, Boston's mayor issued a call for two companies of artillery. People were still milling up and down Washington Street, standing in shop doorways and in knots on the sidewalks. Rumor ran riot among friends and foes: there was going to be another attempt to free Burns; the "kidnappers" were to be sought out in their lodging at the Revere House; there was going to be an attempt on the life of Wendell Phillips.

At midnight, the Boston Artillery and the Columbia Artillery arrived—one stationed at City Hall, the other in front of the courthouse. At 2 a.m., a detachment of federal troops from Fort Independence and a company of marines from the Charlestown Navy Yard arrived. The marshal had also organized a special guard, of whose membership the jailer remarked that among those ranks he saw many of his regular customers.

That morning, after he'd read the cable sent by Marshal Freedman concerning the incident and what he had done, President Pierce replied, "Your conduct is approved. The law must be executed." Later in the morning Pierce ordered the U.S. Attorney for Boston to "incur any expense deemed necessary . . . to insure the execution of the law." The president and his secretary of war, Jefferson Davis, now saw that they could enforce the law as a political manifestation against further defiance originating in the North.

When the examination of Burns began on May 29, the streets around the courthouse and the square were thronged as never before. Nine hundred persons had come in from Worcester alone. Ranks of soldiers with fixed bayonets and lines of policemen stood before the courthouse, with soldiers lining the halls and clogging the stairs. Colonel Suttle, who'd been feted by Harvard professors, appeared at court with a bodyguard of Harvard students, all Southerners, but that group was not admitted into court. With commissioner Loring determined to execute the law in Suttle's favor, all arguments put by Burns's counsel were of no avail. The ruling came June 2, and President Pierce had seen to it that a U.S. Navy warship was in port to transport Burns back to Virginia.

On the day of Anthony Burns's rendition twenty-two companies of Massachusetts soldiers, an entire brigade, were on hand to guard against disturbance, together with a large body of Boston police, and the two batteries of artillery. Soldiers had their guns loaded and capped, with bayonets fixed; officers carried side-arms. A separate body of soldiers, each armed with a Roman sword and with a revolver hanging from his belt, surrounded the prisoner.

When the procession began, a company of cavalry went ahead to clear the streets, which were then lined all the way to the wharf with soldiers shouldering bayoneted arms. Windows along their tramp were draped in mourning, as streams of crepe crisscrossed the street, and at the corner of Washington and State Streets, a coffin was suspended from a window and labeled "The Funeral of Liberty." A few paces beyond, edged in black was an American flag hung "the Union down."

The object of all this—Anthony Burns—remarked the following year when again a free man, "There was lots of folks to see a colored man walk down the street."[44] It was estimated, amidst groans and hisses, as many as 50,000 persons crowded the streets to watch the rendition of Burns. A shower of cayenne pepper, with other irritants, wafted in a cloud from the Commonwealth Building as the procession passed State Street. When the throng surged forward, lancers charged into them, striking some with the flats of sabers; a company with fixed bayonets ran into the mass. Some people were trampled in the crush, others pushed up stairs or into basements; many were pressed against walls.

As the troops marched past the Custom House, a military band struck up "Carry Me Back to Old Virginia," which soldiers sang as they proceeded down the length of the wharf. There the fugitive boarded the U.S. revenue cutter *Morris*. The *Liberator*'s headline cried, "Triumph of the Slave Power—THE KIDNAPPING LAW ENFORCED AT THE POINT OF BAYONET—Massachusetts in Disgraceful Vassalage."

As the Kansas-Nebraska bill was being enacted and as the movement of settlers from New England sponsored by the Emigrant Aid Company was beginning, Missouri residents passed over the line to register claims on the books of some "Squatter Association." Kansas's first territorial governor, Andrew Reeder, arrived in October 1854; a lawyer from Easton, Pennsylvania, he had no previous political experience. The election for the territorial delegate to Congress, held November 29, was carried by J.W. Whitfield, a pro-slavery man who previously had been appointed Indian agent for Kansas by Senator David Rice Atchison. Whitfield's victory had been helped by an inundation of an estimated 1,700 votes cast by Missouri residents.

Despite the irregularity of the balloting, Reeder ordered that elections for a territorial legislature be held March 30, 1855. Again, men poured over the border, 4,000 to 5,000 all told; rough, unkempt, brutal-looking, they swaggered in with music playing and banners flying, armed with bowie knives and revolvers, pistols, and rifles. With many wearing the pro-slavery badge—a white or blue ribbon—they pitched tents, camping near polling places and intimidating free-state voters. "Border ruffians," James Redpath christened them in an apt expression in the *Tribune*, and they easily succeeded in electing an overwhelmingly pro-slavery legislature.

The "brush fire" fretting the undulating long grasses, wood-lined streams, and plains of eastern Kansas likewise loomed ominously over the political panorama in the North. Shortly after the Kansas-Nebraska bill was introduced, a group of anxious "anti-Nebraska" politicians—Conscience Whigs, Democrats, and American and Free-Soil adherents—first came together on February 28, 1854, in a schoolhouse in Ripon, Wisconsin, solely to address the issue of opposing the extension of slavery. When partisans of the same sort began holding meetings in Illinois, they drew among them Abraham Lincoln, showing him to be one of the principal politicians of the emerging movement. This was followed by a meeting in Jackson, Michigan, on June 13, the anniversary of the Northwest Ordinance of 1787. Conventions under the banner of a new party were held in Ohio, Indiana, Wisconsin, and Vermont.

Editorializing in the *Tribune* on what might constitute an appropriate moniker to encompass these new political alliances comprised of otherwise disparate factions, Horace Greeley had written in June, "We should not care much whether those thus united were designated 'Whig,' 'Free Democrat' or something else; though we think some simple name like 'Republican' would more fitly designate those who had united to restore the Union to its true mission of champion and promulgator of Liberty rather than propagandist of slavery."[45]

Chapter Four

"WE NEED ARMS MORE THAN WE DO BREAD"

When the territorial legislature for Kansas began its sessions at Shawnee Mission, a mile or two beyond the Missouri border, Governor Reeder notified members of both houses that he would not recognize their legality nor approve their legislation. He became the first of the territorial governors to vacate the platform. Reeder was succeeded in that office by Wilson Shannon, a former congressman from Ohio and minister to Mexico; tall, rough-featured, and gray-headed, he shared the ruffians' taste for spirits.

From August to September this "bogus legislature" proceeded to enact the most stringent slave code seen anywhere in the South. The code provided that anyone holding office in the territory—judges, sheriffs, justices of the peace, or whatever—had to swear to uphold slavery. Dr. J.H. Stringfellow, a pillar of Weston, Missouri, and editor of the *Squatter Sovereign*, when elected speaker of the house, offered the following resolution: "Be it resolved by the House of Representatives, the Council concerning therein, That it is the duty of the proslavery party, the Union-loving men of Kansas Territory, to know but one issue, Slavery; and that any party making, or attempting to make, any other is and should be held as an ally of Abolitionism and Disunion."[1]

Pressed by poor prospects on their farms in Ohio, prompted by the surge of emigration from the North to the Kansas Territory, and envisioning opportunities as well as the prospect of making Kansas a free state, five of John Brown's sons and their families were considering settling in the untried region. In a letter of August 21, 1854, from Akron, Ohio, to John Jr., their father wrote, "If you or any of my family are disposed to go to Kansas or Nebraska, with a view to help defeat Satan and his legions in that direction, I have not a word to say; but I feel committed to operate in another part of the field. If I were not so committed, I would be on my way this fall."[2]

That other "part of the field" Brown mentioned was in the Adirondack Mountains region of upstate New York. On the twelfth anniversary of Britain's West Indian emancipation, August 1, 1846, Gerrit Smith—an abolitionist free thinker, inheritor of vast tracts of land in the continental United States, and early supporter of Frederick Douglass and John Brown—had offered to free Blacks 100,000 acres he owned in Franklin and Essex counties in the Adirondacks on easy terms. Smith was aiming to give these settlers an opportunity to become self-sustaining farmers and to give them standing to meet New York's $250 property ownership threshold, enabling them to become voters. "It was not a well-thought-out scheme," W. E. B. Du Bois wrote—the climate was bleak for Negroes and the methods of agriculture then suitable were unknown to them; in addition, the surveyor who laid out these farms cheated purchasers as cheerily as though philanthropy had no concern with the project.[3]

The remote region was most expeditiously reached by taking a train to Rutland, Vermont, crossing Lake Champlain to Westport, New York, from there taking conveyance to Keene, and finally traveling the steep wooded road across Keene Mountain into North Elba. Most of those accepting Smith's offer were city dwellers accustomed to working as waiters and barbers, maids and laborers, and as coachmen. The settlement soon began to fail. Hearing of this, Brown visited the Smith estate in Peterboro in the Finger Lakes district of New York on April 8, 1848. Proposing to Smith that he was disposed to put the settlement on a better footing, Franklin Sanborn wrote, in his *Life and Letters of John Brown, Liberator of Kansas, and Martyr of Virginia*, published in 1885, Brown said, "I am something of a pioneer; I grew up among the woods and wild Indians of Ohio, and am used to the climate and the way of life that your colony find so trying. I will take one of your farms myself, clear it up and plant it, and show my colored neighbors how such work should be done, will give them work as I have occasion, look after them in all needful ways and be a kind of father to them."[4] On November 9, 1849, Brown signed a deed for 244 acres at $1 an acre with Gerrit Smith.

Brown's wife Mary, the couple's younger children, and Owen, the third of Brown's older sons, had moved there the year before to lease a farm on which stood a small one-story frame house, a daunting move for nine members of the family. Daughter Ruth wrote, "The day we crossed the mountains from Keene was rainy and dreary and father wanted us to notice now fragrant the air was with the perfume of the pines, hemlocks and balsams." Ruth no doubt was wondering how the tiny abode they beheld was going to accommodate their numbers. After a night's rest in their new home, the family had a visitor. "Before noon a bright, pleasant colored boy came to our gate, (or rather, our bars) and inquired if John Brown lived there," she wrote. "'Here is where he stays,' was father's reply. The boy had been a slave in Virginia, and was sold and sent to St. Augustine, Fla. From there he ran away, and came to Springfield, where by his industry and good habits he had acquired some property. Father hired him to help carry on the farm, so there were ten of us in the little house; but Cyrus did not take more than his share of room, and was always good Natured."[5]

This anecdote recalls Brown's discussion with Frederick Douglass in May 1847 in Springfield, Massachusetts; the Adirondack colony must have figured in Brown's "plan of Negro emancipation" as he then conceived that project—a potential base of retreat and refuge for those and their families freed in the endeavor, a place of recruitment, and a setting where troops could be drilled in a mountainous environment.

In October 1854, John Jr., Owen, Frederick, and Salmon Brown began making preparations to immigrate to the Kansas Territory in two parties; Owen, Frederick, and Salmon going first, driving their animals, arriving in spring 1855, followed by Jason and John Jr., and their families, traveling by rail to St. Louis and continuing by steamboat up the Missouri River, also arriving that spring. On the latter voyage the boat was crowded with men from the South, also journeying to Kansas, drinking and full of profanity, while displaying revolvers and bowie knives. John Jr. wrote that it was then for the first time there "arose in our minds the query: Must the fertile prairies of Kansas through a struggle of arms, be first secured to freedom before free men can sow and reap?"[6]

Hard pressed by matters in Kansas and pondering whether he should join his children there, John Brown wrote his eldest daughter, Ruth, and her husband, Henry Thompson, a letter dated September 30, 1854. Would a commitment to Kansas be "more likely to benefit the colored people on the whole than to return with them to North Elba," he queried. Asking his daughter's advice, he was anxious to learn the opinion, too, of "Mr. Epps & all the colored people. . . . As I volunteered in their service (or the service of the colored people); they have a right to vote, as to the course I take." He had written similarly to Gerrit Smith, Frederick Douglass, and Dr. James McCune Smith for advice. Smith held a medical degree from the University of Glasgow in Scotland, had completed an internship in Paris, and opened a medical office and pharmacy on West Broadway in New York City, serving an intra-racial clientele; and had been among the handful of early Black confidants of John Brown.

A month after the first of his sons set out, Brown informed Ruth and Henry that he was "pretty much determined to go back to North Elba. . . . Gerrit Smith wishes me to go back to North Elba; from Douglass and Dr. McCune Smith I have not yet heard."[7] But after John Jr.'s arrival in Kansas, he wrote his father a letter dated May 20, 1855, giving a harrowing rendition of the plight of the free-state settlers, and John Brown began to perceive where his "duty" lay.

Kansas men were deficient in arms and intimidated by the "ruffians," his son had written, with the result being "that the people here exhibit the most abject and cowardly spirit, whenever their dearest rights are invaded and trampled down by the lawless bands of Miscreants which Missouri has ready at a moment's call to pour in upon them." Could not his father obtain and send arms and ammunition, as war of "some magnitude" seemed inevitable?

"We need them more than we do bread," John Jr. wrote.

That spring, Gerrit Smith and a handful of Liberty Party members, seeing the deficiencies of the movement to form a new party opposed to slavery's extension in the territories but willing to let the odious practice remain in the states where it was acknowledged—began discussing holding a convention which would call for "a clean sweep of slavery everywhere." Douglass was enthusiastic and endorsed the proposal, issuing a call in his paper on April 20 and expressing the opinion that as the so-called "Republican" party grew in numbers, it would "also grow 'in the knowledge of the Truth.'"[8]

The Liberty Party convened in Syracuse on June 26, holding three days of meetings under its newly adopted title as the Radical Abolition Party. With James McCune Smith elected chairman and Douglass serving on the business committee, an "Exposition of the Constitutional Duty of the Federal Government to Abolish Slavery" and an "Address to the Public" were drawn up and adopted as elements of a program calling for the use of the political power of the nation "to overthrow every part and parcel of American Slavery." Both were published as pamphlets and distributed to the wider public.

John Brown was among those arriving on the first day of the convention and was invited to speak on its final day. When he rose to address the gathering, Brown announced his intention to go out to Kansas but only if he could go armed. He had four sons in the territory now, with three others expected to join them, he said, and he wished to arm these as well. Poverty prevented him from obtaining weapons; he appealed to the convention for aid.[9] Gerrit Smith read two of John Jr.'s letters, "with such effect . . . as to draw tears from numerous eyes." Some present, including two retired military men from Europe, contributed on the spot, "amounting," as Brown reported to his wife, "to a little over sixty dollars."

That men were willing publicly to approve of his intentions was a great revelation to John Brown, and he informed his wife in a letter dated June 28 from Syracuse, "The convention has been one of the most interesting meetings I ever attended in my life; and I made a great addition to the number of warm-hearted and honest friends."[10]

To purchase his arms Brown went to Springfield, Massachusetts, and was given a generous discount by the manufacturer. In August he was in Akron; again, he spoke publicly, obtaining donations of ammunition, clothing, a crate of muskets, and ten double-edged swords. In Cleveland, he collected his son-in-law Henry Thompson, and the two traveled to Detroit to pick up sixteen-year-old Oliver Brown, whose older brother Watson had remained at North Elba. From Chicago, in a wagon laden with arms and supplies drawn by "a nice young horse" for which they had paid $120, the trio made for Kansas. Walking much of the time to relieve the burden on the animal, the arms carefully concealed and his surveying implements conspicuously displayed, Brown and his companions arrived in Kansas on October 7, 1855.

The procuring of arms for the free-state settlers in Kansas extended to the new territory as well. In April Charles Robinson, as the agent of the Emigrant Aid Company, sent G.W. Deitzler to Massachusetts to obtain weapons; with the financial assistance of Amos Lawrence, treasurer of the aid company and a wealthy mill owner, Deitzler did so. In July another agent was sent on a similar mission, and he also obtained weapons. In both instances, the armaments were specimens of the Sharp's rifle, a new breech-loading carbine with an effective range of 1,700 yards. These arms were bought with the pecuniary aid of Frederick Law Olmsted and the Rev. Henry Ward Beecher and shipped in crates marked "Books"—the famous Beecher's Bibles. By spring 1855 the population of Kansas had doubled as free-state settlements were coming into predominance. Sitting in convention at Big Spring on September 5, 1855, after a series of meetings at Lawrence in which John Brown Jr. participated, the free-state settlers repudiated the fraudulently elected legislature and vowed not to obey its "bogus enactments." That "bogus" territorial legislature in its first session had selected as its capital Lecompton, about twelve miles west of Lawrence and named after Judge Samuel D. Lecompte, a pro-slavery jurist accommodating to the pro-slavery faction under the leadership of David Rice Atchison and James H. Stringfellow, the nominal heads of the political clique or machine that was seeking control of Kansas in the interests of the South. To even the growing imbalance in settlement, appeals had gone out and meetings had been convened across the South early in 1855, principally in South Carolina, Georgia, and Alabama, with the goal of sending men to Kansas; these entities went under various names, but usually "Sons of Liberty" or, in Missouri, the "Blue Lodge," organized specifically to secure slavery in the Kansas Territory. Stringfellow published an appeal in the *Montgomery Advertiser*: "Not only is it profitable for slaveholders to go to Kansas, but politically it is all-important."[11] Senator Robert Toombs of Georgia heard the call and urged a meeting in Columbus to organize and send settlers. In Eufaula, Alabama, a slaveholder named Jefferson Buford began campaigning for recruits, opening offices to support this southern "Kansas emigration," from the Carolinas to Louisiana.[12]

On arrival, the Browns had taken claims on several parcels about eight miles from Osawatomie, where a half-sister of John Brown, Florilla, and her husband, the Rev. Samuel Adair, had settled and built a home. The country in eastern Kansas was well-crossed by streams and rivers, clotted and thick with woodlands, and cut by deep ravines, with undulating hills as well. The Browns chose land near Pottawatomie Creek, on a sort of swell in the prairie which gently sloped toward the horizon giving a spectacular view all around into the far distance. The brothers' claims were all within two miles of each other. As they arrived of necessity they put their whole effort into clearing land, plowing, and planting, so as to have provisions ready for winter. Construction of dwellings, even of a semi-permanent nature, had been neglected; they and their families were living in tents and wagons.

When John Brown and companions arrived, they found those who had come earlier in "the most uncomfortable situation," shivering by little fires and exposed to cutting wind. Since midsummer nearly all of the original party had been prostrated with fever and the ague, which they now found difficult to break. In addition, although it was the least of their worries in the circumstances, the men's boots were all nearly worn out. Their crops—corn, beans, squash, turnips, and grain—had not been fully reaped or prepared for winter. It is here we see John Brown's true mettle, and that of his large family. As soon as he was on the ground, he set to work lifting everyone up—felling and limbing trees and hewing logs so as to begin building permanent structures, gathering in the animals, some of which were exposed in the fields, gathering fodder, etc. With this work begun, after several weeks, he could report to his wife in North Elba that after beginning work on a house for John Jr. and his family, he had labored at Jason's place, constructing a shanty three logs high, chinked and mudded, roofed using their tent and outfitted with "a chimney so far advanced [as] to keep a fire in it."[13] None of the families had brought stoves. Construction elsewhere in these prairie towns would begin proceeding rapidly, with new commercial structures and dwellings constantly being built. Northern settlers and their outfitters and supporters had made it the first order of business to import and assemble sawmills, and a number of these had sprung into active existence, as had entrepreneurs trading in hardware. But farm settlers still had to rely on the ax, the hoe, and other rudimentary tools.

In the succeeding months, the free-state movement began organizing a state government, selecting Topeka as that government's capital and sending an appeal to the Congress and the nation. When a free-state man was brutally murdered by pro-slavery ruffians, one in a continuing series of such slayings, the sheriff of Douglas County, Samuel Jones, to demonstrate the weakness of the free-state position and to keep free-staters supine, arrested not the suspect but the only free-state witness to the crime. With all territorial officials and the federal government arrayed against the free-state movement, Jones was determined to ride the arrested man through Lawrence, hoping to provoke a rescue attempt that would offer him the pretext to destroy the town. But before reaching the free-state stronghold, Jones—who resided in Weston, Missouri—and his posse were met by eight men carrying Sharp's rifles. Freeing the prisoner, the riflemen carried the witness to safety in Lawrence, where he gave a full recital of the episode.

John Brown had entered Kansas armed and ready to see the territory through to status as a free state. But he had also come, as Sanborn emphasizes, with the intention "to attack slavery by force in the States themselves, and to destroy it."[14] Here was a man then, all commentators agree, of determined, even inexorable will, fortified by his faith in God, and obedient, as ever, to His voice which he heard within and without him, who was about to make his startling, ever memorable, debut.

To force the free-state settlers to submit to the territorial laws, Governor Shannon called out the militia, with Missouri's Platte County Rifles among those answering the summons as Shannon appealed for federal troops at Fort Leavenworth to be deployed. That appeal, however, was refused by the federals' commander, Colonel Edwin Sumner—a cousin of Massachusetts senator Charles Sumner—who said he would not deploy his men unless he was so ordered by the president. Before receiving this answer, nevertheless 1,500 amply armed pro-slavery men with cannon in tow, coming from as far away as Jefferson City, as well as from Lexington and Waverly in Missouri, began wrangling over the border toward Lawrence, determined to quash the abolitionism they saw as jeopardizing Southern slave hegemony and unsettling, in their view, the peace of the Union.

In Lawrence James H. Lane had been elected "major general," and began drilling five hundred men, with others laboring in details digging trenches, throwing up redoubts, and building barricades. When word of the impending clash reached the Brown settlement near Osawatomie, the men there began making preparations to march to the relief of Lawrence. To authenticate the reports they were receiving about the state of things, John Jr. started for Lawrence on horseback, just as word reached them that their help "was immediately wanted." "[I]t was at once agreed," John's father soon thereafter wrote to his wife, "to break up at John's camp . . . and that all the men but Henry, Jason, and Oliver should at once set off for Lawrence under arms; those three being wholly unfit for duty. . . . The five set off in the afternoon, and after a short rest in the night (which was quite dark), continued our march until after daylight; next morning, when we got our breakfast, started again, and reached Lawrence in the forenoon, all of us more or less lamed by our tramp."[15]

Drawn by a lean horse led by a tall slim-faced man of fifty-five, a rough-hewn wagon lumbered into Lawrence. Dark-complexioned, with blue-gray eyes, the man had a bristle of thick gray hair growing low on his forehead. With spare arms lying in the bed, four stalwart-looking men stood at each corner of the wagon. Armed with pikes and swords, each had a rifle slung over a shoulder, two revolvers tucked into a belt, with a spare pistol resting in one or another of their pockets. All weapons were loaded and ready to discharge, enough to fire a hundred rounds in aggregate.

The elder Brown at once became a conspicuous figure, this being the advent of Captain John Brown of Osawatomie.[16] One of the two free-state newspapers published in Lawrence, the *Herald of Freedom*, reported on December 7, 1855: "About noon, Mr. John Brown, an aged gentleman from Essex County, N.Y., who had been a resident of the Territory for several months, arrived with four of his sons . . . bringing a quantity of arms with him, which were placed in his hands by Eastern friends for the defense of the cause of freedom. Having more than he could use to advantage, a portion of them were placed in the hands of those more destitute. A company was organized and the command given to Mr. Brown for the zeal he had exhibited in the cause of freedom both before and since his arrival in the territory."

Five hundred variously armed "abolitionist" men in Lawrence were now opposing 1,500 "border ruffians" encamped in nearby Franklin, a stand-off unbroken for several days. Not wanting a large demonstration that would draw the attention of the nation to his and the administration's underhanded tilt toward the pro-slavery camp, Governor Shannon began "negotiations" with the most prominent free-state leaders, Charles Robinson and James Lane, in the Eldridge House, also known as the Free State Hotel, an unfinished fortified structure purposely being built in view of the struggle. After the governor had been plied with liquor, it was announced that an agreement had been reached averting further conflict. The invading force was to withdraw, and in exchange the free-state leaders had agreed not to resist the execution of any legal process of the elected legislature.

When Brown heard of this, he was livid. He came "into our council room the maddest man I ever saw," E.A. Coleman wrote. "He told Robinson that what he had done was all a farce; that in less than six months the Missourians would find out the deception, and things would be worse than they were that day (and so it was); that he came up to help them fight, but if that was the way Robinson meant to do, not send for him again."[17]

As Shannon and Robinson and Lane came out to the street to address a crowd, John Brown continued his harangue. In his *Reminiscences of Old Brown*, G.W. Brown (no relation) wrote: "If he [John Brown] understood Governor Shannon's speech, something had been conceded, and he conveyed the idea that the territorial laws were to be observed. Those laws he denounced and spit upon, and would never obey—no! The crowd was fired by this earnestness and a great echoing shout arose: 'No! No! Down with the bogus laws. Lead us out to fight first!'"

Proposing to take the fight to the border ruffian encampment at Franklin, Brown said he was prepared to lead a night attack and called for ten men armed with Sharp's rifles. Imagining these rifles firing on their opponents as they bivouacked around campfires—all could see it might have had a salutary effect! "For a moment," G.W. Brown's *Reminiscences* continues, "matters looked serious to the free state leaders who had so ingeniously engineered the compromise, and they hastened to assure Brown that he was mistaken; that there had been no surrendering of principles on their side."[18]

James Lane was a lawyer who had been a congressman representing Indiana. A Democrat and supporter of Franklin Pierce, Lane had helped to pass the Kansas bill. Coming out to the territory himself and seeing the state of things, he switched sides, becoming a figure as large as any in early Kansas history, both before and during the war of 1861-1865. A gifted stump speaker, he suffered as a leader from a temperamental and mercurial disposition. Robinson was a Massachusetts man who had been out to California in '49, crossing the Nebraska Territory on his way. Returning by ship, he studied medicine and became a doctor. Writing a few anti-Nebraska articles for the *Worcester Spy*, he came to the attention of Eli Thayer and Amos Lawrence, the respective organizer and financier of the Emigrant Aid Company, seeing in Robinson just the man for their company. Austere, with a Calvinist constitution, Robinson would increasingly be seen as the conservative, in contrast to Lane's radicalism.

On December 15, 1855, a vote was held on a "free-state" constitution, which was passed with pro-slavery voters abstaining. In January, elections for the legislature for this "illegal"—in the view of the territorial authorities—free-state government were held. Robinson was elected "governor," as Stringfellow's *Squatter Sovereign* recommended every "black and poisonous" abolitionist in Kansas be hung or shot. Giving a thorough report in Akron's *Summit Beacon*, dated December 20, 1855, but published in early January 1856, John Brown wrote optimistically of the effective consequences of the "Wakarusa war," as the stand-off at Lawrence was being called, forecasting that the free-state settlers in the territory now had only to hold the ground, and Kansas was free. Of the "strong, hardy farmers and mechanics" assembled in Lawrence's defense, Brown noted warmly, "Here were developed such a set of determined men as I had no idea this Territory could boast of, in any such numbers. They now know their own members, and their condition for self-government and self-defense. They have now become acquainted, and in their feelings, strongly knit together, the result of having shared together some of the conditions of war in actual service."[19]

Severe weather brought a comparative lull to hostilities. In February, President Franklin Pierce arrayed the power of the federal government behind the pro-slavery territorial officials, issuing a proclamation that the free-state legislature was illegal and the free-state movement treasonous. That Topeka legislature met on March 4, 1856, approving a memorial addressed to Congress seeking admission as a state under the just approved constitution; Lane and Robinson set out for Washington to shepherd the initiative. The House of Representatives, with its anti-Nebraska majority, voted in favor, while in the Senate Lewis Cass introduced an enabling act. On April 6, New York's Whig senator and an emerging leader of the new anti-slavery coalition, William H. Seward, spoke for the Kansas memorial's immediate acceptance while Illinois Democratic senator Stephen Douglas spoke against. There was insufficient population for statehood, Douglas maintained, urging that the much-publicized Southern aid societies be allowed to let their emigrants reach the territory, whereupon Congress could follow the will of the "squatters." But Douglas had another objection, asserting that the document submitted was partially forged by Lane. When a vote was taken, the memorial was denied.

Thwarted, the House resolved to send a committee of three, complete with clerks and secretaries, to the territory to learn the true condition of affairs.

With spring two regiments made up of men from Alabama, Georgia, and South Carolina arrived "to see Kansas through." The first of these, led by Jefferson Buford, came on a single boat, four hundred men in all, waving state banners as they disembarked. Henry Clay Pate, a rising newspaperman at the Westport *Border Star* originally from Virginia, welcomed them in his paper, describing the motley assemblage as "valiant men of the South." There would be no less than 1,000 and as many as 1,500 of these pro-slavery stalwarts in the Kansas Territory, for a time having the entire eastern border in their grip, and blockading the Missouri River to northern emigration, while they held a series of "forts" ringing Lawrence.[20] There came too, the men to lead them—Harry Titus, Claibourne Jackson, Pate, and Buford, the planter from Alabama, who had departed Montgomery with a Bible inscribed "Providence, many change our relations to the inferior race, but the principle is eternal—supremacy of the white race."[21]

The House committee had arrived at Kansas City the week prior, opening its sessions in Lecompton April 18 and scheduling its session in Lawrence to begin April 21. Concurrent with this, John Brown, his sons, and other free-state settlers, meeting in public at Osawatomie, agreed not to pay taxes to the "usurping" Lecompton legislature and in a resolution repudiated that body as one "forced upon us by a foreign vote."

The previous fall and winter free-state men had formed a secret "League of Freedom," organized in units of ten known as councils for mutual protection and to facilitate the task of gathering rapidly for self-defense by enabling each free-state man to know the other. Robinson became its first commander, or chief; the league's badge of recognition was a small piece of black tape or black ribbon worn in a buttonhole or at the throat.[22]

John Brown had anticipated the conditions then extant, observed Richard Hinton, the last of the John Brown biographers who knew him and who along with Redpath and Sanborn are being principally followed in this narrative, publishing *John Brown and His Men; with some account of the roads they traveled to reach Harper's Ferry* in 1893. Hinton wrote that Brown's "close study of current American history taught him the existence of a deliberate design to work the overthrow of the Federal Union"; in resisting this design he believed he was "obeying the highest obligations of citizenship and fulfilling . . . the obligation due from a man to his God, his fellows, and to his country."[23] By this time Brown had organized men under arms, steeping himself in the military use of weaponry, and had been studying the military arts for more than a decade. Already, too, he had formulated a definite view on how best to attack the "slave power" with a settled military policy. A small number of men, well-armed and organized, were sufficient in his view to initiate the anti-slavery war he proposed to introduce on the American scene. His practice would be to bring a clash of arms as quickly as possible, and, once the fighting began, press his adversaries to close quarters. In Brown's theory, any action justly carried out would have the effect of spreading as quickly as a contagion among the like-minded.

Earlier that winter he had written, "We are very anxious to know what Congress is doing. We hear that Frank Pierce means to crush the men of Kansas. I do not know how well he may succeed; but I think he may find his hands full before it is over." A letter from John Brown Jr. to Frederick Douglass was published in *Frederick Douglass' Paper* of May 2, 1856. In his letter, the younger Brown gave Douglass's readers a portent of this program: "From recent developments, it is now evident that our enemies are determined of prosecuting a series of oppressive measures in the form of vexatious suits in conformity with the Border Legislature, and to either compel us into slavish submission to the execution of these hated enactments—into acknowledgement in word or deed of the binding authority from which they emanate, or drive us into forcible resistance, and there by involve us in a quarrel with the general government. This . . . is to be the machinery at present to be employed for crushing us out."[24]

On May 14, Judge S.D. Lecompte in federal court charged a grand jury to issue subpoenas to the free-state leaders instrumental in forming the Topeka government. The territory, Lecompte said in his instructions, was organized by an act of Congress and the legislature, being an instrument of Congress, had enacted laws that therefore reflected federal authority; all who resisted those laws were guilty of high treason.

This tactic had been employed, so the objects of the process held, not to get indictments, but to frighten these men out of the territory before they could testify before the House committee appointed by speaker Nathaniel Banks and chaired by Ohio's representative, John Sherman. Meeting with Robinson, Sherman urged him to leave

Kansas, taking with him a copy of the committee's findings thus far, and to deliver them to the House speaker. Robinson did flee with his wife, but was arrested as his boat was docking in Lexington and charged with escaping from an indictment for treason, although none had yet been issued. He was brought back to Lecompton and jailed; his wife continued eastward carrying the incriminating deposition. Ex-governor Reeder, also leaving the territory, peacefully resisted arrest by sidestepping a deputy marshal in Leavenworth and traveling east on a steamboat disguised as a woodsman. That summer and during the presidential canvass Robinson's wife became an effective witness for the free-state cause.

Arrests of "treason prisoners" went on, amounting to 107 in all. As rumors began to circulate that indictments were being prepared by Judge Sterling Cato, a former Alabama Supreme Court jurist, at Dutch Henry's Crossing near the Brown settlement, John Brown sent his son Salmon and his son-in-law Henry Thompson into the court tempting arrest. They were to go without arms, but to ease their apprehension he had promised that if an arrest occurred he would rescue them. With no action forthcoming, John Jr. announced, as commander of the Pottawatomie Rifles, that the company would meet later at a parade grounds. That evening Cato abandoned the court, leaving for the safety afforded by pro-slavery Lecompton.

To show that the pro-slavery territorial laws would be enforced, Sheriff Jones now attempted an arrest of the man alleged to have participated in releasing a free-state prisoner in Lawrence the previous December. That man was rescued by youths led by a young printer, Charles Lenhart. The next day, a Sunday, Jones's ten-man posse again attempted an arrest but again were thwarted, this time by parishioners emptying out of a church. Appealing to Governor Shannon, Jones was given a detail of U.S Army dragoons but, returning to Lawrence, found that the culprit had absconded. That night, as Jones was standing near a trough, a shot harmlessly penetrated the water. Later, as he was in his tent bedding down, another shot ripped through the canvas, tearing the sheriff's jacket and inflicting a superficial wound. No culprit was found for either discharge, but later Charles Lenhart said he had fired the shot causing the splash; the second shot remains a mystery.

A grand jury was now convened under the chief justice of the Territorial Court. In his instructions to the jury, the judge insisted the derided "bogus enactments" had federal authority, and all who resisted them were "guilty of high treason." The jury promptly indicted most prominent free-state leaders and ordered "abatement" of the two newspapers in Lawrence, commanding the destruction of the Free State Hotel because that edifice "could only have been designed as a stronghold for resistance to law." At Dutch Henry's Crossing, Judge Cato's court reconvened, preparing secret indictments for the arrest of all the Browns.

By this time Jefferson Buford and his partisans were on hand, and Brown rode out on reconnaissance in his wagon with his surveying instruments to meet them. This episode was narrated by Brown to E.A. Coleman, and later appeared in Sanborn's book. As only pro-slavery men could hold title and thus be employed as surveyors, "the old man" was thought to be "sound on the goose," in the parlance of the time for those espousing pro-slavery opinions. Taking four of his sons to act as chain carriers, axman, and marker, Brown found a section line that ran through the Alabamans' camp. Without recognizing him, the men in the camp "indulged in the utmost freedom of expression" with him, Brown related; noting everything down in his jotter. One of them, apparently Buford, said, "We've come here to stay. We won't make no war on them as minds their own business; but all the Abolitionists, such as them damned Browns over there, we're going to whip, drive out, or kill—any way to get shut of them by God!"[25]

As Sherman's congressional investigating committee was moving on to Leavenworth, Sheriff Jones called on the U.S. marshal in Lecompton, Israel Donaldson, for help, and the marshal issued a call for "law-abiding citizens" to muster and enforce the charges of the grand jury. On the morning of May 21, the people of Lawrence awoke to the sight of eight hundred armed men on Mount Oread overlooking the town. At the urging of eastern politicians, Robinson and the other free-state leaders under arrest for "treason" and being held twelve miles away in Lecompton, had decreed that there be no resistance. Accordingly, there had been no preparation for a fight.

Taking positions at the head of the "Southern" columns were David R. Atchison, co-author of the Kansas-Nebraska bill; George W. Clarke, Territorial Delegate for Kansas and Indian agent; Dr. J.H. Stringfellow, editor of the *Squatter Sovereign* and pillar of the community in Weston, Missouri; Henry Clay Pate, editor of the *Border Star* in Westport, Missouri; Jefferson Buford, pro-slavery filibuster; and Harry Titus, ostentatious and grandiose slave baron from Florida.

After Marshal Donaldson and his posse had descended into Lawrence, made their arrests, and had had breakfast at the Free State Hotel, and Sheriff Jones and his posse had confiscated a few arms, Atchison addressed the throng. "Boys, this day. . . . We have entered the damned town and taught the damned Abolitionists a Southern lesson they will remember until the day they die." Then Atchison said, "And now, boys, we will go in again with our highly honorable Jones and test the strength of the damned Free State Hotel and teach the Emigrant Aid Company that Kansas will be ours. If man or woman dare stand before you, blow them to hell with a chunk of cold lead."[26]

Hoisting a flag with the inscription "Southern Rights," the pro-slavery flock descended into the town. Entering the two buildings housing the *Kansas Free State* and the *Herald of Freedom*, they smashed presses, throwing type into the Wakarusa River and books and other pilfered articles into the streets. The next target was the Free State Hotel, on which an artillery piece was trained from a distance, Atchison sighting the gun. The first round sailed cleanly over the building; and more shots were fired, having negligible effect. Finally, it was decided the building should be blown up, and four kegs of gunpowder were placed inside. When these exploded, the hotel remained standing, but the resulting fire gutted the structure. Robinson's home was burned, citizens were robbed, and the town plundered. The charge of the grand jury was complete, as the banner "Southern Rights" waved from the corner of the building formerly housing the *Herald of Freedom*. This was the famous sacking of Lawrence.

The next day, as John Jr. was working in his cornfield, news of the attack on Lawrence roused the Brown settlement near Osawatomie. Hurriedly rallying the men of the Pottawatomie Rifles, John Jr. was joined as well by his father and brothers. By 6 p.m. their party was ready to march in relief of the beleaguered town—until word came that Lawrence had been razed and that free-state men had offered no resistance to this Southern outrage. John Brown, an observer wrote, became "indignant that there had been no resistance; that Lawrence was not defended; and denounced the . . . leading free state men as cowards, or worse."[27]

Camping that night near Prairie City, the company was joined the next day by the Pomeroy Guards and a smaller company under the command of Samuel Shore. They had marched twenty-five miles, with Lawrence still twelve miles away, and saw it was pointless to travel farther. As a council was being held, a young boy rode in on horseback, announcing that border ruffians on the Pottawatomie Creek had warned the free-state settlers that they'd better clear off or they would be burned out and driven away or killed. John Brown said, "Something must be done to show these barbarians that we too have rights."[28] Who was willing, he asked, to go back to the Pottawatomie with him and act under his command? At this point, it could be said, John Brown had crossed his Rubicon: A blow must be struck, he now resolved, and it must fall in such a way as to instill a restraining fear in the foe. Calling his sons together—Watson, Frederick, Owen, Salmon, and Oliver and son-in-law Henry Thompson—he and they were joined by an Austrian-Jewish immigrant, Theodore Weiner, whose house was smoldering in ashes on Pottawatomie Creek, and James Townsley, a member of John Jr.'s company, who offered his lumber wagon to carry the troop, and to act as guide to the neighborhood upon which the intended retaliation was to fall. He knew all the pro-slavery families there, he said. Salmon Brown, the longest-lived of the Brown sons, related decades later, "The general purport of our intentions—some radical retaliatory measure—some killing was well understood by the whole camp."[29] John Brown took his accomplices aside individually, talking earnestly with each. For the remainder of the morning and on into the day the men were busy sharpening the double-edged broadswords Brown had obtained in Akron the previous year. With these weapons, the contemplated blow would be silent, and as the swords would be wielded in the darkness of night, they would fall unseen, thus raising maximal terror.

A day after the sacking of Lawrence, "One shout of exultation went up from the slave-holding States" as Massachusetts senator Charles Sumner, who had taken the seat vacated with Webster's resignation, was brutally attacked as he sat at his desk in the Senate by Representative Preston Brooks of South Carolina.[30] On May 19 Sumner had delivered his controversial address titled "The Crime Against Kansas" in the Senate chamber. The day before, South Carolina's Andrew Butler had called those denouncing the Southern "usurpation" in Kansas as having "an uncalculating fanaticism," while he and Stephen Douglas sought to shut down debate on Lewis Cass's Kansas enabling act. It was too late to dam or divert the tide, said Sumner: "The muster has begun. The strife is no longer local, but national. Even now, while I speak, portents lower in the horizon, threatening to darken the land, which already palpitates with the mutterings of civil war." In repartee after the conclusion of his two-day speech, Sumner characterized his colleague from Illinois as a "noise-some, squat, and nameless animal. . . . not a proper model for an American senator"; of his colleague from South Carolina, Andrew Butler, Sumner had said during his speech, "The senator from South Carolina has read many books of chivalry, and believes himself a chivalrous knight, with sentiments of honor and courage. Of course he has chosen a mistress to whom he has made vows, and who, though ugly to others, is always lovely to him; though polluted in the sight of the world, is chaste in his sight. I mean the harlot, Slavery. For her, his tongue is always profuse in words."

Preston Brooks was a nephew of Andrew Butler. A representative in the House for South Carolina, he had entered the Senate chamber after adjournment bringing with him a fellow South Carolinian, Representative Lawrence Keitt, to stand guard lest anyone try to come to Sumner's aid. Brooks had broached the notion of challenging the Massachusetts senator to a duel as a gentleman, but Keitt counseled that Sumner merited beating as one would a rabid dog. Accordingly, Brooks stepped up to the desk where Sumner was writing and, announcing his relation to his offended relative, savagely struck the top of Sumner's skull with his gutta-percha—a gold-handled cane. Repeatedly struck, Sumner tried to rise but found his legs wedged under the desk; bleeding profusely and unconscious, he slumped into the aisle.

As the ill-omened tidings of the sacking of Lawrence and the caning of Sumner pulsed simultaneously through an anguished North, on the afternoon of May 26 a man came riding over the Kansas plains, his horse reeking with sweat, Jason Brown was to recount. The fellow reported, "Five men have been killed on the Pottawatomie, horribly cut and mangled; and they say old John Brown did it."[31] Those killed had not been among the leadership openly encouraging violence by pro-slavery partisans; they had only been their enablers and abettors, men who allowed the "terror" against free-state settlers to occur in the first place. The dead were James Doyle and his sons William and Dury and their neighbors William Sherman and Allen Wilkinson. But with this joust, as John Brown's son Salmon put it, came recognition "there was as much room to give blows as to take them."[32] Characterizing the finality of the blow about to be given, John Brown said to an onlooker as they began to drive off in Townsley's lumber wagon, indicating the inexorability of his course—"Williams, I mean to steal a march on the slave hounds!"

More than two decades later, and in memory of all that had passed between that generative deed and his book's publication, Sanborn wrote, "Upon the swift and secret vengeance of John Brown in that midnight raid hinged the future of Kansas, as we can now see; and on that future again hinged the destinies of the whole country."[33] When news of the reprisal spread through eastern Kansas, Henry Clay Pate, at the head of the Westport, Missouri, Sharpshooters, was breaking camp at Franklin. Pate—a "butterfly man," as Redpath christened him—who had aspired to a literary career, now vowed in his capacity as deputy marshal to capture John Brown. As Pate started on this errand with forty stalwart pro-slavery men, his only fear, he crowed, was that he would not find the elderly man. Pillaging a free-state store for supplies at Prairie City, this "posse" headed toward Osawatomie, on the way despoiling the cabins of free-state settlers. Arresting two of John Brown's sons, John Jr. and Jason, on Judge Lecompte's "constructive treason" warrants, Pate turned them over to U.S. Army dragoons, who marched the men at a brisk pace, heavily bound and manacled, to Lecompton. John Jr., mentally distressed, and with his arms tightly pinned behind him, came away with permanent scars on his biceps that he afterwards called his "slavery bracelet."

When free-state military leaders Samuel Shore and Orellius Carpenter visited his camp, Brown was to hear the details of Pate's depredations. The three decided to call a council of free-state settlers for the next day at Prairie City. At that meeting some of the men present would decline to join in the resistance Brown was urging. "Why did you send Carpenter after us?" Brown asked. "I am not willing to sacrifice my men without having some hope of accomplishing something." Then he suggested, in an utterance recorded later by one of his company, the course he evidently was already considering: "If the cowardice and indifference of the free state people compel us to leave Kansas, what do you say, men, if we start south, for instance to Louisiana, and get up a Negro insurrection, and thereby compel them to let go their grip on Kansas, and so bring relief to our friends here?"[34]

Learning of Pate's whereabouts, Brown set out after him with a small troop on horseback joined by Shore's company. Having drawn his wagons and tents out on the prairie a dozen yards from a deep ravine, at the bottom of which was a thick stand of timber known as Black Jack, the Virginian had made his night encampment a strong one. The two free-state companies arrived there at about 6 a.m., immediately going on the attack, led by Brown. Posting Shore's company on the left, in the lower part of the ravine, Brown went to the right with seven men, gaining the ravine's head, thus snaring his opponent in crossfire.

A spirited fight ensued, and after a few minutes, with some seven or eight wounded, the Missourians were compelled to seek cover in the ravine. After several hours, Shore's company, its ammunition spent, was compelled to abandon the ground, as Brown continued pressing the fight. Sustaining more casualties, Pate finally sent out his lieutenant behind a free-state prisoner under a flag of truce.

As they were coming up, Brown demanded whether the man walking behind the man carrying the flag of truce was captain of the company.

"No," came the reply.

"Then you stay with me, and let your companion go and bring him out," Brown said. "I will talk with him."

As Pate approached, he was saying that he was a U.S. deputy marshal when Brown cut him short.

"Captain, I understand exactly what you are; and do not want to hear more about it. Have you a proposition to make to me?"

As the Virginian floundered in his response, Brown said, "Very well, Captain, I have one to make to you; your unconditional surrender."

Pate had no other resort than to comply.

Calling the skirmish the best fight he'd seen in Kansas, Brown ascribed his besting Pate to his selection of ground. Shortly afterwards he provided a detailed account of the action in a letter addressed to "wife and children," asking that a copy be made and sent to Gerrit Smith: "I know of no other way to get these facts and our situation before the world, nor when I can write you again."[35]

In his *The Conquest of Kansas by Missouri and Her Allies*, compiled from his articles as a *Tribune* correspondent and published in 1857, William Addison Phillips provided this assessment: "It was at this time that the Free State guerrilla companies sprang up. Finding that armed bands of pro-slavery men were prowling about the Territory, a handful of persons, chiefly youths, took the field. One company, under a young printer named Lenhart, was particularly active and bold. Capt. John Brown, senior, who lived near Osawatomie, immediately on the sacking of Lawrence concluded that the war was begun, and that it ought not to terminate." Black Jack had an electrifying effect on the free-state cause, Phillips wrote, its fighters augmented in the days following by youths, who, "with no recognized leaders, or temporary leaders," engaged in skirmishes with remnants of the invading Southern army.

It was Phillips's view that these guerrillas could have secured freedom for Kansas had they not been dispersed in the early weeks of June by federal soldiers. The direct involvement of government troops in backing the pro-slavery territorial officials came amid developing concern on the part of the Pierce administration, whose secretary of war was Jefferson Davis. The commander of the Department of the West, General Persifor Smith, wrote, "Patriotism and humanity alike require that rebellion be promptly crushed."[36]

Pate and Brown dueled again in the pages of the New York *Tribune*, Pate appearing on June 13, and Brown with a rejoinder on July 11. The Virginian alleged his capture had been the result of duplicity, as his flag of truce was disregarded, although he had praise for his subordinate who had carried it, albeit holding it behind the back of a free-state prisoner. Brown dismissed the complaint as one with "personal cognizance of what then occurred." He wrote of Pate's lieutenant, "I think him as brave as Capt. Pate represents. Of his disposition and character in other respects I say nothing now. The country and the world may probably know more here-after."

Shortly after the battle at Black Jack, Brown made his encampment in nearly impenetrable thickets on an island in Middle Creek that he had been ingeniously fortifying. He was there with his prisoners in early June when Colonel Edwin Sumner, commander of the 1st United State Cavalry, and Lieut. J.E.B. Stuart, advanced with fifty dragoons. By proclamation of President Pierce, Sumner declared he was authorized to command "all illegally formed companies" to disperse and that he had brought with him a U.S. deputy marshal with warrants for Brown's arrest for murder.

Brown met the officers outside his camp, as was to be verified by subsequent biographers. Attempting to parley, he said he wanted to arrange an exchange of prisoners, having in mind in particular his two sons. Sumner replied he was not there to discuss terms but to enforce dispersal of Brown's party and to secure the release of Brown's own prisoners. Having too few men on hand to contest the matter, Brown acquiesced, leading the two officers into his camp and allowing the release of Pate, his men, and their horses and arms. The deputy marshal was then told he should make his arrest. Evidently losing his nerve, the marshal said he couldn't find the warrants. "You are a damn liar and a coward!" Sumner said. "I saw the warrants in your hand last night." Pate began a harangue to the effect that Brown was getting away with murder. Sumner silenced Pate, saying, "I don't want to hear a word from you, sir, not a word."[37] Brown objected that Sumner was commanding him and his men to disperse but what of the Missourians encamped at Osawatomie? Sumner replied that he had also read the president's proclamation there.

Brown afterwards learned that his two sons, chained and padlocked at the ankles, had been marched twenty-five miles under sweltering sun to Lecompton. "What a humiliating, disgusting sight in a free government!" wired a *New York Times* correspondent.[38] Colonel Sumner later attempted to justify not seizing John Brown by saying his island base "could have held against a thousand men, as, from the peculiar nature of the ground, artillery could not be brought to bear on it."[39] With both sides of the internecine struggle now depleted of their provender and the federal government interceding militarily, fighting diminished for many weeks. Buford would post men on the border and blockade the Missouri River, with cannon placed on both sides of the river above Lexington, as mobs of armed men bent upon "lynching" boarded steamers searching for and turning back northern emigrants.

"Bleeding Kansas" and anti-slavery extensionism were the paramount issues roiling that summer in 1856. As the "Republicans" met in Bloomfield, Illinois, on May 29, those at the convention were in such a state over usurpations in Kansas by the territorial government, backed by the president and the federal army, that when Abraham Lincoln spoke, his remarks were so compelling and their effect on his listeners so mesmerizing that even reporters present failed to record them as he uttered them. Ex-governor Reeder was on hand, as was the wife of Charles Robinson, to add their affecting first-hand testimony.

At the Democratic national convention, which started in Cincinnati on June 2, delegates heard ample evidence of the threat posed by a growing rival party. Dismissing the sacking of Lawrence as partisan propaganda, they cited telegrams telling of a terrible massacre of "innocent" settlers on Pottawatomie Creek—evidence of the fanaticism of abolitionism! This new political party was a "sectional" party the Democratic platform asserted, and was itself culpable for "treason and armed resistance!"

Franklin Pierce was denied another run to seek the presidency on the seventeenth ballot when the nomination went to James Buchanan. A sixty-five-year-old bachelor from Pennsylvania, where he'd been a congressman and senator, Buchanan had served at a crucial time as secretary of state for Polk and as minister to Great Britain for Pierce. He had the advantage of having been out of the country during the tribulations of the Kansas-Nebraska bill on which Pierce had staked his leadership and failed. Buchanan, a more seasoned candidate, could now come in to manage the rollback of rising antislavery sentiment in the North and mollify the South. One Virginia newspaper editor murmured approvingly that Buchanan "never uttered a word which could pain the most sensitive Southern heart."[40]

In his father's fifty-sixth year of life, Salmon Brown wrote, "paternalism of necessity gave way to comradeship." Many have marveled too at John Brown's remarkable gamesmanship in the field, which enabled him to improvise tactically while keeping opponents off balance. An expert surveyor, he undoubtedly had a keen sense of topography that allowed him to screen his movements and surprise ever-wary opponents. Moving in parallel to the force transporting his captive sons, whom he hoped to rescue, Brown ordered a raid on a store owned by a man with pro-slavery sympathies, obtaining clothing, blankets, and provisions. From time to time his father would show himself, Jason Brown later wrote, so that the officer leading that company would order dragoons after him; those pursuing invariably returning exhausted and fuming after a rough ride through river bottoms and tangled thickets, their horses done in.

One of the most distinctive characteristics Brown displayed, and the one that gave him the potency uniformly discerned, was his thorough military organization and command of the men enlisted under him. This is attributable to his decades-long study of military arts, and the intense attention he must have devoted to these matters even in the months before his Kansas actions commenced. Although his company is often regarded as having sprung into existence in the space of the week between Pottawatomie and Black Jack, the very alacrity of that process itself stemmed from the fact that for his cadre he looked first to his own family.

James Redpath, a journalist and the first correspondent to happen upon Brown's encampment as he was about to confront Pate, wrote of that May 31, 1856, encounter in a panegyric published in January

1860. "I shall not soon forget the scene that here opened to my view," Redpath wrote. "Near the edge of the creek a dozen horses were tied, all ready saddled for a ride for life, or a hunt after Southern invaders. A dozen rifles and sabers were stacked against the trees."[41] Brown stood near a fire, Redpath reported, over which he was cooking a pig, his shirt sleeves rolled up, with a large piece of pork in his hand. Brown had taken as much care to study the arts of subsisting in the field as he had to commanding men, and it was he who prepared the company's food. "I would rather have the smallpox, yellow fever, and cholera all together in my camp, than a man without principles," Brown had told Redpath. "It's a mistake, sir, that our people make, when they think that bullies are the best fighters, or that they are the men fit to oppose those Southerners. Give me men of good principles; god-fearing men, men who respect themselves; and, with a dozen of them, I will oppose any hundred such men as those Buford ruffians."

Recounting their first meeting in April 1857, Sanborn wrote of seeing a copy of Brown's orderly book titled, "Articles of Enlistment and By-Laws of the Kansas Regulars, made and established by the commander, A.D. 1856." Thirty-five names were written on its pages, along with notes on dates of enlistment, the engagements fought by each, any wounds, and the deaths of a few. This information was followed by a score of by-laws providing for the election of officers, for the deportment and conduct of troops under arms, for orderly camp life, and for trial by jury in instances of infractions, etc., along with rules regarding the treatment and trial of prisoners, and for the receipt and disposal of captured property.

Among those listed in the book were three German immigrants with experience fighting in revolutionary Europe. One of these was Charles Kaiser, often referred to as "Charley the Hungarian," a Bavarian who settled in Hungary in his youth and in 1849 served in the Hungarian revolutionary army as a Hussar.[42] Kaiser's face, said August Bondi, a Viennese Jew himself a member of the company, was marked with lance and saber cuts. "He had a taste for war," Bondi remarked. The most informed description of life in Brown's camp and of the disposition of its commander comes from Bondi, who was an engineer by training. He wrote of his experiences for Kansas papers in 1879 in both German and English, and his testimony is recorded in *Transactions of the Kansas State Historical Society*, volume 8.

Roughing it in the bush, Bondi recalled, "We had come down to wearing ideas, suspicions, and memories of what had once been boots and hats."[43] He further related, "Many and various were the instructions [Brown] gave: . . . [W]e should never allow ourselves to be tempted by any consideration to acknowledge laws and institutions to exist as of right, if our conscience and reason condemned them. . . . He admonished us not to care whether a majority, no matter how large, opposed our principles and opinions. The largest majorities were sometimes only organized mobs, who's howling never changed black into white, or night into day. A minority conscious of its rights, based on moral principles, would, under a republican government, sooner or later become the majority. . . . Regarding the curse and crimes of the institution of slavery, he declared that the outrages committed in Kansas to further its extension had directed the attention of all intelligent citizens of the United States and of the world to the necessity of its abolishment."[44]

Redpath was told by one of the company that Brown would often "retire to the densest solitudes, to wrestle with his God in secret prayer." Concluding his letter to "wife and children," composed within days of his Potawatomie retaliation, Brown had written, "God, who has not given us over to the will of our enemies, but has moreover delivered them into our hand, will, we humbly trust, still keep and deliver us. We feel assured that He who sees not as men see, does not lay the guilt of innocent blood to our charge."

The Republican Party began its first national convention in Philadelphia on June 17. On the first ballot the nomination went to a candidate with no political record because he was as attractive to the public as he was to free-state Democrats, and the new political group advocating denationalizing of slavery. John C. Frèmont was known as the "Pathfinder," an appellation bestowed for his mapping of routes used by the inundation of farers flowing west to California in the previous decade when "gold-fever" had swept parts of the globe. Frèmont's credentials included promoting a free California in 1849 and supporting a free Kansas in 1856. The campaign slogan for the emergent coalition was "Free Soil, Free Speech, Freemen, Frèmont." His wife was the socially prominent Jessie Benton, daughter of Thomas Hart Benton, an enemy of the Atchison faction in Missouri, who as a Missouri senator had championed agrarian interests from 1820 to 1851.

Kansas was a major item in the convention oratory in Philadelphia, and the Democratic administration's failure there was sure to be exploited in the presidential canvass coming that fall. Concomitant with this, Pierce's secretary of war, Jefferson Davis, wrote to General Smith, commanding the Department of the West at Fort Leavenworth, Kansas Territory: "The position of the insurgents is that of open rebellion against the Laws and Constitutional authorities, with such manifestation of purpose to spread devastation over the land as no longer justifies further hesitation or indulgence."[45] The original intent of the Atchison-Stringfellow faction had been to lead an army from Missouri to break up the free-state legislature, a program that now appeared daunting. The border was seventy-five miles away, and it would be difficult to get an army safely over and even more hazardous to get one back. The "Topeka legislature" scheduled to meet July 4 would not be allowed to convene, and Col. Sumner was ordered by proclamation of the president and of the governor of Kansas to be on hand to prevent that body from gathering. Accordingly, by July 3 five companies of dragoons with two pieces of artillery were encamped on the edge of Topeka, while another large force under Colonel Philip St. George Cooke moved in from Fort Riley to encamp northwest of Topeka. Augmenting the federal troops were various territorial officials, marshals, and deputy marshals. Governor Shannon, who had been advised to be out of the territory, boarded a steamboat at Leavenworth bound for St. Louis, so that he would be discreetly absent when the edict was enforced.

John Brown, leaving his company of twenty-two men camped with their mounts on the bank of the Wakarusa River, on July 2 sent word to William Addison Phillips that he wanted to see Phillips at the Eastern House in Lawrence. There was a supply of arms and ammunition at Topeka, and it was expected that 1,000 free-state men might be on hand to protect their government. John Brown's movement was part of this general plan.

Phillips, a Scotsman, had immigrated to the United States with his parents in 1838. Admitted to the bar in 1855, he began to practice law in Illinois and then went to Kansas as special correspondent for the New York *Tribune*. His dispatches detailing events in Kansas would be lauded by Higginson when compiled into a volume as "altogether the best and fairest book upon the confused history of that time and place," which became, along with Sara Robinson's testimony and authentication, an important element that fall among the Republican party's campaign literature. But those influences were then yet to come. In 1879 Phillips's "Three Interviews with Old John Brown" was published in the *Atlantic Monthly*; he also detailed Brown's interactions in Kansas in *The Martyr of Harper's Ferry*.

Phillips was expected in Topeka the next day to report on the situation there for the *Tribune*, and when Brown invited the journalist to travel with him Phillips consented. Riding down Massachusetts Street as one of Brown's men fell in behind them, they proceeded up Mount Oread and waited for the remainder of the company. Climbing the hill in pairs, giving no overt recognition to their commander or of Phillips, the men closely trailed them, riding up the California road as darkness settled in. Phillips wrote years afterward that he could never forget their conversation as they lay down on blankets spread on the ground under the stars, their saddles together so that their heads were only feet apart. That night spent in conversation with Brown, Phillips wrote, was his first "good opportunity to judge the old man's character. I had seen him in his camp, had seen him in the field, and he was always an enigma.... He told me of his experiences as a wool merchant and a manufacturer in Ohio, and of his travels in Europe. I soon discovered that his tastes ran in a military rather than a commercial channel.[46]

"In his ordinary moods," Phillips continued, "the man seemed so rigid, stern, and unimpressible when I first knew him that I never thought a poetic and impulsive nature lay behind that cold exterior. The whispers of the wind on the prairie was full of voices to him, and the stars as they shone in the firmament of God seemed to inspire him." In discussing the men of Kansas, Brown was not wont to criticize both parties, Phillips wrote, "The pro-slavery men he censured bitterly—slavery besotted everything, making men coarse and brutal—and while there were many among the free-state men that were admirable and sincere, there were too many broken-down politicians who would rather pass resolutions than act. These men would always be found to sacrifice their principles for their advantage.

"One of the most interesting things in his conversation that night, and one that marked him as a theorist (and perhaps to some extent he might be styled a visionary), was his treatment of our forms of social and political life," Phillips maintained. "He thought society ought to be organized on a less selfish basis; for while material interests gained something by the deification of pure selfishness, men and women lost much by it. He said that all great reforms, like the Christian religion, were based on broad, generous, self-sacrificing principles. He condemned the sale of land as a chattel, and thought that there was an infinite number of wrongs to right before society would be what it should be, but that in our country slavery was the 'sum of all villainies,' and its abolition the first essential work. If the American people did not take courage and end it speedily, human freedom and republican liberty would soon be empty names in these United States."

On the morning of July 4, to the sound of fifes and marching feet as crowds jostled in the streets, members of the free-state legislature filed into Constitution Hall in Topeka. Marshal Donaldson, too, walked up its steps, reported Redpath in the Chicago *Tribune,* describing the lawman as having "imbecile looking eyes."[47] Donaldson was there to serve the presiding officer with the president's proclamation.

At noon, standing in martial columns before the hall as a free-state battalion was receiving a banner inscribed "OUR LIVES FOR OUR RIGHTS," Col. Sumner arrived leading his troop and cannon. The ceremony concluding, dragoons occupied the square, unlimbering their artillery pieces and lighting slow matches.

With his sword sheathed at his side, Sumner strode to the desk of the clerk where the roll was being tallied. "No quorum," the clerk announced. The speaker ordered the sergeant-at-arms to go out and bring in the other members. Sumner would wait no longer. "Gentlemen, this is the most disagreeable duty of my whole life," he announced. "My orders are to disperse the legislature, and I am here to tell you that it cannot meet. God knows I have no partisan feelings in the matter. I have just returned from the border where I have been driving out bands of Missourians. You must disperse. This body cannot be permitted to meet. Disperse."[48]

As Sumner strode out of the building, the brogue of W.A. Phillips trailed after him, "Colonel, you have robbed Oliver Cromwell of his Laurels."[49] With the legislature complying with the order, as the federal officer rode off, the crowd in the street gave three cheers for "Frèmont" and three groans for "Pierce."[50]

Less than a week after the pitiless caning of Charles Sumner and a week after the sacking of Lawrence, the Radical Abolition Party met in Syracuse to nominate candidates for president and vice president Gerrit Smith and Samuel McFarland. As Douglass announced his support for them, placing their names at the head of the editorial column in his paper, he said the platform of the new Republican Party was too narrow to admit true anti-slavery voters. Criticized for maintaining an abstract position and for obstructing the newly formed coalition, another of the anti-slavery papers called upon Douglass to join in the Republican ranks. Should he and other abolitionists become Republicans, Douglass retorted, "we should feel that we were retrograding instead of advancing." To the charge that by shunning the Republican candidate Radical Abolition Party adherents would aid in the election of a Democratic president and assure the loss of Kansas, Douglass replied, "We deliberately prefer the loss of Kansas to the loss of our anti-slavery integrity," but added that that was arguing at a disadvantage: "It is by no means certain that Kansas can be saved even with the votes of abolitionists."[51]

Five days prior to the convention in Syracuse its importance for Douglass could be gauged in the contents of a letter he wrote to Smith: "Now I want your counsel. Your unceasing interest in me and in my paper, and in the cause to which it is devoted, makes it right that I should seek your counsel." Given the strain of balancing the demands of the lecture circuit and editing a weekly with dwindling subscribership while struggling against mounting debt, Douglass argued that he was "almost convinced" his paper could not be sustained. His credit was still good, but he felt he had done all he could, deep into the paper's ninth year, "toward putting it on a permanent footing." He asked, "Shall the paper go down and be a total wreck—or shall it be saved—by being merged into the Radical Abolitionist?"

Failure was a galling prospect, said Douglass, particularly as no "Negro" paper had yet managed to sustain itself on a long-term basis. He was suggesting nothing for himself in terms of a new enterprise, not even a place on the paper, but simply seeking help in averting its "positive failure." And yet, Douglass conceded, it might be "an element of strength to the concern to have me in some way connected with it."[52]

Nevertheless, by August, even at his most vulnerable, Douglass had abruptly removed the names of the candidates of the Radical Abolition Party from the banner of his paper and endorsed the Republican candidates Frèmont and Dayton, opening a breach in the cordial relations between himself and Smith. In defending this changed outlook, Douglass announced "that upon radical Abolition grounds, the final battle against slavery must be fought out." The divergence in his paper "this week and last week, is a difference of Policy, not of Principle."

As Douglass now saw, the struggle for Kansas had brought about a fundamental realignment in the American political landscape that would only admit two parties. Since this was the case, even despite the limited vision of the Republican politicians, he said, it was his duty "to be with the natural division for freedom, in form, as well as in fact." In doing so, Douglass felt, he could "uphold the Radical Abolition platform in the very ranks of the Republican Party."[53]

Despite the precarious situation of his paper, Douglass continued publishing as an independent editor and as sole proprietor, and by September he and Smith were again acting as colleagues, Smith continuing to provide "generous donations" to the paper. "I am just home from Ohio, where I have been lecturing, and find your kind letters for which please accept my thanks," Douglas wrote. "What I think of your letter to our friend William Goodell, will be seen in my paper of yesterday.... Yes! I get it all around. Mr. Garrison tries his hand upon my case this week, the most skillful of them all. The Liberator and Standard seem more shocked at my apostasy from the Radical Abolition Society, than at Mr. May's apostasy from the American Society."[54]

In spring 1856, deeming the Emigrant Aid Company insufficient to raise the required flow of settlers to the Kansas Territory, Eli Thayer proposed the creation of a National Kansas Committee for the support and relief of free-state settlers, announcing a meeting on June 20 in Cleveland, Ohio. His plan called for an outfitting depot to be located at Chicago, with officers and directors also located there. A national committee would see to it that state, city, and district committees formed to carry out that work. Ex-governor Reeder proposed that 5,000 armed settlers be sent to Kansas, and that they be provisioned for a year, supported from a fund to be raised, with emigration conducted through Iowa and Nebraska.

This effort was followed by a meeting at Buffalo, New York, on July 11, 1856, at which the National Kansas Committee formed, with Thaddeus Hyatt as president. An executive committee began holding sessions on July 19 and by mid-August had the necessary organizational work completed in twelve of the fifteen northern states. One of the most energetic states in this activity was Massachusetts, where the Emigrant Aid Company folded its work, becoming the Massachusetts State Kansas Committee, whose outstanding members were George Luther Stearns, Dr. Samuel Gridley Howe, Theodore Parker, and Thomas Wentworth Higginson, with Franklin Sanborn as secretary. Higginson's steadfast friend, Martin Stowell, of the attempted Anthony Burns rescue, would lead the first contingent organized from the state.

All through the summer a spontaneous popular outpouring spread through the major population centers of the North—Boston, New Haven, New York, Buffalo, Philadelphia, Cleveland, and Milwaukee, along with scores of towns and rural communities. The effort raised $200,000 throughout the North, with Massachusetts alone contributing $80,000. Finding he could no longer raise money among the wealthy and the business class, Stearns turned to common workers, who donated this sum from meager earnings. The popular response had been so broad as even to be astonishing to many receptive eyes and ears. National committee members were given use of telegraph wires gratis by telegraph companies, and the Burlington and Missouri Railroad donated 1,000 fares to settlers traveling from Burlington, Vermont, to Mt. Pleasant, Iowa; that line's fare from Chicago to Mt. Pleasant was set at $3, with other railroads responding with the same.

From New Haven, Connecticut, a company armed with "Beecher's Bibles" departed for Kansas as emigrants from Massachusetts joined hundreds from New York congregating at Buffalo. A Chicago saloon-keeper, James Harvey, sold his business to lead a train of Illinois emigrants; that bustling metropolis became the hub for embarkation, with covered wagons loaded onto flatcars to be unloaded at railheads in Iowa for the final leg. Higginson wrote of this remarkable response in summer 1856 that "it was all really a rehearsal in advance of the great enlistments of the Civil War."[55]

To encourage immigration to Kansas from the Midwest, into this maelstrom now strode James Lane, who had left Kansas after the "treason warrants" had been issued. Eastern newspapers reported on his progress, as the immigrants he gathered became a marching demonstration for "Free Soil, Free Men and Frémont." On the steps of the Chicago courthouse Lane eulogized the new territory. That territory was not the home of derided "Massachusetts Yankees," as border ruffians were alleging, he maintained, but the home of people from Illinois, from Indiana, and from Ohio—who were now shackled under the tyranny of slavocrats. Recalling his service during the Mexican War at Buena Vista, he described how he had sat on his horse next to Illinois' own General J.J. Hardin and that state's current candidate for governor, nominated at the Bloomington convention, William H. Bissell: "It did not occur to me that I should be indicted for treason because I loved liberty better than slavery."[56] When he had finished, his audience rushed up to donate their hard-earned coin and cash—working men, sailors, boys, widows, seamstresses.

A great obstacle had been thrown up before this northern immigration into Kansas when the Missouri River was closed to northern traffic. Now those making the trek, after disembarking from the nearest railhead at Iowa City, needed to toil week after week over three hundred miles of seemingly endless open prairie, exposed but for their tents and wagon covers to the weather and the sun. Days would pass where not a single dwelling was seen, wood and brush for fires was scarce; in addition, they needed to carry every edible thing. The first attempt over this route was by the Massachusetts party under the charge of Martin Stowell, closely followed by Lane's "Northern Emigrant Army"—who were marking their trail through Iowa to Nebraska City with cairns, or "Lane's chimneys," to guide later parties. Richard Hinton, another Scotsman and enterprising journalist who became a noted partisan figure, was among Stowell's company. Also participating, having joined them in Buffalo, was another of John Brown's sons-in-law, William Thompson.

Sitting idly in camp just over the Nebraska-Kansas line in the hottest hour of the day, Hinton had been watching a wagon and a single horse toiling northward along the trail stretching toward Topeka. As the wagon rolled into camp, he could see a wounded man lying on its bed and beside the wagon an elderly man riding a gaunt gray horse. "Have you a man in your camp named William Thompson?" the old man asked as he approached. "You are from Massachusetts, young man, I believe, and Mr. Thompson joined you at Buffalo."

"As I heard the question, I looked up and met the full, strong gaze of a pair of luminous, questioning eyes," Hinton later wrote. "Somehow I instinctively knew this was John Brown, and with that name I replied, saying Thompson was in our company."[57]

The man in the bed of the wagon was Henry Thompson, William's brother, wounded at Black Jack. Also with Brown were his sons Owen and Salmon, both injured in accidents. They were headed back to the Adirondack farm or to Ohio, excepting Owen, each determined to "learn and practice war no more."

Also riding with Brown was Samuel Walker, a lightly framed man from the Midwest with a hip impediment, who had been one of the commanders of the free-state companies in the "Wakarusa War." Walker had brought fifteen of "his boys" to meet Lane at the border and warn him that he was liable to arrest if he entered the territory. Lane had been issuing high-sounding titles under his own authority but had no standing with the National Kansas Committee, whose leading members, Thaddeus Hyatt and Dr. Howe, were in Nebraska City. Meeting Lane at Nebraska City, Walker handed him a letter requesting he leave his "army" at the border. "The Grim Chieftain," as Lane came to be called, became disconsolate; he "could never go back to the states and look the people in the face and tell them that as soon as I got these Kansas friends of mine fairly into danger, I had to abandon them." (He blew his brains out in 1866.)[58]

Walker changed from being an emissary of political interest to a partisan. "General, the people of Kansas would rather have you than all the party at Nebraska City," he told Lane. "I have fifteen good boys that are my own. If you will put yourself under my orders, I'll take you through all right."

Also in Nebraska City, provided with new clothes, hat, and horse, compliments of Thaddeus Hyatt, was John Brown. "The Captain was riding a splendid horse, and was dressed in plain white summer clothing," Redpath wrote. "He wore a large straw hat, and was closely shaven: everything about him was scrupulously clean." Some youths, without knowing who he was, the journalist added, thought he must be a "distinguished man."[59]

Lane, Walker, and Brown, together with Walker's boys, would now ride back into Kansas with the intention of reigniting the flames of civil war, covering the 160 miles to Lawrence in thirty hours.

The principal pro-slavery towns in Kansas were Leavenworth and Lecompton, along with Atchison in the north, with an arc of border ruffian settlements in Paola, Franklin, Indianola, Ozawkee, Hickory Point, and Kickapoo. These hubs flanked the principal free-state towns, Osawatomie, Lawrence, and Topeka, and the accompanying scattering of settlements and farms surrounding them. "The line thus indicated," wrote Richard Hinton, regarding the conditions in summer 1856, "was almost completed and held by fortified camps occupied by Buford's Alabamians and Georgians; Atchison's, Stringfellow's, and Reid's Missourians."[60] In the south, Fort Scott became the rendezvous of several smaller bodies from Arkansas, Texas, and Louisiana, "not as well known and conspicuous as their confreres in the central and northern sections," Hinton wrote.[61]

The trail stretching north from Topeka to Nebraska City had been opened for free-state transit by Aaron Dwight Stevens, then known under the *nom de guerre* Colonel Whipple. Stevens had been a sergeant in the U.S. Army dragoons who was court-martialed for striking an officer who had abused a soldier; imprisoned, Stevens escaped and became one of the fighting free-state leaders in Topeka. He was "engaged in opening a road from the Kaw River (at Topeka due north to the Nebraska line)," wrote Hinton. "It was only by this flanking movement that the free-state settlements, then blockaded and surrounded, could be succored."[62]

In the third week of August a furious campaign beleaguered all the pro-slavery forts ringing Lawrence in the space of a few days. The first attack came at Franklin where a cannon called "old Sacramento," captured in the Mexican War by a Missouri volunteer militia company, was seized. At that time a well-known photograph of the weapon being manned by a free-state battery was undoubtedly taken, since the cannon was returned to the pro-slavery side in Lecompton as a truce was arranged and prisoners exchanged upon the campaign's successful conclusion. Appearing left to right in the photograph are James Redpath, Richard Realf, Augustus Wattles, John T. "Ottawa" Jones, George Gill, and John Brown's son Owen.[63]

After the assault at Franklin in which Lane did not participate, he summoned the "old man" with his company for a combined assault on Fort Saunders. Sanborn reported, "General Lane drew his forces up in front of the fort while Captain Brown occupied the right wing with his cavalry."[64] John Jr., receiving reports through the grapevine as they came into the jail in Lecompton, wrote to "Brother Jason and others" on August 16 that their father had been in the fight at Franklin, and also "aided in routing the gang on Washington Creek, as well as in the capture of Titus and his crew. . . . He is an omnipresent dread to the ruffians."[65] Jason wrote to his sister Ruth on August 13 with a similar assessment: "Old Capt. Brown can now be raised from every prairie and thicket."

Notwithstanding these testimonies, it has often been difficult to explain in detail John Brown's agency in the fighting because he typically took a "step back." Although he surely and effectively put his hand to the work, he kept his own counsel, assisting in the general result while maintaining an independence of action for himself and for his company. He never sought overall command, as Lane did, but kept his keen eyes trained toward the stirrings of the larger and more extensive war he saw looming across the national panorama.

After the capture of Titus's blockhouse near Lecompton, where Harry Titus had built a pillared mansion with slave quarters, Walker brought the prisoner into Lawrence. "The citizens swarmed around us, clamoring for the blood of our prisoner," Walker wrote. "The committee of safety had a meeting and decided that Titus should be hanged, John Brown and other distinguished men urging the measure strongly."[66] Walker told the committee that Titus was his prisoner, and that he had promised Titus his life, and now would defend it with his own.

"Captain Brown and Doctor Avery were outside haranguing the mob to hang Titus despite my objections," Walker continued. "They said I had resisted the committee of safety and was, myself, therefore a public enemy. The crowd was terribly excited, but the sight of my three hundred solid bayonets held them in check."

As his last act in the territory as governor, on August 17 Shannon arranged the release of Titus and other prisoners held on both sides. Brown addressed forty Missourians paroled in the exchange, urging that the men acknowledge their "error" and that they return to their homes and desist from their attacks, becoming loyal, law-abiding, and liberty-loving citizens of the republic. Had their leaders been here in those men's stead, they would have received no leniency, although Brown had been made to relinquish Titus. Evidently, these partisans of slavery were eager to see and to hear from their vanquisher. That speech, recorded in Johnathan Winkely's *John Brown the Hero* published in 1905, began: "Men of Missouri, one of your number has asked to see John Brown. Here he is. Look at him, and hereafter remember that he is the enemy of all evil doers."[67]

Shannon returned to Lecompton to report to General Smith and to write his resignation letter to the president, even as pro-slavery vigilantes were seeking to even the score. Seven free-state cabins were burned, including that of Samuel Walker. Before Shannon's letter could reach Washington, President Pierce's letter removing him from office reached Kansas. With pro-slavery figure Daniel Woodson temporarily stepping in as acting governor, as he had done after Reeder's firing, Atchison and Stringfellow called for a meeting in Kansas City "to rally instantly to the rescue" as a mass meeting convened at Lexington, Missouri.

In the Southern states newspaper reports were drawing a harrowing portrait of conditions in Kansas—Lane and his marauders were in the territory, while another 2,000 Northerners waited on the border to enter the fray. "Kansas is now in a state of open war," the Chicago *Tribune* wrote. "It is not a war in which the interests of Kansas are alone at stake, but the cause of freedom in the whole country."[68] Missouri's *Weston Argus* chimed in, "Civil War has begun. . . . Let the watchword be extermination total and complete."[69]

On August 20 Brown was back in Osawatomie, Bondi related: "with a spic and span four-mule team, the wagon loaded with provisions; besides he was well supplied with money and all contributed by the Northern friends of Free State Kansas, men like Thaddeus Hyatt."[70] Brown joined in with the war parties of Captain James B. Cline and James H. Holmes; on August 25 Cline swept into Linn County to the south, capturing twelve prisoners and some military equipment, while the next day Brown led a raid on a pro-slavery settlement to the east, returning two nights later with a hundred and fifty cattle. Even dumb animals at this time were referred to as "pro-slavery" or "free-state." It was Brown's policy to attack the economy that undergirded the enemy, with the "property" distributed to reimburse the costs of levying war.

A horde of 2,000 men began mustering in Westport under the command of Atchison, Reid, and Clarke. They crossed the border in what was to be the last of the border ruffian invasions into Kansas from Missouri until 1863, when Charles Quantrill led a massacre at Lawrence in retaliation for Lincoln's Emancipation Proclamation. One detachment under George Washington Clarke rode into Linn County to overrun free-state settlements there. The larger wing under Atchison set out to destroy Lawrence. John W. Reid, a veteran of the Mexican War with the rank of general, led four hundred mounted men to "wipe out" John Brown.

As he paused to take his noon rest, Clarke was overtaken by a free-state company commanded by James Montgomery, a diminutive black-bearded preacher and member of a sect known as the Disciples of Christ founded by Alexander Campbell. Montgomery had already made a reputation as a fighter; thoroughly surprised, the enemy fled, leaving most of its horses. On the morning of August 31 Atchison's columns parried with the "army" commanded by James Lane under the alias "General Joe Cook." The determining skirmish of this campaign had occurred a day before as Reid's force swept into Osawatomie, overwhelming and all but destroying it. But Reid's had been a Pyrrhic victory, achieved under scourging violence directed by John Brown.

Reid had wheeled his mounted column with cannon around Osawatomie, halting on a ridge northwest of the town. Farther west,

Brown was in his encampment when he received word from a young messenger of the Missourians' arrival. The boy also brought shocking news for a father that the enemy's advance guard had just shot and killed his son Frederick and Frederick's cousin. With fifteen men of his newly enlisted company, Brown hurried into the town, determined, as he later wrote his wife, to "save the women and children first, and then ourselves if we can." With Reid's metal bearing down on them and glistening in the morning sun— and outnumbered ten to one—Brown could do little more against the foe than "to annoy them" from a thick timber on the south bank of the Osage River. Instructing the men to keep out of sight as they spread out forty feet to conceal their number, he cautioned, "Keep cool, take good aim, shoot low." As the enemy approached, Brown directed a withering fire, sending Reid's column reeling, then retreating. After fifteen to twenty minutes, as many as thirty-two of the enemy had been killed; forty to fifty were wounded. Regrouping and discharging their cannon with grape shot into the trees, they again charged, as Brown and his men withdrew by wading across the river; Brown was seen with raised pistols, his long linen duster floating in the water behind him, wearing his straw hat.

Several free-state men were killed in this retreat; and as the town's thirty dwellings were fired, the free-state prisoners taken were summarily shot. At this time, the dwelling of John Jr. was pillaged and the four-hundred-volume library he had spent decades compiling was destroyed in the flames. The story told later in the Missouri press by Reid was much different. Said he, "the abolitionists had been shot down, thirty-one in all, as easily as 'shooting quail.'" It was reported the "notorious John Brown was also killed . . . in attempting to cross the river," and "the pro-slavery party have five wounded."

But the three wagons piled high with bloody corpses had a chastening effect on Missouri bravado. "The battle of Osawatomie was the most brilliant and important episode of the Kansas war," Senator John J. Ingalls of Kansas (1873-1891) wrote. "It was the high divide of the contest. It was our Thermopylae. John Brown was our Leonidas with his Spartan band."

One of the new immigrants to the territory and the free-state cause was a 22-year-old Ohioan, Edward Bridgman, who settled near Osawatomie on May 1, 1856. He had taken a claim about a mile from the town, adjacent to that of "Win" Anthony, a brother of Susan B. Anthony. The men became fast friends. Bridgman later recalled in his *With John Brown in Kansas*, published in 1915, that Brown and his troop had alighted on his doorstep the evening before the battle, and as the men had dismounted they promptly fell to the ground and to their rest without even bothering with dinner. This veteran of many campaigns of the Army of the Potomac 1861-1865 well understood their condition, having felt the same after a day's march of thirty miles in the sweltering Virginia sun. Their captain had finished his day, he wrote, "reading his Bible by candlelight" on the step of his cabin, and he found book and candle in the morning still on the step where Brown had left them. Casting an eye into Brown's Bible it was evident to Bridgman that Brown was a continual consultant to the volume, heavily annotating it in its margins, particularly in the chapters relating to the Gospels and the Psalms. Bridgman also remarked on the significance of Osawatomie: "[T]he first battle of the war was fought at Osawatomie, and the war was begun on August 30, 1856, with five years intermission;—the war ending April 9, 1865, in which we had over two thousand engagements."[71]

For Brown, "Bleeding Kansas" had reached its nadir or perhaps its apogee, from which for the nation there would be no turning back. Standing on the opposite bank of the Osage River overlooking the smoke and flames, his breast heaving, tears streaming from his eyes, his son Jason (who had been released from the Lecompton prison), at his side, Brown vowed, as Oswald Garrison Villard quoted him as saying in his *John Brown 1800-1859, A Biography Fifty Years After*, published in 1910, "God sees it. I have only a short time to live—only one death to die, and I will die fighting for this cause. There will be no more peace in this land until slavery is done for. I will give them something else to do than to extend slave territory. I will carry the war into Africa."

At midnight, Brown was at the Adair cabin, where the body of his son Frederick was laid. Jonathan Winkley, later a physician, was there when the elder Brown arrived. Winkely said that Brown approached his son's body without a word, tears glistening on his cheeks and in his eyes, his face a profound visage of sadness. Giving instructions on how to dispose of his son's body, after a few moments he was gone.

New territorial governor John W. Geary, riding in from Leavenworth, was soon afterward to write U.S. secretary of state William Marcy: "Desolation and ruin reigned on every hand; homes and firesides were deserted; the smoke of burning dwellings darkened the atmosphere; women and children, driven from the habitations wandered over the prairies; the highways were infested with numerous predatory bands and the towns were fortified and garrisoned by armies of conflicting partisans, each excited almost to frenzy, and determined upon mutual extermination."[72] Days earlier, steaming up the Missouri, Geary's boat had passed Shannon's as he was heading east. At Lexington, a large crowd had been waiting for Geary on the dock; an even bigger crowd awaited at Kansas City. Striding down the gangplank at Leavenworth, Geary was an impressive sight: balding and bearded with a resemblance to Presbyterian leader John Knox. At six feet, six inches and two hundred and sixty pounds, Geary was powerfully built. A Pennsylvania Democrat, he had led troops in the Mexican War and been lionized. He had employed slaves in mines he owned in Virginia and had helped bring California into the Union as a free state, serving in 1850 as San Francisco's first mayor. He was not thought a good choice in the South, but he was Pierce's man, sent to grapple with a seemingly intractable quandary before the presidential election.

In Lawrence, as the new governor was still on the way, the moment was seen as an auspicious one to attack Lecompton, ending the pro-slavery government there and freeing the "treason prisoners." A plan was set: Harvey, the Chicagoan, was to march up the north bank of the Kaw River with his men to the ferry to prevent retreat from the pro-slavery capital, while Lane was to lead a column and attack the town from the south. Harvey's contingent was in position and waited twelve hours before withdrawing. Only then did Lane's column advance to be met by Lieutenant Colonel Philip St. George Cooke and the U.S. Army troops. Recognizing Walker, the federal officer called out, "What in hell are you doing here?"

"We are after our prisoners and our rights," answered Walker.

"How many men have you?"

"About four hundred foot and two hundred horseback."

"Well, I have six hundred men and six cannon, and you can't fight here—except with me."

"I don't care a damn how many men you have," Walker told Cooke. "We are going to have our prisoners, or a big fight!"

Dismissing Walker's contestations, Cooke insisted upon seeing General Lane. Lane was not in command, said Walker; if Cooke wanted to parley, he would call a council of war. Soon a half a dozen free-state officers had drawn their horses around the lieutenant colonel.

"You have made a most unfortunate move for yourselves," said Cooke. "The Missourians, you know, have gone and the militia have nearly gone, having commenced crossing yesterday to my knowledge. As to the prisoners, whilst I will make no terms with you, I can inform you that they were promised to be released yesterday morning."

Lane, seeing the federal officer, had disappeared into the free-state ranks, grabbing a private's rifle as Walker faced down Cooke. The day Geary landed at Leavenworth, Lane was on his way to the Iowa border to avoid arrest. He would be escorted out at a rapid pace by Colonel Whipple (Stevens) and his company.

Geary arrived in Lecompton on September 10. Meeting the same crowds of rowdies in the streets as he had seen in Missouri and in Leavenworth, he established his headquarters as he sought the dismissal of three hated federal officials—Judge Lecompte, Marshal Donaldson, and "General" Clarke. Rebuffing the proffered services of Henry Clay Pate, Geary ordered the militia and all other armed bands to disperse, while the "treason prisoners" were released on bail. He would serve no faction, Geary announced, and would rely on federal troops to maintain order.

That evening Charles Robinson was back in Lawrence, which teemed with people he had not known before his arrest. A celebration in honor of all the released prisoners took place that night; John Brown was there for a joyous reunion with his son, John Jr., and was included among those delivering speeches.

Four days later, despite Geary's attempt at reconciliation, it was reported that Atchison and his entourage of pro-slavery stalwarts—Reid, Whitfield, and Stringfellow among them—had an army of 2,500 infantry and cavalry combined, with a howitzer and a six-pounder, and were again assembling at Franklin. Intent on administering a decisive retribution on Lawrence, they also intended to demonstrate to the new governor the permanence of the pro-slavery reign.

In Lawrence, couriers were dispatched along three routes in order to summon Geary from Lecompton. But he and Lieutenant Colonel Cooke would not set out in relief of the town until two o'clock the following morning. The number of fighting men in Lawrence that day was negligible; Lane and his contingent were on the northern border. Colonel Whipple, Harvey's Chicagoans, and others were out on raids, as many fighters had gone home to their families and farms. With the townspeople laboring on redoubts and other defensive barricades in a desultory fashion, some merchants distributed pitchforks in lieu of rifles. Only about two hundred men were on hand, along with a few women, to bear arms; women also were running cartridges. But John Brown was among these Lawrence stalwarts and was asked to take command in the event of an attack. This role he declined, consenting instead to act as "advisor." As in previous actions, it is difficult to gauge the exact impact of his presence, and many commentators have discounted its significance altogether. Another of those on his way into Lawrence, on a fact-finding tour for the Massachusetts State Kansas Committee, was Thomas Wentworth Higginson, who would serialize his observations in a series of articles entitled "A Ride Through Kanzas [sic]" that ran in the New York *Tribune* in September and October 1856, and was carried as well in the *Liberator*.

In his dispatch dated October 4, Higginson described Brown bucking up the defenders of Lawrence: "They had no regular commander, any more than at Bunker Hill, but the famous 'Old John Brown,' moved among them saying 'Fire low boys; be sure to bring down your eye to the hinder sight of your rifle, and aim at the feet rather than the head.' It was for lack of diligence in this, he said, that he himself had 'so many times escaped; for if all the bullets which have ever been aimed at me had hit me, I would have been as full of holes as a riddle.'"[73]

Walking among the barricades and redoubts, Brown conferred with men and women, offering encouragement. "Now is probably the last opportunity you will have of seeing a fight, so that you had better do your best," he said. At five o'clock four hundred enemy horsemen presented themselves in line of battle at two miles' distance. "Brown's movement now was a little on the offensive order; for he ordered out all the Sharp's riflemen from every part of the town . . . marched them a half mile into the prairie, and arranged them three paces apart, in a line parallel with that of the enemy; and then they lay down upon their faces in the grass, awaiting the order to fire," Redpath wrote. "As a single scout dashed forward, when within range, a shot rang out, raising the sod in front of his horse. In a few moments the firing became general and in the darkness and otherwise stillness of the night, the continued flash, flash, flash, of these engines of death along the line of living fire presented a scene the appearance of which was at once not only terrible but sublimely beautiful."[74] Sanborn, in his account, wrote of riderless horses crossing paths in the night.

The following morning Geary arrived with his escort of four hundred dragoons towing four cannon. In a dawn outdoor conclave he,

Robinson, and Brown, with a few others, conferred amidst the ash and detritus of war. Robinson excused the warlike display as being necessary for the protection of the town; Geary acknowledged that Americans of spirit would protect their property. As the conference terminated, word came that Atchison's army had decamped and was returning to Missouri. Addressing a mass assemblage, Geary reminded everyone of his proclamation, commanding "armed partisans of both sides to lay down their arms;" he would make sure, he emphasized, that "Missouri obeyed it too." Urging everyone to return "to peaceful fields and benches in this fair and blooming land of opportunity," the governor mounted his carriage and headed for Lecompton with his military escort.[75]

The next day, as word came that the Missourians were again marching on Lawrence, Geary wheeled his carriage about, ordering Lieutenant Colonel Joseph E. Johnston to occupy Mount Oread. Geary then whipped his horses and drove straight for Atchison's lines. The governor and the former Democratic senator met in a room of a small clapboard house in Franklin. "Though held in a board house," Geary said to the entourage of pro-slavery leaders, "the present is the most important council since the days of the Revolution, as its issues involve the fate of the Union now formed."[76] He said he was making his appeal to them as a member of the Democratic Party; another attack on Lawrence would injure the Democrats' chances in the coming election, possibly throwing it to the Republican candidate. Atchison maintained that their forces were only marching on Lawrence to apprehend an "organized band of murderers and robbers said to be under the command of Lane, who have plundered and butchered large numbers of our fellow-citizens."[77] Lane was not in Lawrence, countered Geary; he knew, the governor said, because he had just been in that town. A new Democratic administration would sort things out, he assured everyone; meanwhile, he would deal with the abolitionists. Satisfied with Geary's declarations, Atchison reported to his confederates regarding Geary, "He promised us all we wanted."[78] John Brown left Lawrence the next day but remained nearby at the home of Augustus Wattles with his sons John Jr. and Jason and their wives, and Owen. On October 1, he was in Osawatomie, bidding farewell to his company, placing them under the command of James H. Holmes and enjoining them to uphold the highest standard in the fight against slavery. With the blockade of the Missouri River lifted, the wives took a steamboat, while the men, loading arms and ammunition and other supplies into a wagon drawn by a four-mule team and another drawn by one horse, took the overland route.

Traveling through Topeka with Owen, Brown welcomed into the smaller wagon a fugitive they found there, riding with the man hiding in the bed under a blanket when necessary, with Brown's surveying instruments on the outside of the wagon. Aaron D. Stevens and his company and Brown's other sons rode north on a parallel course as an escort, keeping out of sight. The entourage experienced no incidents before reaching Nebraska City, but Lieutenant Colonel Cooke reported October 7, "I arrived here yesterday at noon. I just missed the arrest of the notorious Osawatomie outlaw, John Brown. The night before, having ascertained that after dark he had stopped for the night at a house six miles from the camp, I sent a party who found at 12 o'clock that he had gone."[79]

Such was the closing scene of John Brown's tumultuous first sojourn in Kansas. Higginson, who was in Topeka as Brown was preparing to depart, wondered years later in his *Cheerful Yesterdays* whether he might have seen the old man there. Higginson recollected being shown into a room where a fugitive slave was sheltered, and that he saw sitting in a corner of that room an elderly White man who was silent while Higginson was present. Could that unassuming presence have been the legendary "Osawatomie Brown"?

What Higginson had seen and reported on while in Kansas had an enlivening effect on his outlook and expectations. As he wrote in "A Ride Through Kanzas," he had been looking for stout-hearted men "ever since the rendition of Anthony Burns, in Boston. . . . I have found them in Kanzas. . . . A single day in Kanzas makes the American Revolution more intelligible all Sparks or Hildreth can do. The same event is still in progress here."[80]

Reverend Theophilus Gould Steward, left, coauthor with his father, William Steward, of *Gouldtown—A Very Remarkable Settlement of Ancient Date*, published in 1913. Right, Rebecca Gould, wife of William Steward. (*New York Public Library*)

The signature of John Brown, left, on stiff paper cut to fit within the case of the timepiece inherited by Rebecca "Becky" Lively of Gouldtown, New Jersey. The date "1839," right, inscribed on another paper in the case, referencing the date of John Brown's historic avowal to eradicate slavery. (*Photographs by Joe Eber*)

Examples of notices for "persons" absconding from their "service of labor." Notices for runaways were commonplace from colonial times to the Civil War. (*New York Public Library*)

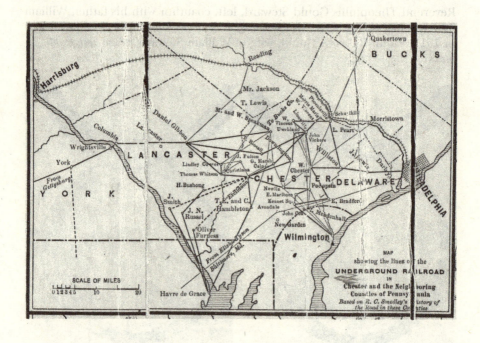

Detail of the Underground Railroad network in eastern Pennsylvania. From William Siebert, *The Underground Railroad from Slavery to Freedom*, published in 1898. In the east, Quakers were effective and practical workers for emancipation. (*New York Public Library*)

"Death of Capt. Ferrer," showing Mende warriors slaying their captors, the frontispiece of *A History of the Amistad Captives* by John Warner Barber, published in 1840. (*Yale University Art Gallery*)

John Rankin's house near Ripley, Ohio. Rankin was a founding member of Ohio's abolitionist society. He and the enslaved he assisted to freedom were inspirations for Harriet Beecher Stowe's *Uncle Tom's Cabin*. (*New York Public Library*)

Left to right: Jermain Wesley Loguen, Martin Delaney, and Henry Highland Garnet. All three men played key roles in the history of Black emancipation and all three were confidants of John Brown. (*Onondaga Historical Association; Wikimedia Commons; National Portrait Gallery*)

From left to right: Henry Clay of Kentucky, John C. Calhoun of South Carolina, and Daniel Webster of Massachusetts, a powerful triumvirate of antebellum politicians. Webster supported Clay's and Stephen A. Douglas's Compromise of 1850 to diffuse tensions between free and slave states, while Calhoun in some of his last remarks before succumbing to tuberculosis, rejected the compromise and affirmed the right of the South to leave the Union. (*Library of Congress*)

William Lloyd Garrison, left, and Frederick Douglass, right. Without their effective, self-sacrificing efforts, the abolition movement in the United State could not have been successful. (*Library of Congress; National Portrait Gallery*)

Harriet Tubman, left, and John Brown, right. Tubman assisted Brown in recruiting and planning the raid on Harper's Ferry. (*National Portrait Gallery; Library of Congress*)

John Brown's Northern supporters, from Oswald G. Villard, *John Brown 1800-1859: A Biography Fifty Years After,* page 396. These men stood most prominently behind John Brown's raid on Harper's Ferry.

"Brown, his son and another of the outlaws awaiting examination." *Harper's Weekly*, 1859. (*Library of Congress*)

"Effect of John Brown's Invasion of the South; A Southern planter arming his slaves to resist invasion." *Harper's Weekly*, v. 3, no. 151 (1859, Nov. 19), p. [737]. Harper's Ferry was the first national news story in an age of steam, iron horses, and electric wires, in which the influence of newspapers had vastly increased. (*Library of Congress*)

W. E. B. Du Bois, left, and Oswald G. Villard. DuBois's biography of John Brown came out a year before Villiard's, written as both men were engaged in the founding of the NAACP. DuBois felt Villard purposely suppressed his book through his media connections in favor of his own biography of Brown. (*Library of Congress; New York Public Library*)

The Gouldtown time-piece disassembled, reminders of a bygone era, shut away for decades in a chest in Gouldtown. (*Photograph by Joe Eber*)

Chapter Five

"'GIVE THEM JESSIE,' AND FRÉMONT BESIDES"

PRECEDED BY THE MONIKER "Osawatomie" and with letters of introduction, John Brown appeared at the headquarters of the National Kansas Committee in Chicago on October 25. Wishing to claim some of the assistances that heretofore had escaped him and his destitute, beggared company, he explained that he had a proposal and wanted to consult about financial support. He wished to arm and equip as many as one hundred "regular volunteers" to operate under his command in furtherance of the free-state cause, and for this he calculated he needed a minimum of $30,000.

Not delegated to consult on such a request, the committee referred Brown to a national meeting to convene in January at the Astor House in New York City. Meanwhile, Horace White, assistant secretary of the National Committee, gave Brown a letter of referral providing him free fare as the committee's agent on three northern railroads, and in addition provided him with a new suit of clothes. White also handed Brown a note reading, "Rev. Theodore Parker, of Boston, is at the Briggs House, and wishes very much to see you."[1]

Theodore Parker was not unknown to Brown, who had been to Parker's church in Boston to hear him preach and would have been familiar with Parker's activities on behalf of fugitive slaves as a member of Boston's Vigilance Committee. A Unitarian minister, Parker was above all the preacher of American Transcendentalism; a reformer and abolitionist, he was of that generation that traced its lineage to the period of the Revolution. Fluent in half a dozen languages, Parker specialized in German theology and thought, drawing his ideas too from Carlyle and Coleridge, as well as from Ralph Waldo Emerson. He saw his career as an orthodox preacher culminate early as he began attending meetings of the Transcendental Club in 1837; breaking with supernatural realism in 1838, he laid out his position the next year in a sermon titled "A Discourse on the Transient and Permanent in Christianity."

Ostracized from preaching, Parker was invited by supporters in December 1845 to become minister of the 28th Congregational Society of Boston—a congregation whose members included Louisa May Alcott, William Lloyd Garrison, Julia Ward Howe, and Elizabeth Cady Stanton and which would grow under Parker's stewardship to 7,000 parishioners. Gradually shifting his emphasis after the Compromise of 1850, Parker devoted his time to combating the Fugitive Slave Law and heading the Vigilance Committee. He was among those at the forefront of the Kansas relief movement, which was contributing money to buy weapons for the free-state militias in Kansas.

Also informed that George Luther Stearns, chairman of the Massachusetts State Kansas Committee, had invited him to visit Boston "to consult with the friends of freedom," and would pay his expenses, Brown traveled east. He included a number of interesting locales on his itinerary; on his way to Ashtabula, Ohio, for a reunion with sons John Jr. and Jason, Brown stopped to see Governor Salmon Chase in Columbus, soliciting a letter of introduction from the governor with the aid of Representative Joshua Giddings. Chase also handed Brown a $25 contribution. In Columbus, Brown explored the possibility of obtaining aid from the state legislature, as reported at the time by the *Cleveland Leader*, whose reporter characterized that overture as provocative and incendiary. In Peterboro, Brown renewed his acquaintance with Gerrit Smith, and consulted with him before traveling on to Rochester, where undoubtedly, he also fully updated Frederick Douglass on his activities and further instantiated their ongoing collaboration. Douglass gives an indication of his interactions with Brown during this period in his autobiography, writing, "In his repeated visits to the East to obtain necessary arms and supplies, he often did me the honor of spending hours and days with me at Rochester." There is also a letter in Douglass's hand, dated December 7, with no year designated, addressing Brown: "I am very busy at home. Will you please come up with my son Fred and take a mouthful with me."[2] Brown's final stop before Boston was in Springfield, where he met with George Walker, whom he had known earlier; Walker, the agent of the Kansas Committee in that city, was brother-in-law to Franklin Sanborn, the secretary of the Massachusetts State Kansas Committee, and had had a brief and tragic marriage to Sanborn's late sister.

Early one January morning in 1857, with his son Owen, Brown walked into the office of the Kansas committee on School Street. He was greeted by the committee's secretary and the sole occupant of the sparsely furnished office, Franklin B. Sanborn. Sanborn, 25, had graduated from Harvard a year and a half before; a protégé of Emerson, he had come to Concord at the philosopher's behest to run a school for the children of that community's well-placed families. Now Sanborn was dividing his time between the school, at which a friend was substituting for him, and the Kansas committee in Boston. At six feet, three inches, he wore his hair shoulder length, and had delicate facial features said to resemble "an early portrait of Raphael." He became an important chronicler of the lives of his friends Henry David Thoreau and A. Bronson Alcott in Concord as well as of John Brown.

Sanborn summarized Brown's January 1857 proposal in an article published in the *Atlantic Monthly* in April 1872. "His theory required fighting in Kansas; it was the only sure way, he thought, to keep that region free from the curse of slavery," Sanborn wrote. "His mission now was to levy war on it, and for that to raise and equip a company of a hundred well-armed men who should resist aggression in Kansas, or occasionally carry the war into Missouri." Besides Sanborn in his role as the body's secretary, the members of the Massachusetts committee hearing Brown's proposal were George L. Stearns of Medford, chairman; Theodore Parker; and Dr. Samuel G. Howe. The other executive committee members were treasurer Patrick T. Jackson, Dr. Samuel Cabot, Dr. William R. Lawrence, and Judge Thomas Russell. Of these, Stearns, Sanborn, Parker, and Howe, together with Thomas Wentworth Higginson in Worcester and Gerrit Smith in Peterboro, were the men who would come to stand prominently behind Brown's

Virginia campaign; in time they were designated in the press "the secret six."

Dr. Samuel Gridley Howe, a noted humanitarian, in 1832 had founded the Asylum for the Blind and, during the Civil War, the Sanitary Commission. Shortly after obtaining his medical degree, inspired by the example of Lord Byron, Howe sailed for Greece, joining the Greek army as a surgeon on the side of the revolutionaries. Bestowed the title "the Lafayette of the Greek Revolution" for his services, he returned to the United States in 1827 and in 1828 published *An Historical Sketch of the Greek Revolution*. In 1843 he married Julia Ward, a suffragist, poet, and in 1861 composer of "The Battle Hymn of the Republic," based on a slower moving John Brown song popular with the Union armies. The couple founded the anti-slavery newspaper the *Daily Commonwealth*.

Thomas Wentworth Higginson was also a Unitarian minister and, like Parker, was active on behalf of fugitive slaves and in the abolitionist movement. Following the lead of Parker on theological matters, Higginson began preaching at the First Religious Society of Newburyport, Massachusetts. Giving prominence to abolition and criticizing the degrading conditions endured by workers in the cotton mills, he invited Parker and Emerson as well as the fugitive slave William Wells Brown, a novelist, historian, and abolitionist, to speak from his pulpit. When his church's pews began to empty, leading to his resignation, he became minister to the Free Church in Worcester in 1852. With a rare combination of literary acumen and commitment to a cause, Higginson was one of the outstanding figures in American letters in the nineteenth and early twentieth centuries. Today he is noted as the liaison and encourager of the Amherst poet Emily Dickinson, a relationship begun in 1862 when she wrote him a letter querying, "are you too busy to say whether my verse is alive?"

The pivotal member in the committee for Brown was George Luther Stearns, without whose support he would not have been able to proceed. An industrialist and merchant, Stearns specialized in ship-chandlery, branching into the manufacture of tin sheeting and lead pipe, eventually supplying plumbers and tinsmiths throughout New England. Identifying with the abolitionist cause after 1848 when he supported the Free-Soilers, Stearns established a branch of the Underground Railroad in Medford, Massachusetts, making a vow after the assault on Charles Sumner "to devote the rest of his life and fortune to the liberation of the slave."[3] With the passage of the

Kansas-Nebraska bill, Stearns became one of the chief financiers of Thayer's Emigrant Aid Company, becoming in the spring of 1856 chairman of the Massachusetts State Kansas Committee. A prodigious fundraiser and tireless worker, he was also a founder of *Daily Commonwealth* with the Howes, and of the *Nation* magazine.

It has been asked what would John Brown have been without these men? That theirs was a pact of paramount, even historic, significance, there has been no doubt. But which side of the transaction was the stronger? As Stearns's son Frank Preston Stearns suggests, that bond was as a magnet catches iron. Ultimately, Sanborn supposes, a thousand men knew Brown meant to harass slaveholders in some part of the South with an armed force, but of these the number at any time intimate with the fullness of his plan was but few. And those knowing in any detail his Harper's Ferry plan did not exceed a hundred "scattered over the whole country, from Boston to Kansas, from Maryland to Canada."[4]

Trying to establish the best date to bring together "the friends of freedom" to consult with Brown, Stearns found that Sunday, January 11, was optimal. Asked if it would be consistent with his religious conviction to attend, Brown replied, "Mr. Stearns, I have a poor little ewe that has fallen into a ditch, and I think the Sabbath is as good a day as any to help her out. I will come." Among those invited to the Stearns residence that day were Doctors Howe and Cabot, Judge Russell and his wife, Pastors Higginson and Parker, John Andrew the lawyer and wartime governor of Massachusetts, and Sanborn. Walking into the parlor as Brown was discoursing with the others present, Mary Stearns wrote in *Reminiscences of Mrs. Mary Stearns*, that she found Brown mesmerizing. "It may not be out of place to describe the impression he made upon the writer on this first visit," she wrote. "When I entered the parlor, he was sitting near the hearth, where glowed a bright, open fire. He rose to greet me, stepping forward with such an erect, military bearing, such fine courtesy of demeanor and grave earnestness, that he seemed to my instant thought some old Cromwellian hero suddenly dropped down before me."[5]

Dressed in a coat of brown broadcloth, with wide-legged brown trousers, Brown had the look of a farmer in his Sunday best or a deacon of a church, and with his patent leather stock, gray surtout, and fur cap, his figure exuded a military air. He was cleanly shaven and scrupulous in his mien. Finding she had interrupted the conversation, Mary Stearns said her initial impression was strengthened, as

Brown turned to finish a thought, saying, "Gentlemen, I consider the Golden Rule and the Declaration of Independence one and inseparable; and it is better that a whole generation of men, women and children should be swept away than that this crime of slavery should exist one day longer." These words were uttered in such an emphatic way, she wrote, that her youngest boy, Carl, then but three years old, standing in the center of the room, his eyes fully absorbing the speaker, remembered the moment as one of his earliest recollections.

Shortly afterward a reception for Brown was held at Theodore Parker's house and attended by William Lloyd Garrison and Wendell Phillips, among others. Phillips was warmly cordial. Not so Garrison. Frank Preston Stearns observed in his *The Life and Public Services of George Luther Stearns,* that while Brown had sincere respect for Garrison, he did not get "an over friendly reception" from him. Stearns wrote that Garrison greatly regretted the course that the anti-slavery movement had taken, for which he held the Free-Soilers chiefly responsible. Garrison thought Sumner's oration "The Crime Against Kansas" very injudicious, and that it would be better to give Kansas to the slaveholders than to offer them armed resistance. John Brown said afterward that "it was difficult to see the difference between Garrison's position, and that of a pro-slavery Democrat."[6] Garrison and Brown then engaged in a colloquy, trading quotes of Scripture, Brown urging attack by force and Garrison moral suasion and nonresistance. One scriptural adjuration Brown liked to cite was "without the shedding of blood there is no remission of sin." He did not believe in moral suasion, he told Garrison, he believed "in putting the thing through." Setting out to raise funds, Brown spoke in succession in New Haven, Hartford, Canton, and Collinsville, Connecticut, and in Worcester, Concord, and Springfield, Massachusetts; he published an appeal for contributions on the editorial page of the New York *Tribune* of March 4, 1857, the day the Buchanan administration was inaugurated and two days before the Supreme Court's decision in *Dred Scott v. Sandford.*

The morning after he gave his lecture at Collinsville, Brown was in the village drug store where he chanced to meet blacksmith Charles Blair. Displaying an eight-inch double-bladed dirk he had taken off Pate at Black Jack, Brown remarked that if he had a number of these attached to six-foot poles "they would be a capital weapon of defense for the settlers of Kansas." Asked what it would cost to produce such weapons in large numbers, Blair said he supposed he could do so at $1.25 apiece for five hundred and $1 apiece for 1,000. Later that day, Brown showed up at the forge master's shop and said he wanted to draw up a contract for 1,000 weapons at $1 apiece.

The opinion in the Dred Scott case, held over from the previous session of the court to avoid igniting dissension that the outcome was sure to raise during the presidential contest, was a comprehensive fifty-five-page ruling addressing three broad issues. Was Scott a citizen with the right to sue; did residence in a free territory confer on Scott his freedom; was the federal post actually free territory—did Congress have the right in 1820 to ban slavery in territories beyond 36 degrees 30 minutes north latitude?

The decision set out a sweeping counterattack upon the anti-slavery movement, asserting that persons of African descent were utterly separate under all the provisions of the Constitution and the rights that that document bestowed on citizens. Slaves, within the framework of the United States, the opinion of Chief Justice Roger Taney maintained, were property, and the right of the slaveholder was secure wherever the writ of the Constitution extended; the Congress had no right to prohibit it. Slaves, therefore, could be taken anywhere under the Stars and Stripes, and they neither were nor could they become citizens. In a stinging phrase, Taney declared that "persons of African descent have no rights a white man is bound to respect."[7]

That spring, Frederick Douglass called the ruling the "judicial incarnation of wolfishness."[8] Casting an eye to the distant future, "the precise speck of time . . . at which . . . the long entombed millions rise from the foul grave of slavery and death," Douglass conceded he could know nothing; all was uncertain—except for the fact that slaveholders would "give up only when they must do that or do worse . . . the slaveholders had the advantage of complete organization over all opposition. The state governments, the church organizations, where the system existed were completely at the service of slavery," while the federal government "is pledged to support, defend, and propagate the crying curse of human bondage."

"But there was another view than this," said Douglass, ". . . the more the slavery question had been thought settled the more it needed settling, and the space between these settlements was decreasing." The first settlement came when Missouri was admitted as a slave state and slavery was prohibited north of its border. Fifteen years later came another settlement, when the right of petition and free discussion in Congress were gagged. In another ten years came renewed settlement with war with Mexico and the annexation of Texas. A seemingly final settlement was reached with the Compromise of 1850, by which "slavery was virtually declared the equal of Liberty." Four years after that, the Kansas-Nebraska bill was enacted, "a settlement which unsettled all former settlements." The first settlement stood fifteen years—the second, ten—the third, five—the fourth, four—the fifth, two years.

Already a gleam of hope had appeared following the presidential election, said Douglass. An unaccountable sickness attributed to the staff had afflicted guests at the National Hotel in Washington, D.C., and an extensive plan of insurrection laid by slaves was uncovered in Lavaca, De Witt, and Victoria Counties in Texas, followed by the demonstration against the Taney decision in St. Louis. "The wedge has entered," Douglass wrote. "Dred Scott, of Missouri, goes into slavery, but St. Louis declares for freedom." A few days after the *Scott* decision, Brown was in Worcester, a guest in the home of Eli Thayer. Brown was entertaining the children of the house on his knee when Dr. Wayland came to call. He was organizing a Frederick Douglass meeting that evening and had gotten agreement from the mayor that the mayor would sit on the platform, the first time in any American city that this honorary courtesy had been bestowed by an elected official, and an acknowledgment of Douglass's increasing importance and potency. Wayland had come to induce Thayer to do the same. "I was then introduced to John Brown of Osawatomie," Wayland wrote. "How little one imagined then that in less than three years the name of this plain homespun man would fill America and Europe! Mr. Brown consented to occupy a place on the platform, and at the urgent request of the audience, spoke briefly."[9]

Brown of course was cognizant that to form and train a force of the size that he was proposing, necessarily aggregated of men for the most part lacking military training, he would need to obtain the assistance of a man versed in these matters. In a letter to John Jr. written as he was concluding his eastern sojourn, Brown wrote, "Your remarks about the value & importance of discipline I fully appreciated; & I have been making arrangements to secure the assistance & instruction of a distinguished Scotch officer & author quite popular in this country, I am quite sanguine of my success in this matter."[10]

In early spring Brown had been introduced to a Briton living in New York who had been involved with Giuseppe Garibaldi and his campaign in Italy. The fellow, Hugh Forbes, had been a silk merchant in Siena and had identified with the "Young Italy" party, becoming a trusted agent of both Garibaldi and Giuseppe Mazzini. Forbes had had notable military experience and had written a multivolume book detailing the European campaigns of 1848. Upon those movements' defeat, he went to Paris where he married and started a family; after being in London alone, he immigrated to New York in 1855. Eking out a living as a translator, editor, and fencing coach, he wrote an occasional article for the *Tribune* and had given a series of lectures under the rubric "On Recent Events in Italy" at New York University.

Impressed with Forbes's erudite yet effete manner, Brown hired him as drill instructor and master-at-arms for his projected company at $100 per month and paid him $600 out of his pocket to translate and prepare for publication a compendium of his book on the partisan fighting under the title *A Manual for the Patriotic Volunteer*.

The rapidity of Brown's response to events had depended heretofore on recruiting his sons as the core of his combatants, but that spring most of these recruits were recuperating in the Adirondack retreat and had, as well, renounced their commitment to their father's warlike cause. Answering a March 21, 1857, letter from his wife ten days after receiving it, Brown wrote, "Your letter of the 21st inst. is just received. I have only to say as regards the resolution of the boys to 'learn, & practice war no more;' that it was not at my solicitation that they engaged in it at the first: & that while I may perhaps feel no more love of the business than they do; still I think there may be possibly in their day that which is more to be dreaded: if such things do not now exist."[11] Owen would remain at his side, and John Jr., living in Ashtabula, Ohio, continued as a valued confidant, performing crucial service as his father's liaison. No longer fit for field service due to his debilitating experiences in Kansas, John Jr. would accompany his father in the future to important meetings. The elder Brown would be joined too by his youngest sons, Oliver and Watson, who had not figured in the Kansas fighting, who were both to be slain at Harper's Ferry.

The results of fundraising had proved to be far less than the $30,000 Brown had projected as adequate. On April 16 from Springfield Brown addressed a letter to Eli Thayer: "One of the US Hounds is on my track; & I have kept myself hid for a few days to let my track get cold." Telling Theodore Parker of his imminent peril, Brown went along as Parker placed him in the home of Judge Russell and his wife from April 6 to April 15. Parker counseled that if he were in a similar position, he would shoot any man dead who should try to arrest him. Passing the time without incident, Brown remained "barricaded" in his room at the Russells' house with a supply of ammunition and two well-tended pistols as a storm blustered over the Massachusetts seacoast. Suffering from his periodic ague and feeling it was too cold to travel, he remained in his room composing his plaintive leave-taking, addressing his shortfall in raising funds: "Old Browns Farewell: to the Plymouth Rocks; Bunker Hill, Monuments; Charter Oaks; and Uncle Toms Cabbins." When he finished the composition, he asked Mrs. Russell if she might summon Mary Stearns from Medford. When Mrs. Stearns arrived, Brown brought the paper down from his room, saying he'd written a text to send to Theodore Parker for possible use in his next morning's sermon, and wanted to know what the women thought.

In April 1885, as Sanborn was putting the finishing touches on his volume on John Brown together with editing Brown's letters, Mary Stearns wrote him in regard to the famous 1857 composition. "The emphasis of his tone and manner I shall never forget," she wrote, "and wish I could picture him as he sat and read, lifting his eyes to mine now and then to see how it impressed me."[12] Delighted with his work, the women thought it should indeed be sent to Parker, even though his parishioners might not appreciate its full context. "This matter being settled, Brown began talking upon the subject always uppermost in his thought, and I may add, action also," she wrote. "Those who remember the power of his moral magnetism will understand how surely and readily he lifted his listener to the level of his own devotion; so that it suddenly seemed mean and unworthy—not to say wicked—to be living in luxury while such a man was struggling for a few thousands to carry out his cherished plan."[13]

"Oh," Brown said, Mary Stearns had written in her *Reminiscences*, "if I could have the money that is smoked away during a single day in Boston, I could strike a blow which would make slavery totter from its foundation." When Mary Stearns awoke that Sunday morning, radiant sunshine had replaced the bleak skies of the previous days—a change with which the birds were happily in accord. Shouldn't she and her family be the ones to help Captain John Brown to attaining his consummation, she asked herself. Couldn't they sell their house, their carriage, their teams? This was the impetus for her 1885 letter to Sanborn. "When Mr. Stearns awoke I told him my morning thoughts," she wrote. Reflecting on the proposition, George Stearns finally said, "Perhaps it would not be just right to the children to do what you suggest; but I will do all I can in justice to them and you."

After he had breakfast, Stearns drove to Judge Russell's residence and placed a letter of credit in Brown's hand authorizing him to draw $7,000. After weeks of unrelenting fundraising and much dejection, on April 15 Brown wrote to John Jr., "My collection I may safely put down at $13,000." The lion behind his apparent success, it is evident, was George Luther Stearns. Answering a query from Frank Preston Stearns, Gerrit Smith, the man second in importance in providing succor for John Brown's plan, wrote on January 3, 1874, "I frequently gave John Brown money to promote his slave-delivering and other benevolent purposes, —in the aggregate, however, only about a thousand dollars. This would have been none too much to compensate him for the self-sacrificing interest in my colony. His dependence for means to execute his Southern undertaking was, as he informed me, mainly on the good and generous Mr. Stearns of Boston."[14]

In the first week of May, Brown arranged to buy two hundred revolvers, on which he was granted a 50 percent discount by the Massachusetts Arms Company in Chicopee for "aiding in your project of protecting the free state settlers of Kansas," spending $1,300 in the transaction. He wrote to Stearns, "Now if Rev. T. Parker & other good people of Boston would make up that amount I might at least be well armed." Stearns had purchased and shipped two hundred Sharp's rifles in fall 1856 which were now sequestered in a basement in Tabor, Iowa; with Stearns as owner of these, the committee had voted to entrust them to Brown's possession, with the stipulation that he hold them subject to committee orders. That body had also voted Brown 4,000 ball carriages, 31,000 percussion caps, and four iron ladles. Few people, Brown had remarked to Thoreau, "had any conception of the cost, even the pecuniary cost, of firing a single bullet in war."[15] Although the funds he had received amounted to less than necessary to equip and mount "one hundred men," he now had ample arms worth over $7,000 and also had received donations of sundry supplies, clothing sufficient for sixty men, blankets, grinding mills, and so on. His efforts finally were amounting to enough to assure a tolerable beginning. A solitary man, John Brown was now moving toward the consummation of a design to which he had devoted twenty years of "silent study, observation, and planning," operating wholly in the public service.[16] While he drew no salary, to allay the needs of his family Gerrit Smith had proposed a subscription be raised to underwrite the purchase of additional land and improvements to the house at North Elba such that the homestead might serve as his retreat "if too hard pressed by his enemies."[17] In a letter dated April 29, 1857, Stearns informed Brown that he and Amos Lawrence had agreed to contribute to such an arrangement, $1,000 being proposed, of which Stearns contributed a fourth and Lawrence nearly a third, with Wendell Phillips and others making up the balance.[18] This was intended to pay off Brown's previous agreement with Smith, and to cover construction expenses payable to William and Henry Thompson, husband of Brown's daughter Ruth, who had built the home. This arrangement, like so many others made during Brown's painstaking canvass in the winter and spring of 1857, went unfulfilled.

Brown was back in North Elba in the second week of May for a poignant visit—he thought it would be his last—with his wife and three minor daughters. On May 27, after making stops with Owen at Gerrit Smith's estate and in Rochester to see Douglass, Brown, on a stopover with John Jr. in Hudson, Ohio, wrote to "Wife and Children" in regard to the memorial that he thought should commemorate both himself and his deceased son, Frederick: "If I should never return, it is my particular request that no other monument be used to keep me in remembrance than the same plain one that records the death of my grandfather and son; and that a short story, like those already on it, be told of John Brown the fifth, under that of grandfather. I think I have several good reasons for this. I would be glad that my posterity should not only remember their parentage, but also the cause they labored in."[19]

Smith and Brown were in Chicago in July, Brown on his way to Kansas, Smith to speak in Illinois and Wisconsin in the wake of *Dred Scott*. Handing Brown $250 for a horse and wagon to carry his supplies and munitions, Smith accompanied him to the office of the National Committee, which had not honored his drafts on money requisitioned at the Astor House meeting in January. Harvey B. Hurd noted the meeting in correspondence decades later with Hinton: "In consequence of the Committee's failure to pay Mr. Brown's drafts on account of the $5000 appropriation, Gerrit Smith came to Chicago to see me. He was very much offended because the Committee did not pay the drafts, but he was told that they had not the means with which to meet them, and there was no other way but to let them be protested."[20]

Throughout that year over 100,000 immigrants moved to Kansas. Largely from Ohio and Missouri, this influx sparked an unprecedented rise in land values—lots that had cost $8 in Leavenworth shot up to $2,000—making that former pro-slavery bastion a free-state harbor. With Leavenworth and other Kansas towns booming, the overland transportation company Russell, Major, and Waddell now employed 20,000 men to work cattle and 2,000 wagons, with teamsters, wagon masters, and blacksmiths, as a macadam road was built from Kansas City Landing to Westport. What remained of the Atchison machine was thoroughly ensconced in the Lecompton legislature but might easily be turned out in the next election by free-state voters. In its last session, instead of bowing out, this legislature passed a bill for a convention to draft a new constitution, specifying that the document be sent to Congress without ratification by the voters of Kansas, and stipulating that county sheriffs and county commissioners be entrusted with registering voters and choosing election judges, in both instances implicitly assuring a pro-slavery vote. When John W. Geary came out to Kansas and assumed office as Territorial Governor he had been warned by Samuel Walker: "Mark my word, you'll take the underground railroad out of Kansas in six months." When Geary vetoed the convention bill, the legislature promptly overrode his veto. On the day James Buchanan took office, Geary's resignation took effect.

With his life threatened, a pistol-wearing Geary told Samuel Walker he was going to Washington; once there he learned that it had been decreed that the Atchison machine must control Kansas, and his resignation became effective. To govern Kansas, Buchanan called upon Robert J. Walker, a man with experience on the southern frontier but originally, like Buchanan, from Pennsylvania. A figure trusted in the South, Walker had served with Buchanan in the Polk administration as secretary of the treasury, had won and lost a fortune in Mississippi, and had been a senator for that state during the nullification crisis. But Walker was doubtful that he could settle the strife in Kansas and refused to accept the proffered appointment unless the president and the leader of the senate, Stephen Douglas, assured him that majority rule would prevail. With that promise made, Walker went out to Kansas. The *Scott* decision too had just set out a sweeping rebuke against the anti-slavery movement and Buchanan hoped it might allay the controversy. That Buchanan expected he had acquired a special pleader and an adroit rationalizer for the Lecompton legislature with his appointment of Walker, none can gainsay. But with his assurances from the president and the majority leader, Walker tried to appear even-handed, urging the free-state party to run delegates in the election to the constitutional convention; any armed resistance would be met by federal troops, he cautioned in his inaugural address. The election for the constitutional convention, held on June 15, was boycotted by free-state voters who had their own convention on July 15 presided over by Lane. This gathering set elections for officers of a free-state government for August 9. These competing elections were to demonstrate a clear preponderance of free-state settlers, with 2,200 votes cast in the first balloting and 7,200 in the latter.

In the months since engaging Forbes, Brown had been checking on his drillmaster's progress through a proxy. On June 1, Brown was informed, "the colonel says he is getting along well in getting the printing done." On June 16 Forbes reported "getting along ... as fast as possible with the book, and will have it ready in about ten days."[21] Brown arrived in Tabor, Iowa, August 9, and a few days later Forbes was on hand. In a letter of August 17 to "Dear Wife and Children," Brown reported, "We are beginning to take lessons, and have (we think) a very capable teacher."[22]

Brown's biographers have dealt with the Forbes/Brown relationship as a cursory affair in which the two came quickly to cross purposes. The imbroglio presents a well-known if only partially analyzed scenario in the chronicle, but is seen to have been, along with other factors, peripherally a contributor to the "failure" of the Harper's Ferry "scheme." Even so, the relationship and rupture merit some scrutiny. Hinton wrote, "At Tabor, in all probability, as to their disagreement, John Brown must have given Colonel Forbes his entire confidence, so far as naming to him, as he had done to Frederick Douglass, in 1847, and a few others of his race before and after that date, the place or region in and from which he designed to attack slavery. It is very evident that this was not at all the idea which Hugh Forbes had associated with the expected movement."[23] In a letter to Dr. Howe dated October 27, 1859, and published in the New York *Herald* after Brown's defeat at Harper's Ferry, Forbes divulged his understanding as to the source of their disagreement. Brown had elaborated on a plan he disclosed to Douglass in the winter of 1858, which Douglass detailed in his *Life and Times* decades later, where Brown again exposed his penchant in regard to Harper's Ferry as a way to rouse the slaves; with Forbes insisting otherwise. Far from eliciting the response Brown was expecting, Forbes had written, "No preparatory notice having been given to the slaves (no notice could or with prudence be given them) the invitation to rise might, unless they were already in a state of agitation, meet with no response, or a feeble one." "To this Brown replied that he was sure of a response"; with Forbes adamantly advocating for getting up "slave stampedes."[24]

Now that he had sufficient arms, equipment, and financial backing, Brown faced two problems militarily: How to generate an effective force from among freed slaves, and how to give that force sufficient impetus to become self-sustaining. Both issues would largely rely upon the organization introduced at the outset. On no point, said Brown, was the South more vulnerable than in its fear of servile insurrection. Sweeping down upon the plantations and farms abutting the Blue Ridge Mountains, the freed slaves would be subdivided into three, four, or five distinct parties under the men he would bring with him. The best of these men would be mounted, he proposed, when they would make a dash on the arms manufactory at Harper's Ferry, on account of the arms there, destroying what they could not carry off. His intention was then to advance into the South, reaching into those counties with an overwhelming predominance of slaves. The arms manufactory was a point to be seized, but not held; still, if retreat became advisable, that facility furnished an ideal egress to the North.

Forbes had, or so he thought, convinced Brown of the foolishness of such a grab; seeming to acquiesce in regard to the U.S. arsenal, Brown agreed, as Forbes suggested, that they would sally out of the mountains to get up "slave stampedes," carrying freed slaves off to safety in the North.[25] The European tactician had argued that "to go anywhere near Harper's Ferry would be folly and would surely bring United States troops down upon them." "What is more," said Forbes, "a slave insurrection being from the very nature of things, deficient in men of education and experience", would under such a system as Brown proposed, ". . . be either a flash in the pan or would leap beyond his control, or any control, when it would become a scene of mere anarchy and would assuredly be suppressed."

Brown initiated his engagement with the drillmaster and tactician, Hinton suggests, because he perceived, after his twelve months of experience of partisan warfare and from his own theorizing, the need for competent men to train and direct the force he projected. He had "a system of his own as to field defenses, drill, and discipline. . . . Such matters would have been at once discussed." Hinton conjectures: "Then all that followed is simple enough. Forbes was familiar with the plans of the European revolutionary organizations and leaders. Among their instrumentalities were plans of street-fighting, guerilla and irregular warfare . . . this system he embodied in a bulky 'Manual.'"[26]

Forbes knew very well who Brown's backers were, and on his way out to Iowa had stopped at Peterboro to confer with Gerrit Smith, soliciting money from him. In Chicago Forbes had gone to the office of the National Committee, conferring with officials there, as he had conferred with Horace Greeley and others on the *Tribune* staff before leaving New York. Later in 1858, when Forbes made his disclosures in regard to Brown's plans to Republican senators Wilson and Seward in Washington, with his demand that Brown be removed as commander of the expedition, it is evident that Forbes's difficulties with Brown's plan arose in part from his misapprehension of the American political context. "He mistook the ferment and sympathetic excitement in favor of Kansas," Hinton wrote, "for a deep-seated revolutionary sentiment in favor of freeing the slave by force of arms, if necessary."[27]

By October relations between the two had clearly soured, and Brown seems to have been at the point of firing Forbes. Despising Brown's ability and feeling defrauded, Forbes was concerned for his family's plight in Paris and demanded pay beyond that already advanced. He would denounce Brown early in the next year to his eastern backers; and he intended to have reparations for his trouble.

When Brown arrived in Tabor that August, he found a letter waiting from the Kansas committee's agent in Kansas, Edmund Whitman. "Your friends are desirous of seeing you," Whitman wrote. "The danger that threatened the Territory and individuals have been removed in the shape of quashed indictments. Your furniture can be brought in and safely stored while you are looking for a location."[28] Brown immediately began sending out correspondence, writing to William Addison Phillips, to James Holmes, and to Augustus Wattles, a long-time friend and abolitionist living outside Lawrence. To Wattles, Brown wrote, "There are some half a dozen men I want a visit from at Tabor, Ia., to come off in a quiet way; I have some very important matters to confer with some of you about."[29]

A reply letter from Wattles reached Brown August 21, stating that Wattles saw no pressing need for resorting to military means, adding, "come as quickly as possible, or not come at present, as you choose." Phillips also replied that he saw no need for military measures and that he would not come to Tabor to confer with Brown and knew no one who would. Holmes, however, wrote, "Several times we have needed you very much." Referring "to business for which I believe you have a stock of material with you," Holmes added. "If you wish other employments, I presume you will find just as profitable ones."[30]

As free-staters gained a majority in the Lecompton legislature in the August voting, the pro-slavery party had resorted to a last line of defense. Completing its handiwork, the constitutional convention emerged with a document declaring, "the right of property is before and higher than any constitutional sanction, and the right of the owner of a slave and its increase is the same and as inviolable as the right of the owner of any property whatever."[31]

The convention decreed the constitution must be sent directly to the U.S. Congress for approval with a petition for statehood. With the free-state press and public infuriated at this brazen attempt to impose slavery, Governor Walker called a special session of the newly elected legislature, suggesting members pass an act for a referendum on the constitution. Jim Lane had written to Brown a bit earlier to be in Kansas by election day, October 5: "We want you with the material you have. I see no objection to you coming to Kansas publicly. I can furnish you just such a force as you may deem necessary for your protection here & ten really ingenious, industrious men (not gassy) with about $110 in cash, could bring it about in the course of eight or ten days." In a message on September 29, Lane disclosed he was sending men, and enclosed $50, saying, "it is all important to Kansas that your things should be in at the earliest possible moment & that you should be much nearer at hand than you are."[32]

"It will be next to impossible in my poor state of health to go through on such very short notice, four days only remaining to get ready, load up & go through," Brown replied. "I think, considering all the uncertainties of the case, want of teams etc. that I should do wrong to set out. I am disappointed in the extreme."[33]

The explanation for Brown's inactivity during this period—when an invasion from Missouri was anticipated before the free-state elections—as Frank Preston Stearns wrote in a biography of his father, "is strongly supported . . . as to Hugh Forbes' conception of Brown's plan."[34] In testimony before the Mason Committee investigating Harper's Ferry, Senator William Seward, whom Forbes had sought out, remarked, "In the course of their conversation as to the plan by which they should more effectually counteract this invasion . . .

[Forbes] suggested the getting up of a stampede of slaves secretly on the borders of Kansas, in Missouri, which Brown disapproved, and on his part suggested an attack upon the border states, with a view to induce slaves to rise and so keep the invaders at home to take care of themselves. He said that in their conversations Brown gave up and abandoned his own project as impracticable."[35]

Brown wrote to Stearns, "I am now waiting further advice from Free State friends in Kansas with whom I have speedy private communications." Then from Brown came the following urgent missive: "I am in immediate want of from Five-Hundred to One Thousand Dollars for secret service and no questions asked." "Rather interesting times" were expected in Kansas, he wrote, "But no great excitement is reported. Our next advices may entirely change the aspect of things, I hope the friends of Freedom will respond to my call & 'prove me here-with'"[36] What this matter referred to has never been ascertained, but in a letter dated October 1, 1857, in regard to any disagreement with Forbes, Brown wrote Sanborn that he and Forbes were still working together. "While waiting here I and my son have been trying to learn a little of the arts of peace from Colonel F., who is still with us," Brown wrote. "That is the school I alluded to."[37]

This was how Frank Preston Stearns appraised the matter: "On September 16 General Lane wrote [Brown] an urgent letter to come to Kansas and assist in the preparations they were making against an expected invasion of the Missourians, but Brown answered in a dilatory manner and did not come until nearly a month later. It is evident that he also intended to act upon it in his own way. Tabor is on the northwest border of Missouri, and would have been a fine strategic position for him. In case of an invasion he could have made a descent into Missouri, and have easily stirred up a slave insurrection while the masters were absent. Brown might have been overpowered by the returning forces of the enemy, but the effect in any case would have been tremendous."[38]

As controversy swirled over the imposition of the Lecompton Constitution, a remedy was proposed. The convention made a modification in its position in line with a suggestion from Stephen Douglas. The change would not allow a referendum on the entire constitution but would allow a vote for a constitution "with Slavery" or "with no Slavery," specifying that if voters choose no slavery "the right of property in slaves now in this Territory shall in no manner be interfered with." This subterfuge signaled that the pro-slavery party had no intention of dealing fairly, and Walker denounced the proposition as "a vile fraud, a bare counterfeit."[39]

On November 5 Brown arrived at the Lawrence home of Edmund Whitman, who forthwith supplied him with money, tents, and bedding. In two days Brown was gone. Two days later Stearns wrote to Brown, "In my opinion the Free State party should wait for the Border-ruffian moves and checkmate them as they are developed. Don't attack them, but if they attack you, 'Give them Jessie' and Frémont besides."

"I find matters quite unsettled; but am decidedly of the opinion that there will be no use for the Arms or ammunition here before another Spring," Brown told Stearns. "I have them all safe . . . & mean to keep them so until I am satisfied they are really needed."[40]

The months following were as crucial as any to the future of the Union, as would be the months following the election of Abraham Lincoln in November 1860. Both periods were merely advances toward a denouement with which the nation had long been struggling. On December 21, when the referendum was voted, free-state voters abstained, thereby seeing it approved "with Slavery" by a vote of 6,226 for and 569 against. This vote was followed on January 4, 1858, by a referendum approved by the free-state majority in the Lecompton legislature, with pro-slavery voters abstaining, whereby a vote was obtained of 138 for the constitution "with Slavery," 24 "with no Slavery," and 10,226 against the constitution altogether. Now Congress had two votes to consider, but the president and his cabinet were not going to let majority rule stand in the way. On February 2, the Lecompton Constitution was submitted to the Congress with the recommendation that Kansas be admitted to the Union as the sixteenth slave state. With his political future hanging in the balance and Congress in the throes of a debate more intense even than the Kansas-Nebraska controversy, Stephen Douglas decided he could no longer support his president, declaring he could not vote to "force this constitution down the throats of the people of Kansas, in opposition to their wishes and in violation of our pledges." For this defection on an issue of paramount importance for the South, Alexander Stephens of Georgia pronounced Douglas "a dead cock in the pit."[41]

The Senate approved the admission of Kansas as a slave state in a vote on March 23, but in the House, as northern Democrats joined Republicans, admission was rejected by a vote of 120 to 112 on April 1. The Democratic Party had split, each faction representing sectional issues.

At Whitman's Brown again met a young man with whom he'd been acquainted the previous summer, an encounter whose context would clearly explain his reluctance to permit the arms committed to his care from falling out of his control, as well as showing Brown's true orientation. The fellow in question was John E. Cook, a 27-year-old hailing from Haddam, Connecticut, who had been a partisan free-state fighter. He had also figured as a journalist on Kansas affairs for the eastern papers, and had studied law at Yale and in New York—he was also, Salmon Brown said of him, "the best pistol shot he had ever seen." Cook later revealed that Brown told him he intended to organize a company "for the purpose of putting a stop to the aggressions of the pro-slavery men" that Cook had agreed to join. Asked if he "knew any other young men of who were perfectly reliable" who might also join, Cook recommended Richard Realf, Luke Parsons, and Richard Hinton. The following Sunday at breakfast in Lawrence, Cook received a note from John Brown requesting that Cook "join [him] at Topeka by Monday night next. Come to Mrs. Sheridan's, two miles south of Topeka, and bring your arms, ammunition, clothing and other articles you may require." He was also to bring Parsons if Parsons could be ready in time. "Please keep very quiet about the matter," the note ended.[42]

Cook was a good-looking youth, with blond curly hair falling on his shoulders; he was also an expert, Salmon Brown said, "in getting into the good graces of the girls." He was "high strung" and "erratic" and often indiscreet in his avowals to others. Much of the information on the John Brown "Harper's Ferry expedition" accordingly is attributable to "John E. Cook's Confession" given to his interrogators after his capture in Maryland after the "raid" was consummated.

Cook's activities in regard to what took place at Harper's Ferry have always loomed large. In the summer of 1858 Cook, given Brown's encompassing preoccupation with the Virginia town at the confluence of the Potomac and Shenandoah Rivers, had relocated there as a sort of advance scout, a role Brown evidently opposed but was unable or unwilling to prevent. Cook would remain at Harper's Ferry for a year before the arrival of Brown and the others adherent to his plans, working in the vicinity as a lock tender on the Baltimore and Erie Canal running along the north bank of the Potomac and as a part time itinerant bookseller. He would take a wife from among the girls he met there and by the time the Brown company began to coalesce at the Kennedy farm, the couple had had a child. With the arrival of the others, Cook undertook on his own volition a survey to find out the number of slaves in the area immediately above Harper's Ferry, in which locale lived one of its most prominent local citizens, proprietor of a plantation and resident of a mansion—and a slaveholder Brown intended to seize as "hostage." This was Col. Lewis Washington, nephew of the great man ranked primus inter pares among the fathers of his country, George Washington. Calling at the nephew's estate on his surreptitious slave census, the voluble Cook conversed with the colonel. Washington, a weapons collector, hearing of his young guest's facility with and interest in sidearms, showed Cook some items among the armaments he owned and treasured: two pistols that had belonged to the Marquis de Lafayette and a sword that had belonged to Germany's Frederick the Great. These artifacts Washington had inherited from his uncle, and, as it would turn out, when Cook mentioned them to Brown, the historical armaments fired the old man's imagination as regarded their utility for symbolic value during his "Harper's Ferry Raid."

In September 1857 George Luther Stearns had written Martin Conway in Lawrence, Kansas, commenting on the "crisis" impinging upon and overriding their current monetary transactions. "Our world is now engrossed with the impending financial crash," Stearns remarked to Conway. "If it would snap the South as well as the North I would welcome it, so much do I hate the present state of affairs."[43]

The September 12, 1857, edition of *Harper's Weekly* reported, "prominent stocks fell eight or ten percent in a day, and fortunes were made and lost between ten o'clock in the morning and four in the afternoon." That same day the steamer *Central America*, carrying fifteen tons or $1.6 million in gold from the San Francisco Mint had foundered in a hurricane off North Carolina—a loss that, together with the deaths of over four hundred passengers, spread panic as it was reported. Half of New York's brokerages, unable to meet specie payments, went bankrupt. In New York, Philadelphia, and Baltimore, banks closed amid a surge in withdrawals that quadrupled in the following weeks. The economic growth set in motion after the United States acquired its western territories in the war with Mexico and the discovery of gold in California had come to a stuttering standstill as the first global financial crisis debuted in the Panic of 1857.

The initial cracks in the new prosperity appeared just after the Supreme Court's *Dred Scott* decision, as the prices of land warrants in Kansas and of western railroad securities declined, signaling the political struggle between slavery and free-soil would now be reprised in western markets.

The basis for the unprecedented economic boom had been railroad construction when, aided by state land grants, government-financed bonds, Wall Street stocks, and foreign investment—particularly British capital—over 20,000 miles of track were laid, a three-fold increase, while between 1850 and 1857 the number of banks doubled, as did the total of notes, loans, and deposits, with reserve funds deposited in New York City branches. As railroads redounded to the benefit of commerce and industry, land speculators sought to capitalize in lucrative real estate markets; with continuing emigration from Europe, farming surged in the West, bringing additional speculation. When Russian grain was lost to Europe during the Crimean War, grain prices in the American West rose to $2.19 a bushel. These economic bounties would begin to reel as a glut in agricultural commodities brought lower prices for farmers, stressing their capacity to repay loans. With European markets opening again to Russian exports, the United States began running a trade imbalance, and gold reserves were drawn out of the country. By the summer of 1857, as banks sought to compensate by raising interest rates, investments in railroad and land, based on speculative credit, became unmanageable.

With this destabilizing news spreading rapidly on the lightning of telegraphed messages and the daily newspaper, a phenomenon enhanced by the new timetables for trains, businesses were shuttered as the railroads, particularly east-west lines, were starved for cash. The Great Lakes region, affected most severely, quickly passed the contagion to the East, which was dependent on western sales. The Illinois Central, Erie, Pittsburgh, Fort Wayne and Chicago, and Reading Railroads were forced to cease operations. The Delaware, Lackawanna, and Fond du Lac Railroad companies went bankrupt, while the Boston and Worcester Railroad "was left straining under its commitments."[44]

When the calamity hit, Karl Marx was in London where he had settled after the failure of the European revolutions of 1848-49. Hard pressed and living with his wife and two children with another on the way, Marx was barely surviving on income from articles he wrote for the New York *Tribune* and for the *New American Cyclopedia*, earning less than a penny a line. He did receive some other income, due to the largess of his friend and collaborator, Frederick Engels, who had settled in as a clerk in a cotton-spinning mill partially owned by his father in Manchester, England, at which he would become a partner. Marx's articles for the *Tribune* would appear for nearly a decade, covering the European scene mostly and economic issues. To research the latter and his own projects, Marx occupied, seemingly as a life sentence, a seat at the British Museum, which had one of the best libraries extant on political economy. His resulting insights, heightened by "the new stage of development" which the Atlantic nations seemed to have entered—epitomized by railroads and steamships and telegraph, and with the discovery of gold in California—these bounties and the subsequent crises, and his reading, induced Marx "to start again from the very beginning and to work carefully through the new material," as he would write in his summation in 1859 of a volume titled *A Contribution to the Critique of Political Economy*.

When the panic struck in fall 1857, Marx acted as if he were a man crossed by a revenant in the night, as this nearly solitary individual plunged into a new historical, political, and economic synthesis of thought. These were the notebooks composed between August 1857 and June 1858 *Grundrisse der Kritik der Politischen Ökonomie* (*Foundations of a Critique of Political Economy*). On November 13, 1857, Marx wrote to Engels, "The American crisis—which we foresaw, in November 1850 of the review, would break out in New York—is fantastic, even though my financial situation is disastrous; I have never felt so 'cosy' since 1849 than with this break out." On December 12, he wrote his friend, "I am working like a madman for whole nights in order to coordinate my work on economics, and to get together the *Grundrisse* before the deluge."

Marx's insight was to reveal to him the essence behind capitalist market relations—the genesis of the social and class workings of a society dominated by the pursuit of surplus value, and the realization that capital itself was a historical phenomenon. This analysis was distinguished by its historical setting, couched in deep philosophical antecedents and afforded by the imminence of crisis. For Marx the moment became the occasion for an historical forecast, with the German philosopher G.F.W. Hegel ensconced over a critical exploration of the categories of political economy from Adam Smith to David Ricardo. On January 14, 1858, Marx wrote to Engels, with whom by way of the railroads he was in daily contact, "For the rest, I am making great progress. For example, I have thrown overboard all the theory of profit that has existed until now. As far as the *method* goes, the fact of having leafed through, once again, by mere accident, Hegel's

Logic rendered me a great service." That the world crisis, and the work undertaken by Marx with his *Grundrisse*, and his *Tribune* articles, and his subsequent *Critique* are linked is undoubtedly true. It was an era—as reflected in its literature, in its philosophy, and in its economic theory, as indeed in Charles Darwin's *On the Origin of Species*, published in 1859—vividly drawn even in the flight of fugitive slaves whose shadows flitted across the American states, a strife roiling the waves like that "great white whale" obsessively pursued by Captain Ahab. These manifestly all contributed to the portentous and combustive atmospherics of the age, promptings that one way or another everyone felt and everyone responded to.

As unemployed workers marched in several American cities demanding "work and bread," the crisis had impacted Europe, South America, South Africa, and the Far East. In New York on November 5, 4,000 persons rallied at Tompkins Square to hear speakers whose demands included that the city government establish public works, guarantee a minimum wage, stop landlords from evicting the unemployed, and build housing for the poor. The next day 5,000 protesters descended on the Merchants' Exchange demanding loans be given to businesses to rehire workers, as an even larger crowd gathered at City Hall on November 9 demanding action.

When another invasion of Kansas did not materialize in October, and elections had come off peacefully, Brown changed his orientation. It is not clear that his relationship with Forbes had degenerated into vituperation. Indeed, Brown accompanied the Garibaldian to Nebraska City to depart by stagecoach, their intention still apparently to begin a military school at West Andover, Ohio, in Ashtabula County, where Brown's sons John Jr. and Jason lived. In November Brown appeared furtively in Lawrence and began recruiting his company. Cook was joined by Stevens (AKA Whipple), Charles Moffat, and John Henry Kagi. This company left Topeka for Nebraska City, camping at night on the prairie. "Here for the first time," Cook recounted, "I learned that we were to leave Kansas to attend a military school during the winter in Ashtabula County, Ohio."[45] As the others continued up to the border, Cook, with an $80 draft from Brown, was sent back to Lawrence with instructions to get Parsons, Realf, and Hinton, and take a steamboat to St. Joseph, Missouri, and the stage to Tabor. Cook found Parson and Realf, but Hinton was away. All united they were Stevens, Kagi, Moffat, Parsons, Realf, C.P. Tidd, William Leeman, and an "intelligent" fugitive slave from Lexington,

Missouri, named Richard Richardson, together with John and Owen Brown. At Tabor these men learned of Captain Brown's long cherished plan and that their "ultimate destination was the state of Virginia."[46] Hinton and Sanborn record that when the project's scope was revealed there was heated discussion; but as they were united, and each individual had scarce means, all resolved to forge on. Two teams were procured for the transport of arms and supplies—two hundred Sharp's rifles and two hundred revolvers, with stores of blankets, clothing, boots, and ammunition. On December 8, four days after leaving Tabor, on a cold, snowy night, with prairie wolves howling around them, the troop engaged, as was recorded by Owen Brown in his diary, in "hot discussion upon the Bible and war . . . warm argument upon the effects of the abolition of slavery upon the Southern States, Northern States, commerce and manufacture, also upon the British provinces and the civilized world; whence came our civilization and origin."[47] The snowbound, windswept prairie made for an arduous, slow march on which the men gathered nightly around campfires, wrapping themselves in blankets and shielding themselves from the weather in tents. During this passage, "Brown's plan in regard to an incursion into Virginia gradually manifested itself," Realf recalled. "It was a matter of discussion between us as to the possibility of effecting a successful insurrection in the mountains, some arguing that it was, some that it was not; myself thinking, and still thinking, that a mountainous country is a very fine country for an insurrection, in which I am borne out by historic evidence."[48]

As the company was trekking through Iowa, Kansas Territorial governor Walker was calling a special session of the newly elected legislature with its free-state majority and asking its members to pass an act for a plebiscite on the Lecompton Constitution. Not able to brook this, Buchanan recalled Walker from office, appointing James W. Denver, his Indian commissioner, as the territory's fifth governor. On the opening day of the legislature, December 7, followed by nine hundred celebrants on foot, horseback, and carriage, Jim Lane marched into Lecompton at the head of the Lawrence Cornet Band, as George Deitzler was elected Speaker of the House.[49]

On Christmas Day Brown's troop passed through Marengo, Iowa, next reaching Iowa City, and on New Year's Eve, the small Quaker community known as the Pedes Settlement, also called Springdale. Some of the men took lodging at Traveler's Rest, an inn in nearby West Branch, while the others moved into the house of William Maxton at Springdale. The trek had taken them across two hundred and fifty miles of wintry landscape, and indoor quarters were a relief. The Quakers were friendly to the man known as "Osawatomie Brown"—although an elder admonished him, "Thou art welcome to tarry among us, but we have no use for thy guns." Brown's intention was to sell the teams and wagons for rail passage through to Ohio from a near-by railhead. But the financial panic was in full swing in the West and the money could not be raised. It was decided the men would winter in Iowa and undertake military training there while Brown went east to develop his agencies. George Gill joined the company, as did his Canadian friend, Steward Taylor, and two Quaker brothers from the town, Barclay and Edwin Coppoc. Charles Moffat observed the broader framework of Brown's design for a military school: "When Brown left he gave Whipple charge of the school, and I had sent Forbes round by water to Ohio. Forbes had been engaged as drill-master at a hundred dollars a month, and when we stopped in Iowa Brown said he would give Forbes the choice of schools: if Forbes would come back to Iowa, Whipple would take the school in Ohio or in Canada. But when he got to Ohio, Brown found that Forbes had gone away, and so gave up the Ohio school."[50]

A makeshift military academy would now be established at Springdale to occupy the men under the superintendence of Stevens. There was study of tactics aided by the Forbes compendium, drill and physical training, with gymnastics and target shooting; along with entrenching, and construction of field fortifications undertaken. On two weekday evenings, a mock legislature was held at one of the homes or in a nearby schoolhouse, where the oratory of Realf, Kagi, Cook, and others was heard with townspeople participating; while on other evenings informal discussions took place.

"There was no attempt to make a secret of their drilling," wrote Richard Hinton. "The neighborhood folks all understood that this band of earnest young men were preparing for something far out of the ordinary. Of course Kansas was presumed to be the objective point. But generally the impression prevailed that when the party moved again, it would be somewhere in the direction of the slave states. The atmosphere of those days was charged with disturbance."[51]

The most important of these cadre lent distinction to the enterprise and occupied a place in the affections of their commander. First, in the second position in a military capacity, was Aaron Dwight Stevens (Colonel Whipple). He was striking-looking, Hinton wrote, "handsome and active as a young Greek gladiator." He was six feet, two inches, with a powerful though graceful frame; his hair raven black, and he wore a full beard. He sang gloriously it was reported, and Gill said of him that he "was the most noble [man] that I ever knew."[52]

John Henry Kagi, of Swiss descent, was born in Bristolville, Ohio. He had taught school in the Shenandoah Valley but had to quit as locals began to notice that every time he left the area a slave would abscond with him. He was second to John Brown in the leadership. He had trained as an attorney, although he was largely self-taught—"an agnostic of the most pronounced type," Gill said, calling him a "tower of strength for John Brown." Because of his journalistic prowess, Brown referred to Kagi as "our Horace Greeley," with a look more of a divinity student than a warrior. His articles were published in the New York *Daily Tribune*, the New York *Evening Post*, and the *National Era*. Admitted to the Nebraska bar in 1855, Kagi joined the fighting in Kansas first under Lane, then enlisted under Colonel Whipple. He was an exceptional debater and speaker, and an expert stenographer. Among these cadres he became John Brown's closest confidant.

Richard Realf, too, had a special place in the affections of the commander. Born in East Sussex, England, of an impoverished working-class family, Realf worked as a boy to pay for his education, astonishing "the village clergyman by his precocity." His chronicler wrote that while "still in his teens he came to the attention of some of the local literati which included Lady Byron, publishing *Guesses at the Beautiful*."[53]

Realf's patroness sent him as steward to one of her country estates, where he had a love affair with one of her relatives, causing a rupture with the eminent lady. He fell into debt soon afterward and became a wanderer indulging in excesses; barefoot and in rags in the streets of Southampton, he sang ballads for pennies that passersby threw into his hat.

Coming to the United States in 1854, he became a missionary in the Five Points district of New York City, assisting in establishing at a low cost a lecture course, and in 1856 he joined an emigrant train going to Kansas. Embroiling himself in Kansas affairs, Realf was also a corresponding journalist. A brilliant talker and orator, his verses were well circulated in newspapers and well received—the nineteenth century's unknown poet. Joining the United States Army in the Civil War, he is credited with having lifted and borne the fallen "colors" during the assault on Lookout Mountain in Tennessee. Realf perhaps never lived down his association with John Brown and his allies, ending his tumultuous life in 1878 at 44 in a hotel room in Oakland, California—a bard *Born unto singing And a burthen lay mightly on him.*

"Liberty! That was the key to his soul; the master-passion that controlled all his other ambitions," James Redpath wrote of Realf. "It swayed him like a frenzy."[54]

Also a member of this coterie, albeit a peripheral one, was Richard Hinton, a Scot born in London who had pursued the stone-cutter's trade as a youth. Crossing the Atlantic in 1851, he resided in New York City, learning the printing trade. He joined an emigrant party at Worcester, Massachusetts, arriving in Kansas in August 1856. He became an important chronicler of Brown and his troops, publishing *John Brown and His Men* in 1895.

Also treasured in his father's affections, and a constant companion, was John Brown's third son, Owen. Six feet in height, he had a fair, somewhat freckled complexion, with red hair and heavy whiskers of the same hue. He was spare in build, his eyes deep blue, and like his father was described as a "host" in battle, even though one of his arms had been mangled in a boyhood accident. Like all the Browns, Owen Brown possessed good humor, ending his days as a hermit on a California mountainside.

In Washington, Charles Sumner, who had retained his seat despite severe debility but not yet returning full-time to the Senate, received two epistles from Colonel Hugh Forbes. Forbes wrote that he had been grossly defrauded by John Brown and was destitute and his family suffering privation in Paris. The letters named well-placed persons in Boston. Sumner forwarded these to Sanborn, who was among those named. Sanborn had received a letter himself intimating that, unless properly compensated, Forbes intended to disclose a plan Brown evidently was developing, but about which Sanborn knew nothing. Forbes had also stopped in Rochester to see Frederick Douglass, who wrote in his autobiography, "I was not favorably impressed with Colonel Forbes, but I 'conquered my prejudice,' took him to a hotel and paid his board while he remained. Just before leaving, he spoke of his family in Europe as in destitute circumstances, and of his desire to send them some money. I gave him a little . . . and through Miss Assing, a German lady, deeply interested in the John Brown scheme, he was introduced to several of my German friends in New York."[55]

These divulgences had come during Christmas week of 1857. Brown left Springdale, Iowa, on January 15, 1858. Those in Boston who had done so much to outfit and to arm a company for him for the support of a free Kansas were mystified by his movements. What could they portend?

Chapter Six

"THERE IS THE MOST ABUNDANT MATERIAL, AND OF THE RIGHT QUALITY, IN THIS QUARTER, BEYOND ALL DOUBT"

IN THE EARLY WINTER OF 1858, when John Brown departed Springdale, Iowa, heading east, he had been contemplating his purpose, as he phrased it, of "Carrying the War into Africa" for nearly twenty years. No one has ever maintained that Brown's oft-expressed belief that he was an "instrument in the hands of God" to destroy slavery in America was the product of rational thought, but the manner in which he fitted himself to become a divine instrument was eminently coherent. John Brown, Sanborn remarked, "knew what he wanted to do," and now he was working on a strict timetable in order to bring off his historic project within the next sixty days.

There is reason to suppose that Brown's months in Tabor, Iowa—from August 7, 1857, to the beginning of November of that year—had been an important period of preparation and study for him. It has been pointed out that there was a noticeable concurrence between the methods commended by Hugh Forbes in his book, *Manual for the Patriotic Volunteer on Active Service in Regular and Irregular War, being the Art and Science of obtaining and maintaining Liberty and Independence,* which Brown had been reading and discussing with the author, and the methods ascribed to him at this time. When juxtaposed with the account in Douglass's autobiography, the similarity is striking. At paragraph thirty of the *Manual*, Forbes had written, "A single band, whether large or small, would have but a poor chance of success—it would be speedily surrounded; but a multiplicity of little bands, some three to ten miles distant from each other, yet in connection and communication, cannot be surrounded, especially in a chain of well wooded mountains, such as the Apennines."[1] Whereas in his autobiography Douglass wrote, "[Brown's] plan . . . [was] to take at first about twenty-five picked men, and begin on a small scale—supply them with arms and ammunition and post them in squads of fives on a line of twenty-five miles. . . . With care and enterprise he thought he could soon gather a force of one hundred hardy men, men who would be content to lead the free and adventurous life to which he proposed to train them; when these were properly drilled, and each man had found the place for which he was best suited, they would run off the slaves in large numbers, train the brave and strong ones in the mountains, and send the weak and timid to the North by the underground railroad. His operations would be enlarged with increasing numbers and would not be confined to one locality."[2]

Douglass places this sketch of Brown's plan in his writing about his initial meeting with John Brown in 1847 in his *Life and Times*, apparently misplacing Brown's insurrectionist idea by more than a decade. An unconscious substitution perhaps, or one necessitated by Douglass's later remarks regarding his own complicity in that plan, and his refusal to join Brown finally at Harper's Ferry?

To complete and complement his military strategizing, Brown began writing a "Provisional Constitution and Ordinances for the People of the United States," which he proposed as the organizational or governmental framework for an oppressed people he was to lead while engaged in this irregular partisan warfare. This document received its first notice "in the literature" again in Douglass's *Life and Times*, published decades later. In that volume Douglass mistakenly maintained that the foundational document was written by Brown in February 1858. "When not writing letters," Douglass suggests, during Brown's three-week stay at his home "he was writing and revising a constitution which he meant to put in operation by means of the men who should go with him into the mountains. . . . I have a copy of this constitution in Captain Brown's own handwriting as prepared by himself at my house." But that composition—a substantial compendium obviously requiring many months of preparation—undoubtedly was begun at Tabor. Passing through Chicago, Brown met with Harvey B. Hurd of the National Kansas Committee, which was then wrapping up its affairs. "I saw [Brown] while he was then in Chicago, at that time, and talked with him to some extent about his operations in Kansas and his future purposes," Hurd told Hinton in a letter dated October 1, 1892. "He had a paper about which he wished to consult me, some parts of which he read to me. I afterwards found that it was a draft of the constitution which he intended to have adopted if it became necessary to form a government, as the result of his prospective operations in Virginia."[3]

Traveling incognito as "Nelson Hawkins" and having adopted the disguise of a full "patriarchal" beard, at the beginning of February John Brown knocked at the door of Frederick Douglass in Rochester. There is no suggestion that Brown wrote prior to his arrival, as he announced upon greeting Douglass that he was in need of lodging for several weeks but would only stay with Douglass, he told his putative host, if allowed to pay board. "Knowing that he was no trifler and meant all he said, and desirous of retaining him under my roof," Douglass wrote. "I charged three dollars a week."[4] Brown was a model guest, occupied in his room writing letters and putting the finishing touches on the "constitution." His correspondents were Franklin Sanborn, George Luther Stearns, Thomas Wentworth Higginson, Theodore Parker, Samuel Howe, and Gerrit Smith. Respondents were to direct posts to "N. Hawkins" care of his host or put a sealed letter inside another addressed to Frederick Douglass. Remittances were to be made out to Douglass. Charles, Douglass's youngest son, was engaged to carry outbound mail and pick up incoming mail. The correspondence centered on an undisclosed plan Brown wanted to discuss with his addressees, from whom he was intent on obtaining further cooperation and commitment, as he had done in the previous year. He was requesting their attendance at a meeting at Smith's estate in Peterboro.

But "his object was not simply to further his campaign for funds, but more especially definitely to organize the Negroes for his work," Du Bois wrote, noting that Brown "particularly had in mind the Negroes of New York and Philadelphia, and those in Canada."[5] Brown's

Black communicants accordingly were Henry Highland Garnet and James N. Gloucester in New York; John Jones and Henry O. Wagoner in Chicago; and Jermain Wesley Loguen of Syracuse—all long-term confidants of Brown. Also in his address book were the names and addresses of George T. Downing of Rhode Island, Martin Delany of Chatham, Ontario, William Still of Philadelphia, and James McCune Smith of New York, among others. Undoubtedly, he expressed to each something of the general tenor of his mission and requested of his addressees their presence at a meeting for consultation in early March at a place to be mutually specified.

James Gloucester offered his endorsement of the project on February 18: "I wish you Godspeed in your glorious work." But in a following letter the next day Gloucester cautioned Brown about being overly sanguine. "You speak of the people," Gloucester wrote. "I fear there is little to be done in the masses. The masses suffer for want of intelligence and it is difficult to reach them in a matter like you propose as far as it is necessary to secure their cooperation. The colored people are impulsive, but they need sagacity, sagacity to distinguish the proper course. They are like a bark at sea without a commander or rudder."[6] Before Brown left Rochester, he and his correspondents determined that those contacted, as well as others including Douglass, would convene in Philadelphia on March 5 at the home of Stephen Smith. After only a few days in the Douglass household Brown had addressed the following in a letter dated June 4 to John Jr. in West Andover, Ohio: "He [Douglass] has promised me $50, and what I value vastly more he seems to appreciate my theories & my labours."[7]

Brown too had piqued the interest and imaginations of his "eastern" correspondents. On February 2, he wrote to Theodore Parker. "I am again out of Kansas, and am at this time concealing my whereabouts," Brown told Parker. "I have nearly perfected arrangements for carrying out an important measure in which the world has a deep interest, as well as Kansas; and only lack from five to eight hundred dollars to enable me to do so."[8] On the same day Brown addressed Higginson about money for "secret service": "Can you be induced to operate at Worcester, & elsewhere during that time to raise from *Antislavery men & women*, (or any other parties) some part of the amount?"[9]

On February 8 Higginson, responding to "N. Hawkins," wrote: "I am always ready to invest money in treason, but at present have none to invest. As for my friends, those who are able are not quite willing, and those who are willing are at present bankrupt."[10] Edwin Morton, a classmate of Sanborn then employed at the Smith estate tutoring Smith's son, had written February 7 to his associate about Brown's letters: "This is news,—he 'expects to overthrow slavery' in a large part of the country." Sanborn sent a query to Higginson on February 11: "I have received two letters from J.B. in which he speaks of a plan but does not say what it is. Still I have confidence enough in him to trust him with the moderate sum he asks for—if I had it."[11]

To Higginson, Brown offered a tantalizing hint: "I have just read your kind letter of the 8th instant, & will now say that Rail Road business on a somewhat extended scale, is the identical object for which I am trying to get means.... I have been operating to some purpose the past season: but now have a measure on foot that I feel sure would awaken in you something more than a common interest; if you could understand it." Brown had just written to "friends G.L. Stearns, F.B. Sanborn" requesting they meet him "for consultation at Gerrit Smith, Peterboro," adding, "I am very anxious to have you come along; certain as I feel; that you will never regret having been one of the council."[12]

In brief, Brown's plan was now calling for an incursion to be made into Virginia in the mountainous region abutting the Blue Ridge. The men coming with him were to act as officers of bands into which freed slaves would be formed. These bands were to act separately or in a concerted way, starting on a line of twenty-five miles under John Brown's general command. At first the movement, Brown suggested, was to have the appearance of a slave stampede or at most a local outbreak. Planters would pursue their fleeing chattels and be defeated; and as militias were called up, they would also be defeated. Gradually expanding, the campaign would "strike terror into the heart of the slave States by the amount of organization it would exhibit, and the strength it gathered."[13] Freed people were to be armed with the weapons they could most effectively use—pikes, scythes, muskets, and shotguns—and would be trained in riflery. The bands would procure provisions by forage and by impressing the property of slaveholders, including arms, horses, wagons, and ammunition. As the force took hold of the region, one of Brown's followers, Richard Realf, remarked later, his commander believed "that the several slave States could be forced (from the position in which they found themselves) to recognize the freedom of those who had been slaves within the respective limits of those States."¹⁴ As regarded Brown's "constitution," Douglass wrote, "He said that, to avoid anarchy and confusion, there should be a regularly constituted government, which each man who came with him should be sworn to honor and support."¹⁵ Douglass also related that, soon after coming to him, Brown asked Douglass to provide "two smoothly planed boards, upon which he could illustrate with a pair of dividers, by a drawing, the plan of fortification which he meant to adopt in the mountains."¹⁶ "These forts were to be so arranged as to connect one with the other by secret passages, so that if one was carried another could easily be fallen back upon and be the means of dealing death to the enemy at the very moment when he might think himself victorious." No doubt signaling his ambivalence about discussing strictly military matters, Douglass confided to his readers that his children were more interested in these drawings than he was. "Once in a while," he added, "he would say he could, with a few resolute men, capture Harper's Ferry and supply himself with arms belonging to the government at that place, but he never announced his intention to do so."¹⁷

On February 20, in a letter to John Jr., Brown wrote, "I am here with our good friends Gerrit Smith and wife, who, I am most happy to tell you, are ready to go in for a share in the whole trade."¹⁸ With none of the Massachusetts "friends" able to make the journey to Smith's estate, Sanborn was delegated to go as their representative. Edward Morton was present, as was "an old officer under Wellington," Charles Stewart. After dinner and a few minutes spent in the parlor with guests, Smith, Brown, Sanborn, and Morton retired to Morton's room. "Here, in the long winter evening which followed, the whole outline of Brown's campaign in Virginia was laid before our little council, to the astonishment and almost the dismay of those present."¹⁹ The constitution was exhibited, the proposed movements of Brown's men indicated, and the middle of May named as the time of the attack. Laying before them his methods of organization and fortification, of settlement on the conquered lands if possible, and of retreat through the North if advisable, Brown anticipated the way in which such a campaign would be received in the country at large. All he was asking to bring off the project was that they collectively raise $800, and he would think it bountiful if he had $1,000.

"We listened until after midnight, proposing objections and raising difficulties; but nothing could shake the purpose of the old Puritan," Sanborn wrote. "Every difficulty had been foreseen and provided against in some manner; the grand difficulty of all,—the manifest hopelessness of undertaking anything so vast with such slender means,—was met with the text of Scripture: "If God be for us, who can be against us?"[20] The dialogue consumed the whole of the following day; in the evening Brown was left by the fire discussing points of theology with Stewart as Smith and Sanborn walked for an hour in the snow-covered woods around the estate. Smith, restating Brown's propositions, finally said, "You see how it is; our dear old friend has made up his mind to this course, and cannot be turned from it. We cannot give him up to die alone, we must support him. I will raise [$500] for him; you must lay the case before your friends in Massachusetts and perhaps they will do the same."[21]

Sanborn returned to Boston February 25, and that day communicated the enterprise to Theodore Parker and Wentworth Higginson. With his meeting in Philadelphia delayed at the request of Douglass, Brown, at the invitation of Parker, visited Boston March 4-8, staying the whole time in his room at the America House. Individually, members of the entire Massachusetts coterie visited him to take part in long discussions. Parker reportedly was deeply interested, but not very sanguine about the mission's success. He wished to see the plan tried, however, believing the exploit would do good even if it failed. Dr. Howe was reported as accepting "the idea with earnestness; within the lines to be worked upon, he saw real military possibilities." George Stearns was reported as accepting the proposition "with an utterly loyal belief in the old covenanter."[22] Holding the middling view with Parker, Higginson believed that nevertheless "with decent temporary success, [it] would do more than anything else to explode our present political platforms."[23]

While at the Smith estate, Sanborn had confided to Morton he was tempted to make "common cause" with Brown. Hearing this, Brown wrote to him as Sanborn, now returned to Boston: "I greatly rejoice at this; for I believe when you come to look at the ample field I labor in, and the rich harvest which not only this entire country but the whole world during the present and future generations may reap from its successful cultivation, you will feel that you are out of your element until you find you are in it, an entire unit."[24] In later years, Sanborn was to write that he was never able to read this letter without emotion, adding that he thought Brown had not until then determined on the seizure of Harper's Ferry. "Yet," Sanborn wrote, "he spoke of it to me beside his coal-fire in the America House, putting it as a question, rather, without expressing his own purpose."[25]

With the world economy only just recovering from the Panic of 1857, and as the Lecompton Constitution was being debated in the Senate, a leading spokesman for slaveholders, James Hammond of South Carolina, rose to deliver a clarion call on March 4, 1858. The Southern economy—its crops and the value of its slaves, its railroads, and its merchant class—had scarcely been affected by the turmoil, Hammond said. Advancing that memorable phrase, "Cotton is king," Hammond went on: "Until lately the Bank of England was king; but she tried to put her screws as usual, the fall before last, upon the cotton crop, and was utterly vanquished. The last power has been conquered. Who can doubt, that has looked at recent events, that cotton is supreme? When the abuse of credit had destroyed credit and annihilated confidence; when thousands of the strongest commercial houses in the world were coming down, and hundreds of millions of dollars of supposed property evaporating in thin air; when you came to a deadlock, and revolutions were threatened, what brought you up? Fortunately for you it was the commencement of the cotton season, and we have poured in upon you one million six hundred thousand bales of cotton just at the crisis to save you from destruction. That cotton, but for the bursting of your speculative bubbles in the North, which produced the whole of this convulsion, saved you. Thirty-five million dollars we, the slaveholders of the South, have put into the charity box for your magnificent financiers, your 'cotton lords,' your 'merchant princes.'"

Who does not know that Cotton is king, crowed Southern propagandists. The basis of this axiom in its most fundamental sense, wrote Frederick Law Olmsted in *The Cotton Kingdom*, was the worth of a prime field hand—not how much work the enslaved man could perform on a plantation in a day's labor—how much wood he could cord or how many acres of grain he could cradle—but whether he would fetch $2,000 from a trader when taken south for sale to a cotton planter. The market value of a slave's labor was determined by what he was worth for producing cotton.

The systematic cultivation of large plots of naturally fertile land worked by large gangs of slaves resembled a "Roman lottery," Olmsted wrote, in which "a few very large prizes were promised" and "many very small ones." With a limited number of tickets, speculators could buy tickets at exorbitant prices "when they know perfectly well that the average chance is not worth a tithe of what they must pay for it." Planters who produced cotton at a rate of seven to ten bales per hand could well afford to buy fresh hands at $1,400 a head. They could even afford to wait for profits a year or two while land was cleared, ditches dug, levees and fences built, and the necessary stocks of corn and bacon, tools and cattle procured, paying 15 percent per annum interest on borrowed capital required to underwrite the expansion. With practically limitless acreage available on which cotton could be grown cheaply, one lucky crop would repay all the outlays for land and improvement, though not the capital needed for acquiring the "hands," as the supply of slaves was limited and could not increase at the same rate as demand for cotton. Olmsted wrote, "If cotton should double in price next year, or become worth its weight in gold, the number of Negroes in the United States would not increase four per cent unless the African slave-trade were re-established."

Olmsted offered this vignette: Step into a dealer's "jail" in Memphis, Montgomery, Vicksburg, or New Orleans, he said, and you will hear the Mezzano of the cotton lottery crying his tickets: "There's a cotton nigger for you! Genuine! Look at his toes! Look at his fingers! There's a pair of legs for you! If you have got the right sile [sic] and the right sort of overseer, buy him, and put your trust in Providence! He's just as good for ten bales as I am for a julep at eleven o'clock."

A cotton bale weighed three hundred seventy-five to four hundred pounds. Half a million bales were being produced annually by 1820. Production reached a million bales in 1831 and doubled by the early part of the next decade. Thereafter census reports show three million bales were gathered in 1852, three and a half million in 1856, and an extraordinary yield of five million bales in 1860. Substantially the whole of the economic activity of the South was thrown into this "cotton lottery" in pursuit of bigger and more luxuriant profits, consequent upon the frightful consumption of human beings and of soil.

Frederick Douglass averred the reality of the American slave trade, invoking the sights and scenes of his boyhood in Baltimore, where he had seen slavery's horrors. In a speech delivered in Corinthian Hall, Rochester, he said:[26] "We are told by the papers, [it] is especially prosperous just now. Ex-Senator Benton tells us that the price of men was never higher. . . . He mentions the fact to show that slavery is in no danger. The trade is one of the peculiarities of American institutions. It is carried on in all the large towns and cities in one-half of this confederacy; and millions are pocketed every year by dealers in this horrid traffic. In several states this trade is a chief source of wealth. It is called (in contradistinction to the foreign slave-trade) 'the internal slave-trade.'" And while this trade between the border slave states and areas of intensive cultivation of cotton in the Deep South proved inadequate, the call was heard for a reopening of the African slave trade to meet the demand. If it was right to buy slaves in Virginia and carry them to New Orleans, why wasn't it right to buy them in Cuba, Brazil, or Africa, and carry them to the Crescent City?

Large-scale mechanized mills had begun to take hold at Lowell and Lawrence in Massachusetts and in towns like Woonsocket in Rhode Island and elsewhere, enlarging the cotton- and wool-spinning sectors in the northeastern United States in the same way that industrialization had in England as much as two generations before. Attacks on the phenomenon of an industrializing capitalism began to be heard in the South because of the fierce social antagonisms occasioned by the exploitation and poverty of the proletarianized workforce up north. Slavery was the superior system, Southerners argued, because it reconciled capital and labor. George Fitzhugh notably articulated this view in *Sociology of the South*, published in 1854 and again in 1857 in *Cannibals All!* The emerging economies of liberal democracies, Fitzhugh said, were possibly only a "little experiment," merely a short-term aberration in world history that could not survive the periodic social and economic paroxysms attendant to them. Experience had shown, Southern propagandists held, that when the black and white races were thrown together in the relationship of slave and master, the result was a society "capable of great development, morally, socially, and politically." Such a relationship was best for both, and if that relationship was destroyed, both elements would decline and decay; abolitionists were only hastening what had already been advanced by political economy, Fitzhugh warned.

In a May 1853 speech in New York before the American and Foreign Anti-Slavery Society, Douglass said that it was becoming increasingly evident that there was in the United States "a purely slavery party." While that party went by no particular name and assumed no definite shape, it was "not intangible" in important respects. That party's objects and its designs and the center around which it was coalescing had been "forcibly presented . . . in the stern logic of passing events." The country was dividing on its issues; old party ties were being broken as like was finding like on both sides, and the battle was at hand. Said Douglass, the Compromise of 1850 had specified all the objects of slave-holder policy. That policy comprehended "first, the complete suppression of all anti-slavery discussion; second, the expulsion of the entire free colored people of the United States; third, the nationalization of slavery; fourth, guarantees for the endless perpetuation of slavery and its extension over Mexico and Central America." But as bad as the case appeared, Douglass said, "I do not despair for my people," as "neither the principle nor the subordinate objects, here declared, can be at all gained by the slave power" for those objects involved "the proposition to padlock the lips of whites, in order to secure the fetters on the limbs of blacks." Free speech could not be suppressed in the end "because God had interposed an insuperable obstacle to any such result," pillowed as the slaveholder was "on the heaving bosoms of ruined souls."[27]

Brown's documentable preoccupation with Harper's Ferry of many years should perhaps be primarily viewed in this context: What he sought above all was something with optimal probative value; something that would thrust wedge-like under the entire foundation of the American political system as that system had evolved in those antebellum years, toppling the precarious equilibrium that system's abettors sought so desperately to maintain to the detriment of the Republic. Such an idea had been expressed to him in a letter at the time of the Lecompton constitutional voting the previous fall in Kansas; Rev. Samuel Adair wrote him about the situation on October 2. "An invasion such as we had in '54 and '55 I do not expect; but doubtless many voters from slave states will be smuggled in. What course things will take if the Free-State men fail," Adair wrote, "I do not know. Some prophesy trouble right along. This would not surprise me were it to occur. But I would deplore a renewal of war. If it is to be commenced again, the boil had better be probed in the centre, at Washington, where the corruption is the worst. The proslavery men in the Territory are but petty tools."[28]

Brown's overriding purpose, then, was to strike at the federal government in the very environs of its national seat; as Adair expressed it, it would be like lancing a boil. Brown intended too, in effect, to raise a "whirlwind" as terrible as any ever seen on the Kansas plains; like that awesome apparition of God's wrath on the north wall of the Kansas state capitol at Topeka. A mural rendered in 1942, eighty years after the events on record, and titled *Tragic Prelude*, was the work of the muralist John Stewart Curry. In the center of Curry's depiction is the figure of a man larger than life, his arms extended; he is wearing the rough-hewn coat and pants of the frontier. With flowing beard, he exerts himself above the noise and agony of battle, as he himself is seen to be shouting at the top of his lungs. In his right hand, he holds an opened Bible, in the other a "Beecher's bible," as the Sharps rifle was known. Towering over fallen Union and Confederate soldiers, symbols of the war of 1861-1865, the figure straddles two groups bearing the flags of the opposing sides. In explaining his principal character to a newspaperman, Curry said: "I wanted to paint him as a fanatic, for John Brown was a fanatic." Enmeshed within these struggling figures are several fugitive slaves; in the background settlers in wagons stream ahead against an ominous prairie-fire; on the opposite horizon, as irrational in effect as Curry's central figure, rages a gigantic tornado. The muralist in making this equivalency has given us not John Brown in his historical determinations but a portrait of bathos.

Brown left Peterboro in late February to confer with his friends among Black leaders in Brooklyn and New York and to prepare for his Philadelphia appointment. Arriving at the home of Rev. James Gloucester and his wife on Bridge Street in the Bedford-Stuyvesant neighborhood of Brooklyn, Brown promptly received a note from Douglass, dated February 27, 1858: "My Dear Friend,—When we parted, we were to meet in Philadelphia on Friday, March 5. I write now to postpone going to Philadelphia until Wednesday, March 10. Please write me at Rochester if this will do, and if you wish me to come at that time. You can, I hope, find work enough in and about New York to that date. Please make my warmest regards to Mrs. and Mr. Gloucester, and accept that and more for yourself."[29]

Since 1848, James Newton Gloucester had been pastor and a founding member of the Siloam Presbyterian Church in Brooklyn, a noted station of the Underground Railroad. Having come from Richmond, Virginia, he and his wife, Elizabeth, had acquired property, and she operated a furniture store. Brown's visit, at the couple's invitation, arose from a decade-long relationship. Cautioned by his friend about his expectation to find recruits among the city's young Black men, Brown did not throttle back his zeal; he wrote his wife in a letter dated March 2: "I find a much more earnest feeling among the colored people than ever before; but that is by no means unusual. On the whole, the language of Providence to me would certainly seem to say, 'Try on.'"[30]

Brown's visitations in the New York environs surely included one or more to Rev. Henry Highland Garnet, who in 1856 had become the pastor of the Shiloh Presbyterian Church in New York City, an appointment occasioned by the death of its former divine and his close friend, the Rev. Theodore Wright, the first Black graduate of the Princeton Theological Seminary. Contacted by John Brown in February 1858 about obtaining his help in "forming societies" to aid in the recruitment of Blacks for his Virginia campaign, Garnet had on his initiative seen to it that the Philadelphia meeting was arranged, attesting to Brown's long-standing reputation among a select but important group of Black abolition and underground leaders.

Garnet had gone abroad in 1850, traveling on the Continent with his wife and family, then to England where they remained for several years. Becoming a sought-after lecturer among anti-slavery societies in Britain, he joined the Free Labor Movement and became active in the West India Committee, organizations that rejected the use of the products of slave labor. In 1851 Garnet was the official American delegate to the World Anti-Slavery Convention in London, at which he gave an address. In 1852 Garnet was sent to Jamaica as a missionary for the United Presbyterian Church of Scotland, presiding in a church near Kingston. Lecturing about the American scene, he gave talks that probed the origins and implications of the Fugitive Slave Law, which was designed, in his view, to assure that markets in Europe, and particularly in England, would be maintained as outlets for the products of the southern American economy. Contracting a fever that lingered for many months, Garnet returned to the United States in 1855; in Boston he proposed to become a "missionary for liberty," but when the pulpit in New York became available, it was hither he went.

On March 7 Brown visited Boston at the invitation of Theodore Parker, taking a room at the America House. Brown asked the preacher to undertake an important literary assignment. He had roughed out an address to be directed at federal troops and officers. The finished message, Brown said, should be brief, or it would not generally be read, and written in the plainest language, "without the least affectation of the scholar about it, and yet be worded with great clearness and power." Brown wanted the communication "particularly adapted to the peculiar circumstances we anticipate, and should look to the actual change of service from that of Satan to the service of God." Certainly no one could calculate in advance, he added, "the value and importance of getting a single nail into old Captain Kidd's chest."[31] Brown possessed among his qualities a literary subtlety, as his writings often attest. Higginson, himself a man of literary merit, wrote of Brown, with whom he had been in close contact that March, that he was "a man whom Sir Walter Scott might have drawn but whom such writers as Nicolay and Hay have utterly failed to delineate."

While in Boston, too, in what was probably his only excursion outside his room, Brown visited Charles Sumner at home, accompanied by the Rev. James Freeman Clarke and James Redpath, who included the episode in his book on Brown in 1860. With Sumner lying abed recuperating from his wounds of nearly two years previous, after some conversation Brown asked, "Do you have the coat you were wearing when you were attacked by Brooks?" "Yes, it is in the closet," Sumner replied. "Do you want to see it?" Redpath wrote: "I recall the scene vividly, Sumner standing slightly bent, supporting himself by keeping his hand on the bed, Brown, erect as a pillar, holding up the blood-besmirched coat in his right hand and examining it intently. The old man said nothing, I believe, but I remember that his lips compressed, and his eyes shone like polished steel."[32]

Before leaving Douglass's home in early February Brown had written his eldest son, "I have been thinking that I would like to have you make a trip to Bedford, Chambersburg, Gettysburg, and Uniontown in Pennsylvania, traveling slowly along, and inquiring of every man on the way, or every family of the right stripe, and getting acquainted with them as much as you could. When you look at the location of those places, you will readily perceive the advantage of getting some acquaintance in those parts."[33] On March 4 Brown again instructed his son to "hunt out friends . . . even at Harper's Ferry." That tour might easily have included a visit to Harrisburg, since it was a rail hub, and he could have included those in the town's growing Black neighborhood on his roster. What was the outcome of this trip, whether accomplished at this time or later? The prescribed route would have taken John Jr. by rail from western Ohio to Pittsburgh, thence to Harrisburg and down to Chambersburg. Traveling across central Pennsylvania by stagecoach, he would have arrived at Philadelphia, where his father's meeting with notables in that city was pending, and which he, too, was to attend. Although the Philadelphia meetings have drawn at most cursory notice, Du Bois correctly indicates their importance: "Brown seems to have stayed nearly a week in that city, and probably had long conferences with all the chief Philadelphia Negro leaders."[34] Convened on Lombard Street at the well-appointed residence of the lumber merchant, abolitionist, and philanthropist Stephen Smith—"headquarters" for Brown and his son during their stay—the meetings gathered attendees, all of them Black except the Browns, including Smith, William Still, and others from the Philadelphia Vigilance Committee, as well from the abolitionist societies and perhaps a few clerics, in addition to Douglass and Garnet. Gloucester, detained, pledged "$25 more" toward the fund-raising in his note of reply; Loguen reported that he was ill.[35] These meetings attest to the significance Brown gave Philadelphia, which contained the largest Black population of any northern city, and to the standing and regard of those under whose auspices the gatherings proceeded. Regarding the reputation of John Brown, Garnet said, he is "the only white man who really understands slavery."[36]

It has been supposed, given that Brown was proposing opening a new avenue of the Underground Railroad that would have direct impact on the Philadelphia area, that Still and others offered detailed remarks imparting knowledge of the operations under their purview. In his treatment Richard Hinton surmises that Brown's interest was "to ascertain the persons who were actually to be relied upon, places to stop, means of conveyance, and especially to learn of the colored who could be trusted. The Philadelphia conference must have gone over this ground with the two Browns."[37] Yet this might not be quite right. Of necessity, these networks were clandestine and had to remain so; details about them could not be committed to writing. More likely the purpose of the meeting was to notify leaders of dramatic changes on the horizon. While Douglass had the most detailed knowledge of his friend's plans, the others would of course have intuited that the action concerned destinations south, in mountainous Virginia retreats. The details of that plan were not something necessarily to be dwelt upon, yet its outline was undoubtedly presented, although such has not been entered in the historical record. Yet Philadelphia had a significant bearing on what ultimately transpired.

If one keeps in mind various accounts given at this time from the Boston coterie to Higginson and Gerrit Smith to Douglass, a picture emerges of Brown conveying that he intended to exploit circumstances to pursue an ascending intensity of operations which, even if moderately successful, would have a withering effect on slavery. On the other hand, a successful demonstration of the kind he was proposing, displaying humanitarian restraint to avoid loss of life and destruction of property, would have a thoroughly salutary effect in the North. Not one effective voice, Brown held, could be raised for the reclamation of that specie in human property to the South once it had been freed. Above all from his listeners, then, Brown sought sanction and cooperation in bringing together selected Black men from their city—and from New York and elsewhere, and from Canada—with his own company to deliberate on and to ratify his proposed constitution and begin to institute, on a continuing basis, the framework and organizational support that such a campaign would entail. For the undertaking to proceed, contact through correspondences needed to be initiated, funds raised, lists of prospective and reliable participants compiled, sites procured at which to convene for deliberations, itineraries proposed, invitations sent out—all these, along with the means for bringing the men together and providing for their subsistence, would have been discussed, with all the connecting channels established and maintained with discretion. Evidently the consensus was that such could not safely be convened in a northern state. Such a conclave and accompanying activities would enrage the South and its northern supporters, were their existence known—and even if it were not, all protested, the reverberations might expose their activities in regard to their underground networks to unwanted scrutiny. It would be impossible to draw into the planning anyone not desiring this unwanted attention; even as some may not have been overly optimistic that Brown's plan could succeed militarily, others undoubtedly felt it ought to be tried.

The thing for Brown to do was to go to Canada, and the man he must seek out was Dr. Martin R. Delany. By involving Delany, his interlocutors were certain, he would be enabled to carry out his plans safely. Later, upon meeting Delany, Brown would express his disapprobation for this reluctance on the part of the Philadelphia men to make a resolute commitment. In his view, respect was only won by compelling it; a blow for freedom was always a victory.[38] In any event it was difficult to wholly oppose the bold notions of John Brown. However, given the difficulties abounding, the "Philadelphia decision" appears suitable. While Brown received this judgment with disappointment—characteristically tracing reluctance to lack of resolve—it had been his intention from the beginning to visit the fugitive slave communities in Canada anyway. Now that trip would be doubly necessary; although his interest in Philadelphia and New York as settings for recruitment would persist, particularly given the easy communication between those locales and the site of his campaign.

Martin Delany had been born in 1812 in Charlestown, Virginia, to a free mother and a slave father. In 1822 the family moved across the Mason-Dixon Line to Chambersburg, Pennsylvania. At 19, Delany crossed the mountains to Pittsburgh, where he found work and education, rising into abolitionism and newspaper editing; he edited the *Mystery* from 1843 to 1847 and co-edited the *North Star* with Douglass from 1847 to 1849. Becoming an important theorist of the African diaspora in the United States, in 1852 Delany published his epochal polemic *The Condition, Elevation, Emigration and Destiny of the Colored People in the United States, Politically Considered*. Attacked as an apostate for vehemently denouncing patronizing and hypocritical attitudes among White abolitionists and for recommending emigration to free Blacks, preferably to Africa, Delany envisioned developing a region that would gain a rising economic and political potency to undermine American slavery. In the winter of 1856, he made his word deed by moving with his family to Chatham, Ontario. Fine looking, with a jet-black complexion, Delany had a clean-shaven head "shining like highly polished Italian marble" to go with a strong bearing asserting racial pride. Frederick Douglass, attending three of Delany's lectures in Rochester in 1861, wrote of him, "He is the intensest embodiment of black Nationality to be met outside the valley of the Niger."[39]

For a decade Delany and Douglass had sparred, each becoming the foil to the other and neither letting the other off without a rejoinder. While Delany was dedicated to the premise that Blacks must wholly rely upon their own resources to overcome the adversity of their condition, and often excoriated other Blacks for looking to Whites for guidance, he was the one man, who, if not quite going all the way with John Brown, nevertheless threw himself wholeheartedly into getting up Brown's Chatham Convention. One participant wrote that Delany was "one of the prominent disputants or debaters."[40]

Brown left Philadelphia for New York City and New Haven. He sent notice to Loguen in Syracuse, who would be accompanying him to Ontario, that "I expect to be on the way by the 28th or 30th inst." Now he took the time to take leave of his family in North Elba.

That visit, so far as he knew, was to be his last, and he took a long walk to reach the settlement, tramping from Keene across the mountain. Among his own sons, the husband of his daughter Ruth, and his brother, Brown now sought the recruits he needed to realize his grand ambition. He had addressed a letter to his eldest daughter about her husband, Henry Thompson, from Rochester, January 30, 1858: "O my daughter Ruth! Could any plan be devised whereby you could let Henry go 'to school' (as you expressed it in your letter to him while in Kansas), I would rather now have him 'for another term' than to have a hundred scholars." In the same letter he wrote, "I would make a similar inquiry to my own dear wife; but I have kept her tumbling here and there over a stormy and tempestuous sea for so many years that I cannot ask her such a question."[41]

On April 2, Brown was in Peterboro, joined by his eldest son. Before they left, Smith handed John Brown a $25 draft for Harriet Tubman, to whom he commended Brown. The next day father and son were in Rochester. As soon as J.W. Loguen came, Brown and his colleague crossed over to the province of Ontario, or Canada West as it was called. Their first stop was in Hamilton, where William Howard Day, a Black printer, resided. Day was an 1847 graduate of Oberlin College who moved to Canada in 1857; it was he who arranged Brown's first meeting with Harriet Tubman, then living in nearby St. Catharines. "Among the slaves she is better known than the Bible, for she circulates more freely," remarked Loguen to Higginson, reported by him in the *Liberator* on May 28, 1858.

Black settlement in Canada had received its first great impetus in the spring of 1829, when 2,000 Cincinnati Blacks emigrated there in reaction to riots organized to drive them out of that city. After bloodletting and the torching of homes, a deputation was sent to Canada, where the governor extended a welcome: "Tell the republicans on your side of the line, that we royalists do not know men of their color." By 1840 the Black population of "Canada West" stood at around 10,000, with another 10,000 joining these by the end of the decade. But most of the refugees in Ontario Province emigrated after the U.S. Congress enacted the Fugitive Slave Law, thereafter adding over 1,000 refugees to its population year upon year. Most of these were newly escaped slaves, or fugitives who had lived in the North for a number of years and no longer felt safe. Of a population of nearly 60,000 Blacks, by 1860 in Ontario fully two-thirds of them were fugitives, making sizable communities in Buxton and Mt. Elgin, Ingersoll, Hamilton, and St. Catharines. The hub of these settlements was Chatham, among whose residents were mechanics and merchants, professionals, and farmers, together with fugitive slaves. In 1861 William Wells Brown wrote, "In my walk from the railroad station to the hotel I was at once impressed that I was in Chatham, for every other person whom I met was colored."[42] The *Provincial Freeman* newspaper was there, the town had a graded school, the Wilberforce Institute, along with several churches, a fire-engine company, and, enhancing community cohesiveness for its Black residents, Du Bois noted, a 400-member self-improvement organization called the True Bands.[43]

Although her reputation was increasing, and she had begun addressing anti-slavery conventions, Harriet Tubman had not yet gained the prominence she was to accrue by 1860. To be sure, she was well known to Douglass, Loguen, and to Thomas Garrett and William Still, as well as to many other abolitionists operating in the eastern branches of the Underground Railroad, but she was unknown in the West and had only furtively appeared in New England. On April 8 Brown wrote to his son, then in Ohio, "I came on here direct with J.W. Loguen the day after you left Rochester. I am succeeding to all appearance beyond expectations. Harriet Tubman hooked on his whole team at once. He is the most of a man, naturally, that I ever met with. There is the most abundant material, and of the right quality, in this quarter, beyond all doubt."[44] Certainly Brown had heard much about Tubman and had come to Canada expressly to meet her; so impressed was he by what he saw on their first meeting that the singular trifurcated in his vision, as he said: "I see General Tubman once, I see General Tubman twice, I see General Tubman three times."[45] Finding there to be complete unanimity between them, Brown stayed two days as a guest in her home, where they held long interviews; he met twice more with her there during his Canadian sojourn. He gave her $15 out of his own purse at the conclusion of their first meeting, and on April 14 gave her the $25 draft from Gerrit Smith, changed for a gold piece.

Loguen seems to have accompanied Brown only as far as Hamilton and St. Catharines, whereupon, having made important introductions to Day and Tubman, he returned to the U.S. side of the border. After several days in St. Catharines, Brown would continue on his tour on his own, with stops at Ingersoll, then Chatham and Buxton, then Toronto, then revisiting Chatham, St. Catharines, and Chatham again. Early on his rounds, he left Ingersoll for Chatham, and the home of Martin Delany. Finding the doctor away for several days, Brown declined to leave his name with Delany's wife, who reported to her husband upon his return that an elderly White man who had the appearance of one of the Hebrew prophets had come seeking him. Brown's hosts while in Chatham included an influential group at the *Provincial Freeman*, an abolitionist and pro-emigration newspaper whose editor at that time was I.D. Shadd. These individuals included Shadd's sister, Mary Shadd Cary, and her husband, Thomas Cary, Thomas Stringer, and the young printer's devil Osborne Perry Anderson. Another inhabitant of Ontario's Black settlements, John M. Jones, having met Brown, wrote, "Mr. Brown did not overestimate the state of education of the colored people. He knew that they would need leaders, and require training. His great hope was that the struggle would be supported by volunteers from Canada, educated and accustomed to self-government. He looked on our fugitives as picked men of sufficient intelligence, which combined with a hatred for the South, would make them willing abettors of any enterprise destined to free their race."[46] In the edition of the *Weekly Anglo African* of October 26, 1861, Mary Shadd Cary noted the tenor of John Brown's reception among those he met: "Some of us who knew dear old John Brown . . . well enough to know his plans, and who were thought 'sound' enough to be entrusted with them by him . . . have the greatest opinion of fighting anti-slavery—give us 'plucky' abolitionism." In a talk she prepared several years later on Brown's relations with people in Chatham, she wrote, "He taught something—he acted. Lessons of endurance, of Charity—of humanity, of zeal in a good cause. He wanted pure politics. Pure religion." It was clear to her that Brown's stroke at Harper's Ferry, when it came, was aimed not only at the strategic vulnerabilities of American slavery but an entire national condition, as he sought to create a break that would become the starting point in revolutionizing American politics.

In Buxton meetings were convened at the homes of Abraham Shadd and Ezikial Cooper, where Brown, it can be reliably surmised, met William Parker of the Christiana fugitive slave resistance, then living in the "bush" nearby. Traveling on to Toronto, Brown found another eager audience; meetings were held there at Temperance Hall and at the home of Dr. A.M. Ross, an abolitionist and naturalist with whom Brown stayed. Returning to Chatham to find Delany still absent, Brown promised Delany's wife he would "be back in two weeks time."[47]

Satisfied that preparations for a convention were in order, Brown had to return to Iowa to bring on his company, whose members would serve as the nucleus of the "fighting emancipationists" that the gathering was to sanction. On April 25, he was in Chicago at the home of his friend John Jones, a well-off tailor, who had been receiving Brown's mail during his two weeks in Canada. Hurrying on, he arrived in Springdale two days later.

Soon after Brown had left for the East the previous winter, the company had moved into a large concrete house owned by William Maxton, who charged each man $1.50 per week for room and board, "not including washing and extra lights." Of their departure, a witness wrote, "The leave-taking, between them and the people of Springdale was one of tears. Ties which had been knitting through many weeks were sundered, and not only so, but the natural sorrow at parting was intensified by the consciousness of all that the future was full of hazard for Brown and his followers."[48]

Traveling through Chicago and Detroit, the company arrived in Chatham and took up lodging at the Villa Mansion, a hotel under Black proprietorship. Soon Brown called at the home of Dr. Delany, who had returned. Delany recollected his initial meeting with Brown to his biographer, Frances Rollin Whipper, who wrote under the pseudonym Frank A. Rollin, for her *Life and Public Service of Martin R. Delany*, published in 1868. "I came to Chatham expressly to see you, this being my third visit on the errand," Brown said, according to Delany as quoted by Rollin. "I must see you at once, sir, and that, too, in private, as I have much to do and but little time before me. If I am to do nothing here, I want to know it at once."

"Going directly to the private parlor of a hotel near by he at once revealed to me that he desired to carry out a great project in his scheme of Kansas emigration, which to be successful, must be aided and countenanced by the influence of a general convention or council," Delany told Rollin. "That he was unable to effect in the United States, but had been advised by distinguished friends of his and mine, that, if he could but see me, his object could be attained at once. On my expressing astonishment at the conclusions to which my friends and himself had arrived, with a nervous impatience, he exclaimed, 'Why should you be surprised? Sir, the people of the Northern states are cowards; slavery has made cowards of them all. The whites are afraid of each other, and the blacks are afraid of the whites. You can effect nothing among such people.' On assuring him if a council was all that was desired, he would readily obtain it, he replied, 'that is all, but that is a great deal to me. It is men I want, and not money; money can come without being seen but men are afraid of identification with me, though they favor my measures. They are cowards, Sir! Cowards,' he reiterated. He then fully revealed his designs. With these I found no fault, but fully favored and aided in getting up the convention."

It had been Brown's desire above all to attract other important Black leaders, and Loguen, Douglass, and Charles Lenox Remond received invitations. While Loguen and Douglass had assisted in crucial ways setting up the proceedings, both declined to attend, Douglass perhaps reasoning that his presence would arouse suspicions, and however sympathetic he might have been he was less than eager to participate in meetings where Delany was a prominent disputant. Remond, a Garrisonian abolitionist but of independent mind and outspoken, received an invitation signed by both Delany and Brown stipulating that his expenses would be paid—but he declined to respond. Neither did Harriet Tubman attend, nor any other woman, though she is said to have sent at least four fugitive slaves to Chatham for the meetings. Loguen's stance vis-a-vis the convention was perhaps indicated in a letter he sent Brown dated May 6, intimating difficulties, financial and otherwise, that other prospective participants were having. "I was glad to learn you and your brave men got to Chatham," Loguen told Brown. "I have seen our friend Gray and find it as I feared—that he was not ready yet. I do not think he will go to War soon. Others that would go have not the money to get there with, and I have concluded to let them rest for the present. . . . Have you got Isaac Williams with you? Have you got Harriet Tubman? Let me hear from you soon. As I cannot get to Chatham, I should like much to see you and your men before you go to the mountains."[49]

The individuals most instrumental after Delany had also emigrated from the United States. James Madison Bell was from Cincinnati; Osborne Perry Anderson, from West Chester, Pennsylvania. Bell, a twenty-eight-year-old poet, was among the circle around the *Provincial Freeman* and was employed as a plasterer. He first met Brown when Brown returned from Iowa, presenting himself at Bell's door in Chatham with a letter of introduction from William Howard Day. Brown stayed several days as a guest in Bell's home, then moved to the Villa Mansion. Bell was at Brown's side throughout the meetings and received all the "old man's" mail. Osborne Anderson, likewise, was at the *Provincial Freeman*, where he was employed as a printer's devil and general assistant. He had immigrated to Canada with a branch of the Shadd family who purchased two farms near Chatham, which Anderson managed for a time.

The only extended treatments in contemporaneous sources of the convention are contained in Anderson's well-known *A Voice from Harper's Ferry* and a monograph titled "John Brown in Canada," published in *Canadian Magazine* by James Cleland Hamilton in 1894, when only one of the participants in John Brown's Chatham convention was still living. The meetings were also dwelt upon by Delany biographer Frances Rollin Whipper and by Richard Realf in his Congressional testimony in 1860. Preparatory to the convention were a series of private talks during which many points arose and were settled. "During one of the sittings Mr. Jones had the floor, and discussed the chances of the success or failure of the slaves rising to support the plan proposed," Hamilton wrote. "Jones expressed fear that he would be disappointed because the slaves did not know enough to rally to his support. The American slaves . . . were different from those of the West India Island of San Domingo, whose successful uprising is a matter of history, as they had there imbibed some of the impetuous character of their French masters, and were not so overawed by white men. 'Mr. Brown, no doubt thought,' said Mr. Jones, 'that I was making an impression on some of the members, if not on him, for he arose suddenly . . . and having become the object of all attention, said 'Friend Jones, you will please say no more on that side. There will be a plenty to defend that side of the question.'" Whereupon a general laugh took place.[50]

Jones, a gunsmith and engraver, had come to Canada from Raleigh, North Carolina. "Mr. Brown called almost daily at my gun shop, and spoke freely of the great subject that lay uppermost in his mind," Jones said. "He submitted his plans, and only asked for their approval by the Convention." John Cook was also a good deal in the gun shop, repairing the revolvers of the company.

At one of the sittings Brown's constitution was examined and the proposition of the organization as a legal and political entity was considered. The point was raised that since Blacks had no rights, they "could have no right to petition and none to sovereignty." Therefore, it would be "a mockery to set up a claim as a fundamental right."

Delany remarked, "To obviate this, and avoid the charge against them as lawless and unorganized, existing without government, it was proposed that an independent community be established, without the state sovereignty of the compact, similar to the Cherokee Nation of Indians, or the Mormons." To these groups, references were made as parallel cases at the time. Also raised was the question of the most opportune time for an attack, one speaker holding that it would be folly to begin while the United States was at peace with other nations; better, he said, to wait until the country was embroiled in a war with a "first class" foreign adversary. One participant wrote, "Mr. Brown listened to the argument for some time, then slowly arose to his full height, and said: 'I would be the last one to take the advantage of my country in the face of a foreign foe.' He seemed to regard it as a great insult."[51]

Some of those attending the meetings, as Jones did, expressed apprehension that Brown's plan would not succeed in effecting much in the South. Delany in particular seems to have strongly questioned some of Brown's views. According to Realf, "Delany, having objected repeatedly to certain proposed measures, the old captain sprang suddenly to his feet, and exclaimed severely, 'Gentlemen, if Dr. Delany is afraid, don't let him make you all cowards!' Dr. Delany replied immediately to this, courteously, yet decidedly. Said he, 'Captain Brown does not know the man of whom he speaks. There exists no one in whose veins the blood of cowardice courses less freely, and it must not be said, even by John Brown of Osawatomie.' As he concluded, the old man bowed approvingly to him, then arose and made explanations."[52]

Among those joining in the preliminary meetings were Isaac Holden, a surveyor, civil engineer, and native of Louisiana, who with friends had built Chatham's No. 3 Fire-Engine House; Israel D. Shadd, publisher of the *Provincial Freeman*; James M. Jones; James M. Bell; Osborne Anderson; Thomas W. Stringer of Buxton, who helped establish the African Methodist Episcopla Church in Chatham; James W. Peunell, 25, a merchant in Chatham; and Martin Delany—all of whom imparted speeches that "conveyed to John Brown that he might rely upon all the colored people in Canada to assist him." Many attending were fugitive slaves, identities unknown, whose eagerness to meet with John Brown "was a reflection of their feeling that the conventional methods of striking at slavery were simply not working well, the times calling for new approaches."[53] Jones remarked, "In his conversations during his stay here, [Brown] appeared intensely American. He never for a moment thought of fighting the United States, as such, but simply the defenders of slavery in the States. Only the ulcer, slavery, he would cut from the body politic."[54]

In Brown's company were twelve men, all White except Richardson, and they had been joined by an equal number of Canadian refugees in the preparatory meetings, at which Delany, Brown, Bell, Anderson, Kagi, and Realf imparted solid oratory. On May 5 invitations went out to some thirty persons in the United States and Canada who had all been apprised of the proceedings. "My Dear Friend: I have called a quiet convention in this place of true friends of freedom," the simple summons read. "Your attendance is earnestly requested. Your friend, John Brown."

Among those attending were William Lambert, head of the Detroit Vigilance Committee in that city and a well-off tailor originally from Trenton, New Jersey; the Rev. William C. Munroe, who had presided over "emigration conventions" held in Cleveland in 1854 and 1856—he was also from Detroit and would serve as president of John Brown's Chatham convention. The Rev. Thomas Kinnard from Toronto came, as did James H. Harris from Cleveland, and Alfred Whipper, a schoolteacher from Pennsylvania. One of the strongest individuals attending was George J. Reynolds, a coppersmith and Underground Railroad leader from Sandusky, Ohio. Among those attending from Chatham were James Bell, I.D. Shadd, Thomas Stringer, Isaac Holden, Osborne Anderson, and Martin Delany. All assembled, forty-four persons were in attendance; many were fugitive slaves now living in St. Catharines, Ingersoll, Chatham, and Buxton. Ten were Black men from the United States, with thirteen attending from Brown's party, one a fugitive slave from Missouri, the balance being Blacks from Chatham and the interspersing settlements in Ontario, with one attendee from Toronto. For a meeting that is most often given only cursory attention, and ultimately is regarded as having accomplished little to supply recruits for John Brown's Harper's Ferry foray, this gathering was in key respects an impressive, swiftly arriving, assembly noteworthy especially for the breadth of participants' experience in Black life and Underground Railroad work. And although they were not present, the peripheral interest of Douglass, Loguen, and Tubman in convening the meeting is also impressive, attesting as it does to the reputation of John Brown. A glimpse into its details is afforded by the recollections and testimony of Delany, Jones, Gill, Realf, and Anderson, and to the circumstance that the meeting minutes were captured with John Brown in Virginia, scrutinized, and published. This exposure led Osborne Anderson to publish them in his *A Voice from Harper's Ferry* in 1861.

On Saturday, May 8, the convention was called to order by John J. Jackson. Munroe was chosen president, and on the motion of Brown,

Kagi was elected secretary. With a crowd of the curious growing outside, Monroe moved the meeting to another building, explaining that the proceedings were for the purpose of organizing a "Masonic lodge." The assembly walked two blocks to No. 3 Engine House, where the participants would be free from outside scrutiny. Newly situated, Delany called for John Brown.

"Mr. Brown unfolded his plans and purpose," Anderson wrote. "He regarded slavery as a state of perpetual war against the slave, and was fully impressed with the idea that himself and his friends had the right to take liberty, and to use arms in defending the same. Being a devout Bible Christian, he sustained his views and shaped his plans in conformity to the Bible ... [and] freely quoted from the Scripture to sustain his position."

Richard Realf's summation of Brown's speech before the Congressional committee in 1860 reads in part: "He stated that for twenty or thirty years the idea had possessed him like a passion of giving liberty to the slaves; that he made a journey to England, during which he made a tour upon the European continent, inspecting all fortifications, and especially all earthwork forts which he could find, with a view of applying the knowledge thus gained, with modifications and inventions of his own, to a mountain warfare in the United States. He stated that he had read all the books upon insurrectionary warfare, that he could lay his hands on: the Roman warfare, the successful opposition of the Spanish chieftains during the period when Spain was a Roman province,—how, with ten thousand men, divided and subdivided into small companies, acting simultaneously, yet separately, they withstood the whole consolidated power of the Roman Empire through a number of years. In addition to this he had become very familiar with the successful warfare waged by Schamyl, the Circassian chief, against the Russians; he had posted himself in relation to the wars of Toussaint L'Ouverture; he had become thoroughly acquainted with the wars in Hayti and the islands round about."[55]

Brown presented his finished handwritten copy for the organization's charter entitled "Provisional Constitution and Ordinances for the People of the United States," and moved for the reading of the document. Thomas Kinnard objected until an oath of secrecy was taken by each member, whereupon Delany moved that an oath be taken. The motion carried and the president administered a collective oath of obligation.

Many observers have mistakenly maintained that the document drawn up by Brown was intended for the overthrow of the U.S. government, with Brown to be installed as commander-in-chief. To the contrary, Brown's design should be seen as eminently adapted to the political ends he had in view as he sought to ensure that the actions of this "provisional government" and its "provisional army," instituted for the duration of the war, adhered to the republican and constitutional forms of the United States. Following Brown's opening remarks the constitution was brought forward, and after a parole of honor, was read aloud. Modeled on the national government with its branches and offices, these forms were adopted, not as mock-historiographical effects, but as an instrument for the governance of isolated guerrilla bands and of oppressed people fighting for their liberty. After that first hearing the document was read again article by article for consideration. There were forty-eight articles, with only the forty-sixth eliciting debate. That article should be seen as providing "the keynote to John Brown's position," wrote Hinton, which is seldom understood in commentary.[56] That article reads: "The foregoing articles shall not be so as in any way to encourage the overthrow of any state government, or the general government of the United States, and looks to no dissolution of the Union, but simply to amendment and repeal, and our flag shall be the same that our fathers fought for under the Revolution."

Reynolds moved to strike that article. He felt no allegiance, he said, to the nation that had robbed and humiliated the Africans in its midst; they already carried their emblem on their backs, he said. Delany, Brown, Kagi, and others advocated on behalf of the article and it passed. Brown said the flag had represented the patriots in the war of the Revolution and he intended to make it perform the same duty for Black men. He would not give up the "stars and stripes."

The Preamble of the document is a succinct and powerful statement and should be looked at from the vantage of the entire political evolution of the antebellum period and of abolitionism, as of Brown's own evolution against the increasing articulations of "his plan of emancipation." Set against the national founding documents to which it refers, the document merits appraisal, too, for its literary qualities: "Whereas slavery, throughout its entire existence in the United States, is none other than a most barbarous, unprovoked, and unjustifiable war of one portion of its citizens upon another portion—the only conditions of which are perpetual imprisonment and hopeless servitude or absolute extermination—in utter disregard and violation of those eternal and self-evident truths set forth in our Declaration of Independence: Thereof we, citizens of the United States, and the oppressed people who, by a recent decision of the Supreme Court, are declared to have no rights which the White man is bound to respect, together with all other people degraded by the laws thereof, do, for the time being, ordain and establish for ourselves the following Provisional Constitution and Ordinances, the better to protect our persons, property, lives, and liberty, and to govern our actions."

Delany motioned that all supporting the constitution as approved should stand to sign the same. Jones, who had not attended all the sessions, had voiced the notion that Brown would be disappointed in his expectation of a "slave rising."

"Now, friend Jones," Brown said as the paper was presented for signature, "Give us John Hancock bold and strong." After congratulatory remarks by Kinnard and Delany, the convention adjourned at a quarter to four that afternoon until six, on a motion by Stevens.

At six p.m. the convention reassembled for the purpose of electing the officers named in the constitution. A committee consisting of Stevens, Kagi, Bell, Cook, and Monroe was chosen to select candidates for the various offices. On reporting, members asked leave to sit again; the request was refused, and the committee discharged. On the motion of Bell, the convention went into the election of officers. As moved by Stevens, John Brown was nominated for commander-in-chief, seconded by Delany, and elected by acclamation. Realf nominated Kagi for secretary of war, he also was elected by acclamation. The convention adjourned until 9 a.m. Monday, May 10.

That Sunday many of the conventioneers joined in services presided over by the Rev. Monroe at the First Baptist Church in Chatham, no doubt in solemnization of the significance of the moment to which many had turned their thoughts—the deliverance of the slave in the South.

The convention reconvened Monday morning for the further election of officers. Stevens nominated Thomas M. Kinnard for president. In a speech of some length, Kinnard declined. Osborne Anderson then nominated J.W. Loguen, who was not present, he having declared that if elected he would not serve, the nomination was withdrawn. Brown moved to postpone the election of president, which carried. This perhaps could be pointed out as a significant and crucial omission, leaving as it did an important functional and organizational capacity unrealized.

The convention took up the election of members of Congress, electing A.M. Ellsworth and Osborne Anderson, both of Chatham; after which Richard Realf was chosen as secretary of state. Adjourning at 1:45 p.m., the convention immediately reconvened for the balloting for the treasurer and secretary of the treasury, electing Owen Brown to the former office and George Gill to the latter. Brown introduced a resolution appointing a committee to fill all the offices named in the Provisional Constitution left vacant. The convention then adjourned.

At this time, another larger committee was organized; Delany set out its scope in his biography: "This organization was an extensive body, holding the same relation to his [Brown's] movements as a state or national executive committee holds to its party principles, directing their adherence to fundamental principles."[57]

On May 12 John Brown ended a brief letter to "wife and children" by writing, "Had a good Abolition convention here, from different parts, on the 8th and 10th inst. Constitution slightly amended and adopted, and society organized. Great unanimity prevailed."[58] He had obtained all he could have wanted or hoped to achieve. But now he would have to bring together all the elements by assembling men—his own company, those in Canada, and those in the states of New York and Pennsylvania, as well as a formidable cadre along the lake states known for resistance to the Fugitive Slave Law—in proximity to the locale in northern Virginia where operations were to commence. Certainly if this process had begun in 1858 instead of 1859 he would have had more than 19 men to conduct the raid.

But by the close of proceedings, Brown had spent all the cash he had and had debts totaling $300 still to be settled. As he waited in Canada for money to cover his receipts, disclosures regarding Forbes that were more troubling to him were coming to his attention. Since November the previous year Forbes had been in New York City spinning his tale for anyone who would listen. Gaining some sympathy along with some cash, Forbes decided to travel to Washington to solicit Republican leaders; there he began denouncing Brown's Boston supporters, of whom he'd evidently learned while in the confidence of Dr. James McCune Smith, as Douglass had surmised. Smith had come to disparage Brown for reasons likely to do with doubts about his soundness, in which he would be joined by countless others. Approaching Senator Henry Wilson at his desk on the Senate floor, Forbes unburdened himself, referring to well-placed persons in Massachusetts. Then he sought out Senator William Seward at his home; Seward said he "found his story incoherent," concluding that Forbes was "a confused man soliciting charity."[59]

Wilson wrote to Dr. Howe, warning him in confidentiality that any arms in Brown's possession should be withheld from his control, implying that Brown intended the weapons for some action in Missouri. Wilson wrote, "If they should be used for other purposes, as rumor says they may be, it might be of disadvantage to the men who were induced to contribute to that very foolish movement." After consultation with Stearns and others, Howe quickly responded, "Prompt measures have been and will resolutely be followed up to prevent any such monstrous perversion of trust." On May 14, Stearns wrote Brown at Chatham that as chairman of the Kansas State Committee he must warn Brown not to use the arms "for any other purpose and to hold them subject to my order as chairman of said committee."

"None of our friends need have any fears in relation to rash steps being taken by us," Brown replied. "As Knowledge is said to be Power, we propose to become possessed of more knowledge. We have many reasons for begging our eastern friends to keep clear of F. personally unless he throws himself upon them. We have those who are thoroughly posted up to be put on his track and we humbly beg to be allowed to do so."[60]

Brown sent Richard Realf to New York City, instructing him to gain Forbes's confidence, find out what he knew, and secure any documents that may have fallen into his hands. Meanwhile, part of the company—including Stevens, Cook, and Owen Brown—left Canada for Cleveland, taking day jobs in the countryside.

In Boston, Brown's supporters were bedeviled by Forbes's disclosures. Sanborn wrote, "It looks as if the project must, for the present, be deferred, for I find by reading Forbes' epistles to the doctor that he knows (what very few do) that the doctor, Mr. Stearns, and myself are informed of it. How he got this knowledge is a mystery." Only Higginson remained steadfast, writing to Parker, "I regard any postponement as simply abandoning the project; for if we give up now at the command or threat of H.F., it will be the same next year. The only way is to circumvent the man somehow (if he cannot be restrained in his malice). When the thing is well started, who cares what he says?"[61]

George Gill, before going on to Cleveland with the others, decided to visit Reynolds in Sandusky. He left a narrative, included in Hinton's treatment, which relates a matter of historical consequence that until now has been little explored. "My object in wishing to see Mr. Reynolds . . . was in regard to a military organization which, I have understood, was in existence among the colored people," Gill wrote. "He assured me that such was the fact, and that its ramifications extended through most, or nearly all, of the slave states. He himself, I think, had been through many of the slave states visiting and organizing. He referred me to many references in the Southern papers, telling of this and that favorite slave being killed or found dead. These, he asserted must be taken care of, being the most dangerous element they had to contend with. He also asserted that they were only waiting for Brown, or someone else, to make a successful initiative move when their forces would be put in motion. None but colored persons could be admitted to membership, and in part to corroborate his assertions, he took me to the room in which they held their meetings and used as their arsenal. He showed me a fine collection of arms. He gave me this under the pledge of secrecy which we gave to each other at the Chatham Convention."[62]

It will be recalled here that Nat Turner was an important precursor for Brown in his projection of his Harper's Ferry plan, and of Brown's entire thinking on the effectiveness of a servile insurrection on the South. In the inaugural issue of the *Anglo-African Magazine*, December 1859, editor Thomas Hamilton, introducing "The Confessions of Nat Turner" which he was publishing, noted to readers that the slave leader and John Brown bore comparison. To Hamilton these comparisons were personal: Both men were idealists who harbored their purposes for years and followed spiritual impulses, one seeking signs in the air, earth, and heavens, the other believing he was preordained in his actions from eternity. But don't the comparisons go beyond this? The Turner experience in fact was an important reference for Brown, so much so that the slave leader, he held, deserved a place in the American patriotic pantheon. Both Turner and Brown were individuals whose actions have come to be viewed through the distorting lenses of apocalyptic events. The fulcrum of fact turns here on concrete historical conditions and tendencies traversing lives with ideas that can only come to animate individual minds after long years of struggle. When Nat Turner was interrogated about a contemporaneous revolt in North Carolina, he disavowed having knowledge of it. Seeing his interrogator probing his face, hoping to penetrate his thoughts, he replied, "I see sir, you doubt my word; but can you not think the same ideas . . . might prompt others, as well as myself." Rather than accept the assumption that the Turner action demonstrated the futility of slave revolts, Brown held that Nat's rebellion had demonstrated the possibility of their success. The former came at the beginning of the South's great antebellum development; Harper's Ferry, with great calculation, came at that development's end.

The prompter for Brown's overriding was a web of secret operations culminating at Cleveland, Sandusky, and Detroit and fed by extensive and distinct pathways running fugitives through Ohio up from the border of Kentucky, at that time one of the most active of the Underground Railroad networks. From Kentucky, the pathways crept through the heart of the Cumberland Mountains into northern Georgia, east Tennessee, and northern Alabama.[63]

"As one may naturally understand, looking at conditions then existing, there existed something of an organization to assist fugitives and of resistance to their masters," Hinton wrote. "It was found all along the Lake borders from Syracuse, New York, to Detroit, Michigan. As none but colored men were admitted into direct and active membership with this 'League of Freedom,' it is quite difficult to trace its workings or know how far its ramifications extended."

The "literature" on this subject understandably is slight, and still little probed; some of it however is contained in an interesting book published in 1859 by James Redpath. *The Roving Editor* is a compendium based on the author's travels in the South starting in spring 1854, with additional trips that autumn and again in 1858 and dedicated to John Brown. "Many extraordinary stories are told by the Southrons themselves of the facility with which negroes learn of all events that transpire in the surrounding country," Redpath wrote. "In spite of strict surveillance of the plantation, and careful watching abroad, by means of numerous and well mounted patrols, the slaves pass freely over large tracts of country. More especially does this state of things exist among the plantations of the cotton growing states. . . . It seems to me that here lies a power by means of which a formidable insurrection, directed by white men, can safely be formed and consummated. And the slaves know this fact. The Canadian fugitives understand it; and are thoroughly systematizing this Underground Telegraph."[64]

These passageways can be regarded as veritable forces of resistance that have never been fully appraised. The fact that two of Brown's cohorts—Redpath and Hinton, both "John Brownists"—comment on its operations argues that Brown himself was fully cognizant of the phenomena. That, it seems to this author, manifestly was the case. That Brown fully expected after the opening salvo to call upon a broad area of south-central Pennsylvania, and that he was expecting increased activity in the form of slaves fleeing along the entire line of the Kentucky border, thereby calling into play the "League of Freedom" or those erstwhile American Mysteries with which, as is suggested, he expected to form concerted and ongoing arrangements to meet the emergency. That the line of the Ohio offered a second front is indubitable, opening as the river does on the interior of Ohio and extending north to the lake region. James Montgomery would have made an obvious choice for leadership in the Cumberland region, but Brown did not think this at all practicable until he had first made a successful and ongoing demonstration in the Virginia Blue Ridge Mountains.

Gill's return to the others in Cleveland was facilitated by Reynolds, who passed him through the network: first to J.J. Pierce in Milan, who paid Gill's bill at a hotel and gave him money, then to E. Moore in Norwalk, who paid for his lodging and purchased his rail fare through to Cleveland. When Gill reached Cleveland, he found Stevens and Cook in a hotel; they had been joined, on his way east, by Realf. With Cook talking loosely and making rash avowals to strangers, Gill confided to his comrades the details of his visit to Sandusky. Unnerved by Cook's indiscretions and Gill's disclosure of his meetings with Reynolds and others, Realf wrote to an uncle in England about his misgivings, stating that one of their number had "disclosed its objects to the members of a Secret Society calling itself the 'American Mysteries,' or some other confounded humbug. I suppose it is likely that these people are good men enough but to make a sort of wholesale divulgement of matters at hazard is too steep even for me, who are not by any means over-cautious."[65]

After two weeks' delay, Brown received money to settle accounts in Canada and immediately went to Cleveland, leaving Kagi in Hamilton to finish the documents using Day's printing press. Five members of the Boston Kansas committee, absent Higginson, met in Boston's Revere House on May 24 to deliberate the situation in regard to Brown. Decisions requiring that he postpone the attack and place the arms under temporary interdict had already been made; the questions remaining were whether Brown should be obliged to go to Kansas, where there had been a new spasm of violence, and how much money should be raised for him. Unanimously resolving that Brown should go to Kansas immediately, both to reinforce the free-state cause and to discredit and mislead Forbes in his meddling—they suggested that Brown's Virginia campaign could safely be brought off in the next winter or spring; they pledging severally a total of $2,000 to $3,000 toward that prospective. Further, they resolved henceforth not to know nor inquire about Brown's plans.

Soon after the meeting at the Revere House, Brown arrived in Boston. Stating his objections in a conversation with Higginson to the decision reached by the others, he said delay was very discouraging to his men and to those in Canada. The others of the committee were not men of action, he said; they had been intimidated by Wilson's letter and magnified the obstacles. The knowledge Forbes had of his plan was injurious, for he wished his adversaries to underrate him; still, the increase in terror might counterbalance this, and it would not make much difference. If he had the means he would not lose a day; it would cost him no more than $25 apiece to get his men from Ohio. Still, as they held the purse it was essential his backers not think him reckless. Faced with being cut off from his financial resources, Brown finally acknowledged he had little choice but to acquiesce.

With all in agreement, Stearns foreclosed on his title to the Sharps rifles and gave them to Brown as a gift with no conditions attached. Henceforth it was agreed: action would be all.

Chapter Seven

"I CONSIDER IT MY DUTY TO DRAW THE SCENE OF EXCITEMENT TO SOME OTHER PART OF THE COUNTRY"

Using the *nom de guerre* Captain Shubel Morgan, on Friday, June 25, 1858, Brown arrived in Lawrence and took a room at a hotel down by the river. Saturday morning, as he sat in the lobby, he was regarded with curiosity by two younger men—James Redpath and Richard Hinton—who soon penetrated his disguise. Hinton left an interesting account of brief interviews with Brown—that Sunday, and of another more substantial one that September. These interviews were published in 1860 in Redpath's *The Public Life of Captain John Brown* and later became part of Hinton's own *John Brown and His Men*, with only slight changes, appearing in 1894.

When he and the journalists met, Brown was principally interested in learning the particulars of "various public men in the Territory, and the condition of political affairs," especially of those with an anti-slavery reputation; he was also keenly interested to hear about James Montgomery. During the conversation, Hinton vented his detestation for slavery and its underlings, while tetchily wishing for some way of injuring it.

"Young men must learn to wait," Brown counseled. "Patience is the hardest lesson to learn. I have waited for twenty years to accomplish my purpose." He reminded Hinton of a message the latter had sent to him in the fall of 1857, saying his heart was with Brown and he would join him, but must decline at that time because of his newspaper commitments.

"I hope you meant what you said, for I shall ask the fulfillment of that promise, and that perhaps very soon," Brown now said. "I caution you against rash promises. Young men are too apt to make them, and should be very careful. The promise given was of great importance, and you must be prepared to stand by it or disavow it now."[1]

By July 1 Brown, accompanied by ten of his men who had come back to Kansas, was on the scene where the murders of May 19, called the Marais des Cygnes Massacre, had occurred. Eleven free-state men had been seized and driven from their fields to be lined up and summarily shot. Five were killed, five were severely wounded and thought to be dead, and one lay under the corpses unhurt but feigning death. The killers, led by the handsome son of a wealthy Georgia planter, Charles A. Hambelton, pillaged their victims' pockets and to cover their tracks rode back into Missouri in multiple directions.

It was during these weeks that Brown gained a valuable ally in James Montgomery. From Ohio's Western Reserve, Montgomery migrated to Kentucky where he took an illiterate but brave woman for a wife; in 1852 they moved to Missouri. Settling in Kansas in 1856, Montgomery, like Brown, was of a religious nature; meeting him in 1860, Sanborn was surprised to find that Montgomery "had an air of elegance and distinction which I hardly expected. He was a slender, courteous person with a gentle cultivated voice and manner of a French chevalier."[2]

By 1858, with northeastern Kansas thoroughly under the standard of Free-Soil, southeast Kansas, with its center of power in an abandoned army outpost, was under the grip of the pro-slavery party. The majority of settlers in Bourbon and Linn Counties were from Missouri, having been driven off claims in the northern counties. As pro-slavery Democrats awaited the vote of Congress on the Lecompton Constitution, ex-Indian agent Clarke and an ex-chief justice of the Iowa Supreme Court, "Fiddling" Williams, administered "justice" at Fort Scott. Living among them was a diminutive man with a refined manner—the black-haired, black-bearded Campbellite preacher James Montgomery. He, along with his followers, had decided to ignore Judge Williams's decisions in land disputes favoring pro-slavery claimants. When the federal marshal was ordered to break up Montgomery's so-called "Self-Protection Company," men from Lawrence came to his assistance, and the new governor ordered U.S. Army dragoons to disperse them, along with Clarke's regulators.

Pursued in April by dragoons, Montgomery posted his men in good position, killing one soldier and wounding half a dozen, leaving a number of dead horses on the field. This impressed Brown. "When he learned the particulars of this engagement," Hinton wrote, "he said the like had not happened before in the Territory, and that the skill with which he conducted the engagement, stamped him as one of the first commanders of the age."[3] Soon after coming on the scene Brown arranged to buy land near Trading Post, the site of the May massacre, and with his company and some of Montgomery's men began to build a fortification that afforded a commanding view across the border into Missouri and of the surrounding country. Undoubtedly, Brown thought it would be efficacious to occupy a strong position, but more likely he had in mind a practical demonstration of building a type of defensive work which, before this, he had largely theorized. Said to be of a design that twenty men would be able to construct in a day without using implements or draft animals, the structure, of hewn logs twelve or fourteen feet in length, had two levels, with loopholes interspaced on each level for firing. Earth and stone were mounded all around the perimeter to a height of four feet, making the bastion a thorny problem to assault and impervious to artillery. Upon its completion Brown wrote his eldest son on August 9, "In Missouri . . . the idea of having such a neighbor improving a Claim (as was the case) right on a conspicuous space and in full view for miles around in Missouri produced a ferment that you can better imagine than I can describe. Which of the passions most predominated, fear or rage, I do not pretend to say."[4]

On August 2, Kansasans went to the polls to vote on the Lecompton Constitution, with Buchanan offering a backhanded inducement of a block of public lands for new settlement to be made available after the Senate had approved the constitution. All but 2,000 of 13,000 votes were cast against the document. "The election of the 2nd Inst. passed off quietly on this part of the line," remarked Brown in a letter to John Jr. Meeting Robinson in Lawrence after the vote,

Brown said, "You have succeeded in what you undertook. You aimed to make Kansas a free state and your plans were skillfully laid for that purpose. But I had another object in view, I meant to strike a blow at slavery."[5]

Brown was ill off and on much of that summer, and in the last weeks of August and early September was convalescing at the cabin of the Adairs near Osawatomie. He was thinking in these weeks of writing a biography and history of the Browns, to be published serially with Augustus Wattles acting as agent. The proposed title was "A Brief History of John Brown; otherwise (Old B) and his family; as connected with Kansas; By one who knows." But illness and other preoccupations precluded his beginning the project. During this time Brown and Kagi met with Richard Hinton for a second interview. Arriving at 10 a.m. one September day, they remained in discussion until three that afternoon. As they began, speaking of his treatment at the hands of "ambitious men" among free-state leaders, Brown said, "They acted up to their instincts. As politicians, they thought every man wanted to lead, and therefore supposed I might be in the way of their schemes. While they had this feeling, of course they opposed me. Many men did not like the manner in which I conducted warfare, and they too opposed me. Committees and councils could not control my movements, therefore they did not like me. But politicians and leaders soon found that I had different purposes, and forgot their jealousy. They have all been kind to me since."[6]

Robinson's actions, Brown said, were those of a "weather-cock character." Of Lane, alluding to his June 1858 slaying of Gainius Jenkins in a claim dispute, Brown said, "I Would not say one word against Lane in his misfortunes. I told General Lane myself he was his own worst enemy." Of Montgomery, Brown said, "[He] is the only soldier I have met among the prominent Kansas men. He understands my system of warfare exactly. He is a natural chieftain, and knows how to lead." Brown said he found Montgomery "kind and gentlemanly . . . and what was infinitely more a lover of Freedom." Hinton criticized the Free State struggle from an antislavery point of view, pronouncing it "An Abortion." He wrote, "Captain Brown, looked at me with a peculiar expression in the eyes, as if struck by the word, and in a musing manner remarked, 'Abortion!—yes, that's the word.'" Bringing up Hinton's intention of embarking on a newspaper enterprise, Brown reminded the younger man of his promise, advising that he not enter into any "entangling engagements." "I think," Brown said, "all engagements should be considered sacred, and would like you to adhere to the one you were committed to. That is why I have not sent for you; but now I hope you will keep yourself free."

All through the conversation, Hinton wrote, he had the feeling that Brown's "blue eyes, mild yet inflexible, and beaming with the steady light of a holy purpose," were probing his inmost thoughts and that he was completely transparent to the older man. "I shall never forget the look," he wrote, "with which he said: 'Young men should have a purpose in life, and adhere to it through all trials. They would be sure to succeed if their purpose is such as to deserve the blessing of God.'"[7]

After dinner Brown and his lieutenant had a conversation apart; then, saying he wanted to do some fishing, Kagi asked Hinton to accompany him to the river. Stopping halfway, the two sat on a fence rail as the conversation turned to Brown's nearer object. Hinton was now given a full account of the meetings in Chatham, as well as of the organization effected there. "The true locale of their operations were to be in the mountains of Virginia," said Kagi; and he went on to describe their mode of operation, sketching a theory of how the campaign would develop and be received in the North and in the South. "Given a country admirably adaptable to guerilla warfare, the freed slaves were to be armed and organized into companies, headed by the men Brown had selected and the Canadian recruits that would be sent down," Hinton wrote. "The southern oligarchy," Kagi continued, "would become alarmed by the discipline maintained and by the show of organization. At no point was the South more vulnerable, he emphasized, "than in its fear of servile insurrection; they would imagine that the whole North was down upon them, as well as their slaves."

"Kagi and Brown had marked out on a series of maps a chain of counties," Hinton related, "extending continuously through South Carolina, Georgia, Alabama, and Mississippi." These counties contained a predominance of Black over White, "and with the assistance of Canadian negroes who had escaped from those States, they had arranged a general plan of attack."

The plan was to make a fight in the Virginia mountains and to hold the egress into the free states as long as possible, in order to retreat north if that became advisable, but their intent was to move southward, toward regions with a predominance of slaves, "extending the fight into North Carolina, Tennessee, and also to the swamps of

South Carolina, if possible."[8] One of the reasons that induced Kagi to go into the enterprise, Hinton wrote, "was a full conviction that at no very distant day forcible efforts for freedom would break out among the slaves, and that slavery might be more speedily abolished by such efforts than by any other means. He knew by observation in the South, that in no point was the system so vulnerable as in its fear of a slave-rising. Believing that such a blow would soon be struck, he wanted to organize it so as to make it more effectual, and also, by directing and controlling the negroes, to prevent some of the atrocities that would necessarily arise from the sudden upheaval of such a mass as the Southern slaves."

Returning to the house the men resumed their conversation, Hinton wrote, centering "mostly upon Brown's movements and the use of arms." Brown expressed his idea of forcible emancipation tersely: "Give a slave a pike and you make him a man. Deprive him of the means of resistance, and you keep him down. . . . The land belongs to the bondman. He has enriched it, and been robbed of its fruits. . . . Any resistance, however bloody, is better than the system which makes every seventh woman a concubine. . . . I would not give Sharpe's rifles to more than ten men in a hundred, and then only when they have learned to use them. It is not every man who knows how to use a rifle. I had one man in my company who was the bravest man and worst marksman I ever knew. . . . A ravine is better than a plain. Woods and mountain sides can be held by resolute men against ten times their force. . . . A few men in the right, and knowing they are, can overturn a king. Twenty men in the Alleghenies could break Slavery to pieces in two years. . . . When the bondmen stand like men, the nation will respect them. It is necessary to teach them this."

Brown ended with an invocation of the storied leader of the 1831 Southampton slave revolt. "Nat Turner, with fifty men, held Virginia five weeks," he said. "The same number, well organized and armed, can shake the system out of the state."[9]

In October Kagi notified *Tribune* readers, "Captain Brown will now, if necessary, take the field in aid of Captain Montgomery." The signal that an offensive had begun came in mid-October when Montgomery and Brown led a force to Fort Scott, seizing and ransacking "Fiddling" Williams's courthouse. As payback, a volley was fired into Montgomery's cabin, but he, his wife, and his children escaped unharmed. Brown proposed that the cabin of Montgomery's mother-in-law be fortified; and he, Stevens, Kagi, and Tidd occupied themselves with this undertaking for much of November. On November 13, after Montgomery was indicted for destroying ballot boxes stuffed with "bogus ballots" in the previous January's election, again Brown and Montgomery led their companies to the town of Paris, overturning it looking for indictments and arrest warrants. Warrants were issued for both leaders, with rewards offered for securing their persons at Fort Scott. To "break up their organization and drive them from the Territory," the sheriff of Linn County and his posse visited "Montgomery's Fort" on November 30, hoping to apprehend Brown. As he was in Osawatomie, and they did not wish to quarrel with Stevens, who was brandishing a shotgun at the door, they left. The next day the sheriff himself was cornered alone, relieved of his arms, and sent home. After this Brown worked out a "peace agreement" between Montgomery and his opponents; the warring factions met at Sugar Mound. In the accord all prisoners held by either side were to be released and all criminal prosecutions against free-state men were to cease; each party was to discontinue acts of "theft or violence against the other on account of their political differences," and all pro-slavery men who had been forcibly expelled from Kansas were to stay out.

No sooner had the agreement been completed than Williams, on trumped-up charges, ordered the jailing of two free-state men at Fort Scott. A force larger than any yet seen, seventy-five men, was raised to set them free. That night in council Brown asked for undivided command, promising the assembly he would lay Fort Scott in ashes. When Montgomery rose to oppose this, saying that the only purpose should be to free the prisoners, Brown stalked out, leaving Kagi and Stevens to participate. In a skirmish the next day Fort Scott was captured and the prisoners held on the third floor of the Fort Scott Hotel freed. A store owner, who was also a deputy marshal, discharged a shotgun into Kagi's breast, but heavy outer clothing saved him from serious injury. His assailant was shot and killed, and his store emptied of merchandise valued at $7,000.

During the autumn, Brown's nearly constant companion was George Gill. More than thirty years after the death of his chief, in a letter dated July 7, 1893, Gill confided his private thoughts to Richard Hinton regarding the elder man's intolerance of the wishes of others and of his "individuality." Gill wrote, "All great men have their foibles or what we in our difference from them call their weakness." Intimate acquaintance had demonstrated to Gill that John Brown was very human, with a love of command and adventure, together with firmness and combativeness sometimes given vent in vindictiveness. Brown's immense egotism, coupled with love of approbation and his God idea, "begot in him a feeling that he was the Moses that was to lead the Exodus of the colored people from their southern taskmasters," Gill told Hinton. "Brooding on this, in time he believed that he was God's chosen instrument, and the only one, and that whatever methods he used, God would be his guard and shield."

"Believing this," Gill wrote, "he could brook no rival, and while at first he was very fond of Montgomery, he loved him no more when he found he had thoughts of his own and could not be dictated to." The day after the Fort Scott expedition Brown and Montgomery were to rendezvous when Brown severely upbraided the commander in front of Gill for carrying along a prisoner. "Montgomery gave him a trial and he was released by general consent as not meriting punishment," Gill wrote. "When we returned Brown was furious because the man was not shot. His Calvinism and general organism would have treated Servetus as Calvin did.... And yet this very concentration on self commanded the grand advance on American slavery."

Of John Brown's personal influence, Richard Realf remarked, "He possessed that strange power which enables one man to impress many with his views, and he so psychologized his associates, that, seeing only through his medium of vision, they consequently were unable to controvert his theories; therefore the movement went blindly on. For myself, too, it is certain that had I not been to New York, where, out of reach of his great mesmeric power, I could in some sort master the questions involved, I should have been with the enterprise to the bitter end. I should, indeed, have had no other choice. Had John Brown sent a man on an errand to Hades he must have started hither, for Brown was one of God's own commanders."[10] And yet both these men, so justly critical in later years of their commander, really believed in the overthrow of slavery by the nucleus of men John Brown brought with him to Harper's Ferry, and Gill was even on the road there as that event transpired.

Realf remained in England until early in 1860, delivering a few lectures on American events. Upon learning of the events at Harper's Ferry, Realf took a cotton ship to New Orleans, arriving in Tyler, Texas. His association with Brown came to the attention of the Congressional committee empaneled to investigate the affair, and in exchange for his testimony his expenses and mileage were paid through to Washington. That testimony brought no recriminations against any individual, and its only relevance was to the historical record. Gill got a striking illustration of the extraordinary union of messianic belief and abhorrence of slavery in his chief late that fall, when Gill came across a Black man ostensibly engaged in the earthly business of selling brooms. After each resolved the propriety of making the other his confidant, Gill learned the man's name was Jim Daniels, and that he had come across from Missouri looking for help. He, his wife, and their children belonged to an estate that was to be sold at an administrator's sale, and Daniels wished to avoid the certain prospect of seeing his family broken up and sold into the Deep South. They immediately hunted up Brown, who devised a plan to bring the needed assistance. Gill wrote in Hinton's *John Brown and His Men*, "I am sure that Brown, in his mind, was just waiting for something to turn up; or, in his way of thinking, was expecting or hoping that God would provide him a basis of action. When this came, he hailed it as heaven sent."[11] The next night seventeen heavily armed horsemen crossed into Missouri. Dividing into columns, Brown with his party, guided by Daniels, rode to the farm where Daniels and his family belonged, while Stevens with his party rode toward neighboring farms. The Brown party approached and surrounded the house of Daniels's proprietor; several men entered with drawn revolvers, while others rounded up animals in corrals and barns. Less than a mile away Stevens did likewise. "We have come after your Negroes and their property," he told the startled slave owner at gunpoint. "Will you surrender or fight?"

In all, Brown's party freed ten slaves and seized horses, oxen, clothing, boots, bedding, and a wagon loaded with bacon, flour, and meal. Stevens freed but one slave after killing her owner, who had resisted, and also seized property that included horses, mules, oxen, and a wagon with provisions. At an early hour the two parties joined, taking three White men as hostages, and hastened back into Kansas. In Brown's view the goods and animals seized belonged by right to the slaves, procured as they had been through unrequited labor; property was taken too, to defray the costs of carrying the Blacks to freedom. As peradventure an act of war, it was meant, too, to weaken the economic basis of slavery.

Once across the border the hostages were released with an admonition that they could follow if they wished. Sheltering in a ravine from the wind and cold, the animals, the armed men, and the newly freed people hunkered throughout the daylight hours. George Gill wrote, referring to the Blacks, "To our contrabands, the conditions produced a genial warmth not endorsed by the thermometer." When night came the entourage resumed its trek, reaching the farm of Augustus Wattles at midnight a day later. Bunked in the loft there with a few of his men, and awakened by the commotion, was James Montgomery, who peered down as Brown was ushering the fugitives into the parlor.

"How is this Captain Brown?" Montgomery exclaimed. "Whom have you here?"

"Allow me to introduce to you a part of my family," Brown replied, gesturing broadly with his straw hat. "Observe, I have carried the war into Africa."

Three of the persons presented were men, five were women—one of them, the wife of Jim Daniels, was pregnant—and three were children, two boys and a girl.

As morning came a covered wagon was drawn up into which the fugitives were secreted; the wagon was packed with provisions and tethered to oxen, with Brown and Gill occupying the driver's seat. On Christmas Eve they reached the Adair home near Osawatomie, where they remained through Christmas Day in the warmth of the kitchen. In the early hours of the following morning all moved into a roughly hewn cabin abandoned on Pottawatomie Creek. As improvements were hastily made to the dwelling, in this setting was born the first of the John Brown namesakes, John Brown Daniels, attended by a physician of the neighborhood, Dr. J. G. Blunt, who was sympathetic to Brown.

As news of the incursion spread, the Missouri press howled, demanding retribution for "Old Brown's" infamy, while the state's governor, amidst denunciations of robbery and assassination, offered $3,000 for his capture, to which President Buchanan personally added $250 and the Kansas territorial governor an equal amount. With calls for the arrest of both Brown and Montgomery, a five-hundred-man posse assembled to ride up from West Point, as Brown notified his ally they should be in readiness to fight. Brown's forcible expropriation of slaveholder property also met with severe condemnation in Kansas. One criticism was that Brown intended to leave the territory, meaning that a retaliatory attack would fall upon other heads than his; another was that the Buchanan administration would now only redouble its effort to impose a pro-slavery constitution on Kansas. To this censure, Brown retorted, "It is no pleasure to me, an old man, to be living in the saddle, away from home and family, exposing my life, and if the Free State men of Kansas feel that they no longer need me, I will be glad to go." To one of his staunchest friends, Augustus Wattles, Brown said, "I have been at your abolition meetings. Your schemes are perfectly futile. You will not release five slaves in a century. Peaceful emancipation is impossible. The thing has gone beyond that point."[12]

As Montgomery, Brown, and Kagi sat debating the situation at Wattles's home in the early weeks of the new year, Brown wrote his famous "Old Brown's Parallels," published on January 22, 1859, in the New York *Tribune*. Contrasting the reaction of the administration and the law enforcement agencies to the May murders, about which nothing had been done, and his own recent exploit, Brown's observations and the keen interest the *Tribune* took in Kansas affairs assured that his foray would be well known in the East. "Old Brown Invades Missouri" had been the caption of a lead story on January 6, while Horace Greeley editorialized, "Captain Brown, who had cooperated with Montgomery and whose property had been destroyed and his son murdered in the former wars, did not wait for invasion. He led a party into Bates County, who retorted on the slaveholders of the vicinity the same system of plunder which the Free state people of Kansas have suffered during the recent invasion." On January 10 Gerrit Smith noted in a letter to his wife, "Do you hear the news from Kansas? Our dear John Brown is invading Missouri and pursuing the policy which he intended to pursue elsewhere."[13] Would that the spur of the Alleghenies extended into Kansas, Smith lamented in a missive on January 22 containing $25 forwarded to Brown.

But Brown's prescription may have been too strong even for Montgomery. With his support waning among men who had sustained him in the past, Montgomery felt a need to distance himself from Brown, and walked into the territorial court in Lawrence on January 18 and turned himself in. Freed on $4,000 bail, Montgomery made an appearance at the territorial legislature then in session at Lecompton. The *New York Times* correspondent described the occasion: "Scores were pressing to grasp him by the hand while he 'looked down' upon the heads of those who but a few days before were branding him as the arch-robber. Firm, fearless, erect, he now stood in the same hall where his name had been traduced and vilified. This must have been to him one of the strange vicissitudes of human life."[14] In this charged atmosphere, with Gill and eleven "contrabands" plus one newborn, on January 20 Brown's ox-drawn wagon lumbered inconspicuously northward toward Lawrence, crisscrossing labyrinthine roads and fields of dried corn stalks and dead sunflowers. Everywhere spies were on the lookout, as armed posses scoured in every direction. In parting Brown gave this assessment to Augustus Wattles: "I considered the matter well. You will probably have no more attacks from Missouri. I shall leave Kansas and probably you will never see me again. I consider it my duty to draw the scene of the excitement to some other part of the country."[15]

Arriving in Lawrence, Brown took a room in the Whitney Hotel and sent Kagi to summon William A. Phillips for a private interview. Phillips was one of a select group of men active among Kansas freestate political circles whom Brown had sought as allies, and he now wished to draw his engagement toward his broader object—the struggle between slavery and freedom that was harrying the nation toward the precipice of war. Showing reticence to engage with Brown, Phillips at first sent back that he would not come, as Brown never took his advice and he saw no reason to offer any now. On being summoned again, Phillips relented, agreeing to an interview in the hotel room where Brown was staying. Ushering Phillips into the room, Kagi posted himself outside to ensure their conversation would not be overheard. This interview, the last of three Phillips conducted with Brown in Kansas, was reported, along with the others, in the *Atlantic Monthly* of December 1879.[16]

Phillips's ambivalence had perhaps been overcome by journalistic curiosity; there was a fascination about the "old man" which he had clearly recognized. Although he was not in agreement with some of Brown's most strongly held convictions, Phillips was not of the view that would come to prevail in later decades—that Brown was "fanatical," or a "monomaniac," to cite two terms often circulating in American scholarship about him. In fact, when they met the previous year, Phillips had tried to placate Brown by recommending that he and his adherents stay in Kansas and take claims, suggesting Salina, one hundred and fifty miles from the border; they could keep their arms for self-defense, but otherwise would assure the territory entered upon statehood as a prosperous and free country. Brown of course would not consider this, but Luke Parsons did—thus Brown lost another highly esteemed recruit for Harper's Ferry.

"He had changed a little," Phillips wrote. "There was in the expression of his face something even more dignified than usual; his eye brighter, and the absorbing and consuming thoughts that were within him seemed to be growing out all over him." Brown began by citing the long career of slavery in the United States. "He recalled many circumstances that I had forgotten, or had never heard of," Phillips wrote. When the republic had been founded, Brown said, the expectation had been that slavery would be shaken off, and this view prevailed for the first twenty-five years of the nation's existence. This was evident in that, even before the Constitutional Convention, the founders had enacted the Ordinance of 1787 under the Articles of Confederation. Known as the Northwest Ordinance, this ordinance excluded the importation of slaves into the Northwest Territory from which the future states of Ohio, Indiana, Michigan, Illinois, and Wisconsin were formed. Meanwhile, in the 1st Congress slavery had been recognized in those territories that became the states of Alabama (1819) and Mississippi (1817), but only after Congress prohibited the continuance of the Atlantic Slave Trade after January 1, 1808. Then, as part of the Missouri Compromise of 1820 prohibiting slavery's expansion north of that state's border, Congress had barred slavery in the remaining Louisiana Territory. These compromises with slavery had been allowed because the new nation could not have come into nor remained in existence otherwise. But the founders had taken care not to use the word "slavery" in the Constitution, believing the very term incompatible with republican governance and the principles of human equality and liberty.

Slavery was thus thought to be on the road to extinction. Only gradually had it become more profitable and been able to extend and to increase itself. This was due first to the invention of the cotton gin in 1794, which brought with it an exponential rise in the demand for slaves. And second, it was due to the abundance of cheap fertile land west of the original Atlantic southern states on which to cultivate cotton, acquired in 1804 with the Louisiana Purchase during the presidency of Thomas Jefferson, a transaction negotiated for sale as the Napoleonic empire was losing its crucial hold on the island of St. Domingo with the revolution there.

When harnessed to a horse, a gin yielded fifty times more cleaned bolls than the older machines then in use. Soon the invention had spread throughout the cotton planting districts of the South and would be applied whenever new cotton planting lands were acquired. The yield of cotton thus was doubled in each decade soon after 1800, as the use of spinning and weaving machines, along with the application of steam, also saw an exponential rise. By 1850 the American South would be growing three-quarters of the world's cotton supply; and as demand for the white fiber increased, demand for land on which to work the enslaved African-derived labor proliferated. By 1860 the states of the South where the system was in use had increased from six states at the founding of the republic to fifteen states. By the end of this period, cotton planting had spread into the Southwest, as slaves were being worked on ever larger plantations, and in increasingly regimented and relentless toil. By the census of 1860 one person in every three counted would be an enslaved person in the South.

Of necessity these developments brought with them, said Brown, an even more despotic system, with rights once accorded slaves taken away. The breeding of Blacks for sale had likewise become profitable. Thereafter, little by little the pecuniary interests that rested on slavery had enabled pro-slavery interests to seize power in the government. Opinion opposed to slavery in the South was placed under ban, and an attempt was made to apply that to the northern states. At length, the politicians of the South had become mere propagandists for slavery, and the northern politicians supporting the system were labeled "trimmers" for changing their opinions and actions to suit the political winds or as interests dictated. When Northerners tried to check slavery's alarming growth, the South threatened secession. Now, said Brown, began an era of compromise—"where for peace, men were willing to sacrifice everything for which the republic was founded."[17] Now the point had been reached with the collision in Kansas where nothing but war could settle the question. The South had just missed the opportunity of permanently getting the upper hand; but its aggressions had only temporarily been checked.

Phillips still recalled despite the years passed much of what Brown had said verbatim: "It has taken them half a century to get the machinery of government into their hands and they know its significance too well to give it up. They will never peacefully relinquish it. If the Republican party elects its president next year there will be war. The moment they are unable to control they will go out, and as a rival nation alongside they will get the countenance and aid of the European nations, until American republicanism and freedom are overthrown."

As astonished by the thrust of Brown's reasoning as by his exposition, Phillips suggested that surely the old man was mistaken. The collision in Kansas would soon die down, and it was in the northern interest to let it do so, he said.

"No, no, the war is not over," Brown said. "It is a treacherous lull before the storm. We are on the eve of one of the greatest wars in history, and I fear slavery will triumph and there will be an end of all aspirations for human freedom. For my part, I drew my sword in Kansas when they attacked us, and I will never sheathe it until this war is over. Our best people do not understand the danger. They are besotted. They have compromised so long that they think principles of right and wrong have no more any power on this earth."

Phillips: "Let us suppose all you say is true. If we keep companies on the one side, they will keep them on the other. Trouble will multiply; there will be collision, which will produce the very state of affairs you depreciate. That would lead to war, and to some extent we should be responsible for it. Better trust events. If there is virtue enough in this people to deserve a free government, they will maintain it."

Brown: "You forget the fearful wrongs that are carried on in the name of government and law."

Phillips: "I do not forget them—I regret them."

Brown: "I regret and will remedy them with all the power that God has given me."

Brown offered the example of the slave revolt leader Spartacus, who had opposed Rome.

Phillips pointed out that Roman slaves were a warlike people, trained in arms and in warfare; American slaves were far more domestic and "in all their sufferings they seem to be incapable of resentment or reprisal."

Brown: "You have not studied them right; and you have not studied them long enough. Human nature is the same everywhere."

Continuing to point out the mistakes of that ancient insurrection, showing he had given it his best study, Brown said, "Instead of wasting his time in Italy, the leader should have struck at Rome, or if not strong enough for that, escape to the northern provinces to build an army. But Rome's armies were able to swoop down on them to destroy them."

Hearing nothing but more talk of war, Phillips finally bridled, predicting Brown would end by bringing himself and his men into a desperate enterprise, where they would be imprisoned and disgraced.

Brown: "Well, I thought I could get you to understand this, I do not wonder at it. The world is very pleasant to you; but when your household gods are broken, as mine have been, you will see all this more clearly."

As Phillips rose to leave, he said, "Captain, if you thought this, why did you send for me?"

Reaching the door, he felt Brown's hand touch his shoulder. As Phillips turned, the old man took Phillips's hands in his, tears showing on his hard, bronzed cheeks.

"No, we must not part thus," Brown told Phillips. "I wanted to see you and tell you how it appeared to me. With the help of God, I will do what I believe to be best."

Holding Phillips's hands firmly in his own, Brown leaned forward and kissed him on the cheek.

"And," Phillips wrote, "I never saw him again."

Leaving George Gill in Lawrence recuperating from frostbite and exhaustion, Brown left for Topeka on January 25, with Stevens sharing the driver's seat. Reaching the edge of town, they stayed for a few days in the Sheridan family cabin, where new shoes were donated for the Blacks and food and money obtained. Three days later the party was some fifteen miles north of Topeka, in Holton. The next day, six miles farther on, they sought refuge after a snowstorm at the cabin of Abram Fuller. By then it was well known that John Brown was passing through the vicinity and an eighty-man posse led by a U.S. marshal rode to apprehend him and his companions, even as the territorial governor wired President Buchanan premature confirmation of that posse's success. As three of the marshal's advance scouts were approaching Fuller's cabin, Stevens stepped out to greet them.

"Gentlemen," he said, "you look as if you were looking for somebody or something?"

"Yes," one scout replied, "We think you have some slaves up in that house."

"Is that so? Well, come on with me and see."

As the scout reached the door, Stevens opened it just enough to grab a shotgun resting inside.

"You want to see slaves, do you?" he asked, pointing the weapon at the men. "Well, just look up those barrels and see if you can find them."

All three ran, but as one had a bead drawn on him, he was captured. Brown had sent word back to Topeka that he needed help, and soon Kagi arrived with twenty well-armed men, leaving the odds still four to one against them. With the marshal and his posse waiting in a strong position of ambush at Fuller's Ford and Governor Medary telegraphing President Buchanan of Brown's imminent capture, one of the men who had come up with Kagi asked what he was going to do.

"Cross the creek and move north."

"But Captain, the water is high and I doubt if we can get through," the man objected. "There is a much better ford five miles up the creek."

"I intend to travel it straight through and there is no use of talk of turning aside," Brown replied. "Those who are afraid may go back. The Lord has marked out a path for me and I intend to follow it. We are ready to move."

George Gill, who had come with the men from Topeka to rejoin the company, wrote, "The scene was ridiculous beyond description." Placing a double row of mounted men before the wagon, giving the outriders room to maneuver, Brown gave the order to charge straight at the enemy. The would-be ambushers found they were under attack. Seeing horsemen bearing down on them, the entire posse along with the marshal sprang for their horses and fled in disarray. One of the freed slaves, Samuel Harper, later said, "Captain Brown and Kagi and some others chased them, and captured five prisoners. There was a doctor and a lawyer amongst them. They all had nice horses. The captain made them get down, then he told five of us slaves to mount the beasts and we rode them while the white men had to walk. . . . The mud on the roads was away over their ankles. I just tell you it was mighty tough walking, and you can believe those fellows had enough of slave-hunting. The next day the captain let them all go."[18]

On February 1 the party was approaching the Nebraska border. With the Memaha River only partially frozen and running too high to cross, they waited through a bitterly cold night. By morning the ice was solid enough to bear the weight of a man, but not that of the team and wagon. Disassembling the wagon, they pushed it across in pieces, and laid a makeshift bridge of lumber, poles, and brush for the horses. Three days later, after eluding another posse, Brown and his party crossed the Missouri River into Iowa.

Reaching Tabor on February 4 they found the news of their exploit had preceded them. The fugitives sheltered in the schoolhouse of a local church and were fed by member families during the week that followed, but there was controversy. At Sunday service a clergyman refused to entertain Brown's petition to the pulpit asking for "public thanksgiving to Almighty God in behalf of himself, & company; and of their rescued captivates," because they had killed a man and taken horses and other property. The following evening, as Brown was giving a recital at a public meeting, he interrupted his remarks when a slaveholder from St. Joseph, Missouri, entered. Brown requested the man withdraw, but the sense of the meeting was to the contrary. As Brown walked out, he remarked to Charles Plummer Tidd, a recruit to the company originally from Maine said to be the only member of the troop who resembled a mechanic in appearance, "There are some there who would give us a halter for our pains. We had best look to our arms and horses." The meeting debated and passed a resolution of support for the fugitives, but stipulated, "We have no sympathy with those who go to slave states to entice away slaves and take property or life when necessary to attain that end."[19] The caravan left Tabor on February 11. Traveling twenty-five miles a day, on February 18 they were in Des Moines, where Kagi paid a visit to the office of the *Register*, giving its editor an account of Brown's Missouri exploit that Brown followed up with in a letter. Two days later they reached the town of Grinnell, where Brown knocked at the door of Josiah Bushnell Grinnell, an abolitionist and the founder of the town and college bearing his name. "This cannot be a social visit," Brown told Grinnell. "I am that terrible Brown of whom you have heard." As he was explaining that he needed a place to stay for himself and his companions, Grinnell threw open the door to his parlor, henceforth called the Liberty Room. "This room is at your service and you can occupy the stables at the barn which are not taken," Grinnell said. "Our hotel will be as safe as any place for part of your company."[20]

The contrast between the reception in Tabor and that in Grinnell was striking, and Brown exulted. On successive nights at full-house meetings Brown and Kagi spoke, and "were loudly cheered; & fully indorsed," Brown wrote. Contributions in clothing, food, and cash were raised for the fugitives, and J.B. Grinnell, now called "John Brown" Grinnell, arranged for rail conveyance to Chicago for them from the railhead at West Liberty, Iowa.

By February 25 the party had moved on to Springdale, where Brown's Quaker friends extended their hospitality. Gill stayed there with his family to recover from an inflammation in his joints; he never saw his companions again. As they were enjoying their reunion with friends and supporters from the previous year, word reached Springdale that a posse was being raised in a nearby town to apprehend the fugitives. Brown and his entourage quickly traveled the seven miles to West Liberty and on March 9 boarded an unbilled boxcar for Chicago. The following morning, as the train reached Chicago, the crew halted a half-mile from the depot, where the car with the fugitives was detached and pushed to a side track where its occupants were released. Brown was soon in touch with Allen Pinkerton, the famed detective, who showed no hesitation whatever in escorting the fugitives to a mill owned by Henry O. Wagner, who put out a sign reading "Closed for Repairs," while Brown went to the home of his friend, John Jones. That afternoon Pinkerton solicited $400 from C.G. Hammond, superintendent of the Michigan Central Railroad, to hire a freshly provisioned boxcar to Detroit.

Brown had boarded an earlier train after telegraphing Frederick Douglass, whose whereabouts he had learned from Jones, requesting that they meet in Detroit. On the afternoon of March 12 in a blizzard the fugitives arrived at the wharf in Detroit to await embarkation for Windsor, Canada. Shortly before they were to board the ferry, John Brown arrived to see them off. "Lord, permit Thy servant to die in peace; for mine eyes have seen Thy salvation!" Brown said. "I could not brook the thought that any ill should befall you—least of all, that you should be taken back to slavery. The Arm of Jehovah protected us."[21]

The trek, beginning to end, had taken eighty-one days. No doubt it had been one full of perils both for Brown and his company, and for the fugitives; but so far as is known, they felt themselves in the hands of benefactors, and none were cognizant of the dangers.

During the winter of 1858-59, Douglass, with John Jones and H. Ford Douglass, had been making an intensive lecturing circuit through Illinois, Wisconsin, and Michigan. Meeting with a generally positive, even enthusiastic reception, Douglass wrote of "Our recent Western Tour" in his April *Monthly*, ". . . a Negro Lecturer [is] an excellent thermometer of the state of public opinion on the subject of slavery." He was much better than a White anti-slavery lecturer, because "a hated opinion is not always in sight—a hated color is. . . . The Negro is the test of American civilization." At the conclusion of the tour Douglass gave special notice in his paper to his co-lecturer, writing, "He has that quality without which all speech is vain—earnestness. He throws his whole soul into what he says, and all he says. His person is fine, his voice musical, and his gestures natural and graceful." This acknowledgment was offered, however, "not as incense offered to vanity," but that he might better serve the cause. "We call upon H. Ford Douglass to put himself unreservedly into the lecturing field, not upon the platform of an African Civilization Society."

Frederick Douglass rejected the necessity of seeking, as others were, a "nationality" far from the shores where the principal struggle had to take place. "We have an African nation on our bodies," he said. "We are contending not for the rights of color, but for the rights of men." Douglass called upon H. Ford Douglass to "stand upon the platform of Radical Abolitionism and go to the people of the country with a tangible issue." What better issue could be made, he advised, than to return to the state of Illinois and agitate for the repeal of its Black laws. "The immediate repeal of these cruel enactments, (which the white [Stephen A.] Douglas is endeavoring to sustain,) should be the demand of the black Douglass of Chicago," Douglass said.

While completing his tour of Michigan—he visited Battle Creek, Marshall, Albion, Jackson, and Ann Arbor—Douglass had received the telegram from John Brown, then with John Jones in Chicago, summoning him to a meeting in Detroit. For this reason an appearance at Detroit's City Hall was added to Douglass's schedule, and he arrived in the city on March 12. The Detroit *Free Press* marveled as to why Frederick Douglass should have come to such an inhospitable region. The reason, to which the editors were not privy, was a closed-door meeting of select persons at the home of William Webb, whose guests included William Lambert, William C. Munroe, George DeBaptista, and at least three other Black Detroiters, and John Brown. Webb, an escapee from slavery in Mississippi, would publish in 1873 *The History of William Webb, Composed by Himself*. He had been part of that interstate transit of information amongst slaves referred to as the "Underground Telegraph." John Brown and John C. Frémont were his heroes, he wrote in his narrative.

While few details of the get-together are available, one can surmise it had an earnest, if congratulatory air. Among other things, Brown's recent exploit was discussed, its implications and incidents narrated. As for Brown's projected campaign, the fact that several of the participants had also been at the Chatham Convention the previous year indicates it too was discussed. Beyond this it is known that DeBaptista, who had taken over leadership of the Detroit Vigilance Committee from Lambert, questioned the efficacy of Brown's plan. In its stead, he is said to have suggested a campaign of bombings across the South to throw the slave oligarchy off-balance and raise a national outcry. Whatever the resolution on the issue, surely Brown demurred from being connected with it on humanitarian grounds. There was indication, too, that disparaging words passed between Brown and Douglass, some supposing that Brown challenged Douglass's courage when he opposed certain measures. But the two were seen working together in the coming months, and any friction had more to do with Brown's aversion to merely "talking" abolitionism. Shortly after the meeting in Detroit, in the columns of his April *Monthly*, Douglass avowed his confidence in Brown. The basis for Brown's idea, Douglass wrote, was that "the enslavement of the humblest human being is an act of injustice and wrong, for which Almighty God will hold all mankind responsible; that a case of the kind is one in which every human being is solemnly bound to interfere; and that he who has the power to do so, and fails to improve it, is involved in the guilt of the original crime. He takes this to be sound morality, and sound Christianity, and we think him not far from the right."

Uppermost on Brown's mind—and another subject likely broached in the discussion at William Webb's house—was not only the gathering of Black recruits for the Virginia campaign, but above all the need to enlist a Black leader of recognized accomplishment who would not shrink from the dangers the action entailed. The setback with the Canadian refugees had to be addressed, a task for which Brown must have expected to rely on Harriet Tubman and Martin Delany. But there had been no contact with either, and Delany—who had corresponded with Kagi in Kansas, assuring him, in a letter dated August 16, 1858, of his and other Chathamites continued support—had other priorities just then. He was preparing to embark to Africa on his Niger Valley expedition, commissioned by the 1854 emigration convention in Cleveland. Others who had been at the Chatham convention, and to whom Brown could have looked, had also turned their attentions elsewhere. Isaac Holden and James Munroe Jones were traveling to the Canadian and U.S. Pacific coast, William Howard Day was sailing for Dublin, Ireland, and Reverend Munroe was to sail for Africa on the same ship with Delany that May, going under church auspices to Liberia.

Others to whom Brown may have looked were Gloucester in Brooklyn, Loguen in Syracuse, and Garnet in New York City. But Garnet had founded his African Civilization Society in 1858 and was thoroughly engaged in controversy. Garnet and Gloucester, moreover, had been skeptical, counseling that they did not think the time was ripe, that slaves were not sufficiently aware of their rights to respond in the way Brown predicted, nor were northern Blacks sufficiently prepared—as they had been shut out in consequence of the discrimination against them "from both the means and the intelligence necessary," as John S. Rock phrased it.[22]

As a result, the office of president under Brown's provisional constitution had been left vacant. That office called for an individual with organizational abilities and extensive contacts who would be able to promote and inspire cooperation between the various societies, associations, and individuals that could be looked to for support. And then too, perhaps none of these, excepting Delany and Tubman—whose commitment remained unshaken—had the military grounding for the enterprise.

Brown next arrived in Cleveland, where the Oberlin-Wellington fugitive slave trial was under way. The case originated in Wellington, Ohio, on September 13, 1858, when a Kentucky slaveholder, searching for a fugitive in nearby Oberlin, recognized a man who had been a slave of his neighbor in Mason County, Kentucky. The visiting Kentuckian obtained the power of attorney to act on the owner's behalf, and a complaint was taken to a commissioner who issued a warrant; a U.S. marshal was sent to Oberlin.

As it would be difficult to affect the man's capture there, a plan was devised whereby he would be captured in Wellington on a subterfuge. Offered a job digging potatoes for a prominent Democrat farmer, the alleged fugitive, John Price, was seized by four men on his way to perform the work and confined in a local tavern to await a train to Columbus. Word that Price had been seized spread "like a flash of lightning," and people were soon converging by every available means upon the building where he was being held. After two hours of wrangling with his captors, the secretary of the Ohio Anti-Slavery Society and an active Underground Railroad operative, Charles H. Langston—the younger brother of the abolitionist John Mercer Langston—led a charge from the growing crowd that freed the fugitive. Spirited away in a wagon driven by Simeon Bushnell to Cleveland to await a ferry to Canada, Price was accompanied on his journey to freedom by a pistol-bearing young man named John Copeland. An outraged Buchanan administration decided to make a signal example of this "villainy," and thirty-seven warrants were issued against residents of Oberlin and Wellington, including professors, clergy, students, free Blacks, and fugitive slaves. Twenty-three of those charged refused bail and were confined *en masse* in Cleveland to await trial. As delegations began arriving from all over the state to show support, the defendants became the object of growing attention and sympathy.

As the trial was set to begin, 12,000 persons rallied to be addressed by Governor Salmon P. Chase and Congressman Joshua Giddings. Demonstrators marched in ranks around the block where the jail stood, carrying banners, as those inside made speeches from cell windows. When Brown arrived on March 20, he took a room at a hotel four blocks from the U.S marshal's office, making no effort to conceal his identity, even as posters were being displayed calling for his arrest. Several days later, broadcasting his defiance, Brown stood before an auction to raise money by the sale of two horses and a mule, despite their "questionable title"; they brought "good prices," he reported. A short time after this a public meeting was called where Brown and Kagi spoke, drawing an audience of fifty at a 25-cent admission charge. The city editor of the *Plain Dealer*, Charles Farrar Browne, an up-and-coming humorist writing under the pseudonym Artemus Ward, wrote for his paper that Brown was, "a medium-sized, compactly built and wiry man, and as quick as a cat in his movements. His hair is of salt and pepper hue and as stiff as bristles. He has a long, waving, milk-white goatee, which gives him a somewhat patriarchal appearance. His eyes are gray and sharp. A man of pluck is Brown. You may bet on that. He shows it in his walk, talk and actions. He must be raising sixty and yet we believed he could lick a yard full of wild cats before breakfast and without taking off his coat."[23]

In his remarks that night, a reporter for the *Cleveland Leader* noted, Brown called attention to the fact that he was "an outlaw," the governor of Missouri having offered a reward of $3000, and James Buchanan $250 for him. The article reported that "John Brown" remarked parenthetically he would give two dollars and fifty cents for the safe delivery of the body of James Buchanan in any jail of the free states. He would never submit to an arrest, he said, as he had nothing to gain from submission; but should settle all questions on the spot if any attempt was made to take him.

The story Brown related of his Missouri incursion in his talk was "refreshingly cool," remarked Ward in his column. Brown "would make his jolly fortune by letting himself out as an Ice Cream Freezer," he suggested.

In the audience that evening was a man from Oberlin named Lewis Sheriand Leary, the uncle of John Copeland, who was being held in the jail awaiting the beginning of the trials with the other rescuers. Like Copeland, who had come to Oberlin to enter its university preparatory school, Leary, a saddle and harness maker, was originally from North Carolina. This uncle and nephew by relation were first among a community where Blacks bore an attitude toward Whites, a contemporary remarked, that said "touch me if you dare," and both quickly developed a keen interest in John Brown.

The first defendant to be tried in the Oberlin-Wellington trials was Simeon Bushnell. He was adjudged guilty and sentenced to sixty days in the county jail, fined $600, and ordered to pay the cost of his prosecution. Charles Langston was the next up. His speech to the court—"Should Colored Men Be Subjected to the Penalties of the Fugitive Slave Law?"—had a powerful effect, both in the court and in wider circulation. Printed in its entirety in the *Cleveland Leader* and the *Columbus State Journal*, it was again published by the *Anglo-African*, where it appeared together with his brother's account of the episode, then circulated as a pamphlet. Langston was also adjudged guilty, but on the strength of his statement the judge meted out a less stringent sentence—twenty days in the county jail and a fine of $100 plus the cost of prosecution.

As Tidd and Kagi, with others from Cleveland and Oberlin, were planning a rescue of those being held for trial, the state of Ohio relieved them of this necessity by arresting the four Kentucky men who had seized John Price, as they appeared to testify. Both sets of prisoners were freed in June as a settlement of the case, with only Bushnell and Langston tried and convicted—recognition that the Fugitive Slave Law had been broken in the Western Reserve. Brown was in Cleveland for only ten days and certainly did not meet with Charles Langston but was surely familiar with his eloquent appeal for justice to the court. Kagi and others of his party did become Langston's intimate, Kagi reporting on the trials as a correspondent to the New York *Tribune* and the *Cleveland Leander*. While in Cleveland, Brown received an invitation from Joshua Giddings to speak at the Congregational Church in Jefferson where Giddings was a member. Receiving donations from the congregation afterward, including money from Giddings, and an invitation to his home for dinner, Brown undoubtedly considered fortuitous this contact with the leader of antislavery opinion in the House of Representatives, which with the addition of Leary, Copeland, and Langston as adherents augured well for his coming campaign.

Leaving Ohio, Brown stopped for a conference with John Jr., in West Andover. His cache of arms, shipped from Springdale, Iowa, in February 1858, had first been stored in a furniture warehouse in nearby Cherry Valley, then after the Chatham convention moved at Brown's urging by his son to where none "but the Keeper & you will know where to find them." Some had been concealed inside a haymow in Wayne, and the remainder in another farm building. They had been cleaned and oiled and were ready for shipment.

Chapter Eight

"HARPER'S FERRY IS THE BEST NEWS THAT AMERICA HAS EVER HEARD"

Toward the second week of April 1859 Horace McGuire, employed by Frederick Douglass in his Rochester printing office, took note of a visitor to that establishment. Douglass was elsewhere but soon to return. The visitor waited. Much later McGuire recalled "a tall, white man, with shaggy whiskers, rather unkempt, a keen piercing eye, and a restlessness of manner" had come asking for his employer. The man gave the appearance of one whose "interview was by appointment," and when Douglass returned, McGuire observed, "the greeting between the white man and the former slave was very cordial" and they "talked freely" and with great "earnestness."[1] It was at this time that Douglass arranged for Brown's appearance at Rochester's City Hall, giving notice of the event in his *Monthly* published April 15 under the heading "Old Brown in Rochester." Upbraiding the self-professed "Republicans" of Rochester for staying away, Douglass wrote, "Even our newly appointed Republican janitor ran off with the key to the bell of the City Hall, and refused to ring it on the occasion! Shame upon his little soul, and upon the little souls who sustained his conduct." During this visit, it would seem, Douglass introduced Brown, as his contribution to recruiting for the Virginia campaign, to an individual who was then a boarder in the Douglass home. A fugitive slave from Charleston, South Carolina, he had arrived in Rochester having escaped aboard a sailing vessel in 1856 after the death of his wife, leaving a son in slavery. He went on to live for several years in St. Catharines, Ontario, working as a house servant and waiter. Returning to Rochester in 1858, he proposed to establish himself in business as a clothes cleaner, having a card printed stating his work would be done "in a manner to suit the most fastidious and on cheaper terms than anyone else." His name had been Esau Brown, which he soon exchanged for another—Shields Green. A full-blooded African, he was twenty-four years old, of slight stature but well built, possessing a self-confident bearing and styling himself in dress and action a "Zouave." Reputedly having the lineage of an African prince, he referred to himself as "Emperor." One of his contemporaries, Lucy Coleman, wrote that the "overseer's lash had cut deeply into his soul." His host described him as "a man of few words," with speech that was singularly broken, "but his courage and self-respect made him quite a dignified character." The convergence between the elderly White and the young Black could not have been greater, Douglass concluded. "John Brown saw at once what 'stuff' Green was made of, and confided to him his plans and purposes. Green easily believed in Brown, and promised to go with him whenever he should be ready to move."[2]

Still, it could be asked just how far Douglass himself was willing to go to sustain John Brown. For two decades he had participated in any number of venues for anti-slavery action; he had been ever ready to publish, to speak, and to combine or to conspire with any individual, society, or party standing against the "desolating tide of slavery." But it was a sad fact, Douglass wrote later that summer, "that in the hands of all these societies and committees, nearly all our anti-slavery instrumentalities have disappeared. . . . The Radical Abolition Society . . . was built on a faultless plan, but where is that Society to-day? Where is its committee? Where is its paper, its lecturers and patrons? All gone!" He was therefore opting, he wrote, to work for the present on the plan of individualism, "uttering our word for freedom and justice, wherever we may find ears to hear, and writing our thoughts for whoever will read them." It is on this ground that one must look for concurrence between Brown and Douglass, noting that the latter supplied the former with a recruit, convened meetings and collected money for him, and also facilitated his contact with Harriet Tubman—all in the service of an attack upon slavery "with the weapons precisely adapted to bring it to the death."[3]

Three days later Brown and Jeremiah Anderson, acting as Brown's adjunct, were in Peterboro at the estate of Gerrit Smith, where Anderson wrote his brother on June 17, announcing unequivocally, "Douglass is to be one of us." This was the assessment in which others in the Brown family later concurred, with Anne Brown remarking, as Hinton quoted her, "Douglass is to be one of us, even unto death." At Smith's that evening Brown addressed a small gathering including Smith and his wife, Edwin Morton, and Harriet Tubman, who often traveled across New York from her parents' home in Auburn to St. Catharines. Tubman assuredly had received word from Douglass that Brown would be at Smith's. After Brown spoke, with an eloquence that moved both Smith and his wife to tears, the philanthropist rose to hail Brown as "the man in all the world I think most truly Christian" whereupon he wrote a pledge for a $400 contribution. Morton later wrote to Franklin Sanborn that Brown had been "tremendous," and that he no longer had any doubts as to the soundness of his course. "I suppose you know where this matter is to be adjudicated," Morton wrote. "Harriet Tubman suggested the 4th of July as a good time to 'raise the mill.'"[4]

From April 9 to May 5 Brown was with his wife and younger daughters in North Elba, mostly convalescing from illness. May 7 to June 2 found him once again in Boston, where Harriet Tubman had also gone. Before arriving in Boston, Brown visited Sanborn in Concord, where he delivered an address. A. Bronson Alcott wrote in his diary, "Our best people listen to his words—Emerson, Thoreau, Judge Hoar, my wife; and some of them contribute something in aid of his plans without asking particulars.... I have a few words with him after his speech, and find him superior to legal traditions, and a disciple of the right in ideality and the affairs of the state. He is Sanborn's guest, and stays a day only. A young man named Anderson accompanies him. They go armed, I am told, and will defend themselves, if necessary."[5] In this speech, while not revealing his plans, Brown did not conceal from listeners "his readiness to strike a blow for freedom at the proper moment." Many could infer his intention when he asserted that it was right to repeat such incursions as his Missouri raid when the opportunity arose, and that in the process it was right to take property and even life. Sanborn noted that those in the audience winced at these remarks, but when Brown concluded his presentation availed him good applause and contributions that he might continue his activities. While in Concord Brown suggested to Sanborn that he undertake a journey to Canada for him, the scholar demurring owing to previous obligations. In a letter to Thomas Wentworth Higginson, Sanborn wrote that Brown was "desirous of getting someone to go to Canada and collect recruits, with H. Tubman, or alone as the case may be & urged me to go. . . . Last year he engaged some persons and heard of others, but he does not want to lose time by going himself now. I suggested you to him. Now is the time to help the movement, if ever, for within the next two months the experiment will be made."[6]

Sanborn already had notified Higginson that Brown informed Smith he would be coming east with new men "to set his mill in operation." Sanborn suggested, "As a reward for what he has done, perhaps money might be raised for him." But Higginson's ardor of the preceding year had cooled; he recalled in his *Cheerful Yesterdays*, "It all began to seem rather chimerical." In his reply to Sanborn at the time, apparently referring to Brown's raid in Missouri, he wrote, "It is hard for me to solicit money for another retreat."[7]

Beginning his visit to Boston the next day, Brown again called on Amos Lawrence, who had also turned decidedly cool to him. "He has been stealing Negroes and running them off from Missouri," Lawrence wrote in his diary. "He has a monomania on that subject, I think, and would be hanged if he were taken in a slave state. . . . He and his companion both have the fever and ague, somewhat, probably, a righteous visitation for their fanaticism."

Samuel Gridley Howe and George Stearns conveyed Brown to dinner at the Bird Club where he met Senator Henry Wilson. When Brown remarked that he understood the senator did not approve of his course, Wilson offered that he did not, saying that if Brown had gone into Missouri two years before there would have been a retaliatory invasion with great resultant bloodshed. With a scathing look Brown replied that he thought he had acted rightly and that the incursion into Missouri had exercised a salutary influence. Howe also introduced Brown to John Murray Forbes, a wealthy clipper trader and railroad financier. Invited to visit Forbes's home in Milton, Brown kept the businessman and a few of his friends up past midnight "with his glittering eye" and talk of the coming war between North and South. Forbes contributed $100 for Brown's "past extravagances, and none for his future."

At another meeting, John A. Andrew, soon to be elected governor of Massachusetts, contributed $25 for Brown and noted, "The old gentleman in conversation scarcely regarded other people, was entirely self-possessed and appeared to have no emotion of any sort but was entirely absorbed in an idea which preoccupied him and put him in a position transcending ordinary thought and ordinary reason."[8]

Spring 1859 found Harriet Tubman in Boston, primarily to arrange for the security of her parents so that she could do "practical work" with John Brown. It was at this time that the woman whose strenuous anti-slavery activity, as Douglass wrote, had been witnessed only "by the midnight sky and the silent stars," began to appear onstage, leaving deep impressions in abolitionist circles and forming lasting friendships with many persons. Sanborn wrote, "Pains were taken to secure her the attention of which her great services to humanity entitled her, and she left New England with a handsome sum of money towards payment of her debt to Mr. Seward."[9]

Wendell Phillips wrote of being called upon by two distinguished visitors: "The last time I ever saw John Brown was under my own roof, as he brought Harriet Tubman to me, saying 'Mr. Phillips, I bring you one of the best persons on this continent—General Tubman as we call her.'" Brown went on to recount her labors and sacrifices on behalf of her people, asserting, "she was a better officer than most whom he had seen, and could command an army as successfully as she had led her small parties of fugitives." After her visit Higginson wrote his mother, "We have had the greatest heroine of the age here, who has been back eight times secretly and brought out in all sixty slaves with her, including all her own family, besides aiding many more in other ways to escape. Her tales of adventure are extraordinary. I have known her for some time and mentioned her in speeches once or twice—the slaves call her Moses. She has had a reward of twelve thousand dollars offered for her in Maryland and will probably be burned alive whenever she is caught, which she probably will be, first or last, as she is going again. She is jet black and cannot read or write, only talk besides acting."[10]

Since February Brown had been preparing his financial backers, or the "secret six" as they were to be called, to begin collecting the money promised after the Chatham convention; he wrote Kagi back in Ohio that the fund-raising "was a delicate and very difficult matter," further complicated by the departure of Theodore Parker. Ill with consumption and no longer able to take New England's winters, Parker had gone to Cuba in December 1858 accompanied by Dr. Howe. After two months he sailed for Rome, dying two years later at age fifty in Florence. Parker's interest in Brown's crusade continued; he wrote Sanborn from Rome, "Tell me how our little speculation in wool goes on, and what dividend accrues there from."[11] But he had to drop all active participation and could contribute nothing financially. Howe, for his part, began to take a more nuanced stance regarding slavery after stopping on his way home from Cuba at Wade Hampton's plantation in South Carolina. His interest in Brown's sanguinary outlook diminished once the doctor had experienced his host's gracious hospitality; Howe felt he had to relinquish his stake in the enterprise after envisioning its consequences for Hampton and his family and others of their ilk.

The amount finally raised for Brown came to something over $2,000; Stearns came in with $1,200, with $750 from Smith; Higginson handed in a mere $20, with similar amounts coming from others. All in all, Brown probably marked his visit to Boston a success. Sauntering down Court Street oblivious to the glances of passersby, Brown nonchalantly peeled an apple with his jackknife and talked with his companion, "Jerry" Anderson. The young man conveyed his excitement at hearing the noted anti-slavery orator Phillips, whom he thought had rendered a particularly apt phrase. Constitutionally under-impressed by abolitionist eloquence as he was, the older man replied, "I supposed I ought to say as the boys say—O shit!"[12]

Leaving his supporters in Boston "much in the dark concerning his destination and designs for the coming months," Brown next appeared at six in the evening on June 3 at the metal-working shop of Charles Blair in Collinsville, Connecticut. Reminding the blacksmith who he was, Brown said he had come to fulfill the contract they had made in the previous year for blades and handles to be used to fashion pikes.

"Mr. Brown, the contract I considered forfeited, and I have business of a different kind now," Blair said. "I do not see how I can do it."

"Well, I want to make you perfectly good in the matter," Brown declared. "I don't want you to lose a cent."

"Why not take the steel and handles just as they are?" asked Blair.

"No, they are not good for anything as they are."

"What good can they be when they are finished? Kansas matters are all settled."

"They might be of some use if they are finished up. I might be able to dispose of them."

Blair agreed, and, when paid the remaining $450, said he would "find a man in the vicinity to do the work."[13] The next day Brown came again, handing Blair $50 and a $100 check; he mailed the balance in a check on June 7 from Troy, New York.

On June 9 Brown was in North Elba for a week for a reunion with his wife and young daughters. Traveling across New York, he arrived on June 18 in West Andover, Ohio, for a consultation with John Jr. As the senior Brown went about setting up his "southern headquarters," his eldest son became his indispensable liaison, shipping arms, collecting money, maintaining contacts with supporters, and gathering and forwarding recruits. Setting out from Akron with sons Owen and Oliver and Jeremiah Anderson, Brown notified Kagi that he was on his way to the Ohio River.

The "old man" and his companions would have traveled by rail through Pittsburgh to Harrisburg, continuing to Chambersburg, Pennsylvania, lodging for the night on East King Street as "Isaac Smith & Sons" at the inn of Mrs. Mary Ritner, who appeared very compatible with her boarders, and at whose establishment members of the company would continue to room until the last days before the Harper's Ferry "raid." The next day they reached Hagerstown, Maryland, where they again took lodgings. At 8 a.m. July 3 the quartet arrived at Harper's Ferry. Surveying the town and taking in the imposing view of the surrounding country, Brown and party would have passed over the Potomac Bridge to Maryland to begin inquiring about land for sale or rent. Before they had gone far, they encountered a man who owned a farm in Maryland, and as they fell into conversation the man suggested that "Mr. Smith" see about renting a farm owned by the heirs of a Dr. Kennedy; that parcel lay three miles to the north of Harper's Ferry and a mile or two east of the Potomac River on the Boonsboro Pike. Three hundred yards from the road, they would see a farmhouse, the fellow said, and on the other side a cabin. Within a day or two of learning of the place Brown rented the buildings and land for $35, an agreement running until March 1, 1860, nine months away.

In 1859 Harper's Ferry was a bustling center of commerce and industry with a population of 3,000. Two rail lines ran through the town: the Baltimore and Ohio, connecting Baltimore and Washington to Ohio west of the mountain ranges, and the Winchester and Harper's Ferry, running some thirty miles into Virginia's Shenandoah Valley. The railroads converged in a Y-junction near the confluence of the rivers, crossing the Potomac to Maryland on a single-truss iron suspension bridge. This bridge was covered and served other traffic, while a second covered bridge, the Shenandoah Bridge, crossed the river a quarter of a mile upstream carrying wagon traffic. The town occupies a narrow spit of land at the convergence of the rivers, the Potomac flowing out of the west and the Shenandoah flowing south to north out of the valley named for it. Harper's Ferry rises beyond the point of this juncture on a great hill known as Bolivar Heights, as another commanding ridge called Loudoun Heights occupies the south bank of the Potomac on the Virginia side, encompassing and sheltering the town as within a deep well.

The United States Congress, at the urging of President George Washington, had established at Harper's Ferry a national arms manufactory and arsenal, which by the 1850s was a substantial works. Lining both sides of a single street lateral to the Potomac and named for that river, two orderly rows of multi-storied buildings ran for 2,000 feet, with stocking and machine shops, smith and forging shops, warehouses for annealing, and storehouses. Fronting these government works was an open area called the Ferry Lot, across from which on the point stood the commercial establishments, the train depot, and a hotel called the Wager House. Along the Shenandoah River on Shenandoah Street was the enclosure of Arsenal Square, site of the superintendent's office and large and small arsenal buildings. These structures housed at any given time as many as 200,000 arms; behind them was the depot of the Winchester and Harper's Ferry Railroad. The stately ridge rising over the Shenandoah on the Virginia side afforded a commanding view of the entirety of Harper's Ferry, and beyond the ridge was the road to the slave-filled interior, or "Africa."

Once preparatory work was done, Oliver was sent to North Elba to bring back his sister Anne and his wife Martha, who was pregnant with their child. The young women would serve as a screen of normality to curious eyes, while also providing sustenance and comforts for the men. Notified of these developments, John Jr. received $100 from his father to cover traveling expenses, along with instructions to "hold back Whipple & Co" until the quarters were ready. John Brown's agent was also told to "be in readiness to make the journey through the country northward," meaning to New York and Canada. Meanwhile Kagi, using the name "John Henri," had arrived in Chambersburg, fifty miles north of Harper's Ferry, with instructions to take lodgings with Mrs. Mary Ritner. He was also to make the acquaintance of Mr. Henry Watson "and his reliable friends," the Underground Railroad operatives in that Pennsylvania town, but was told in no way to appear "fast" with them.

The Kennedy farm was an excellent location in every respect. Kagi received and dispatched "freight" and men as they arrived. Oliver and Owen Brown received anything and anyone sent down, while to maintain communications, John Brown often traveled between the two locations, seeing "that matters might be arranged in due season." September 1, 1859, had originally been designated as the date to begin operations, but the time-consuming and cumbersome arrangements, the slowness with which some of the men were being mustered, and the crucial work that remained to be done in Canada soon led to the realization that more time would be required. On July 27 Brown sent notice to North Elba that his son Watson and one of the Thompson boys, Dauphin, could delay their departure "to allow more time for haying."[14]

As these arrangements were being completed, Brown could at last turn his attention to the formidable tasks still at hand. Of necessity his primary focus had been on the funds that had been promised, without which he could not do anything. The men from his Kansas company and those recruited along the way could now be contacted, and if they needed assistance, money could be forwarded. But Brown had been out of touch with the crucial Canadian sector; moreover, some principals in Chatham who had attended the convention the previous year were no longer on the scene. John Jr. was poised to begin an important journey to renew and vitalize these contacts and would look to the assistance of Harriet Tubman and others. On July 22 Brown reported to his wife that "Oliver, Martha & Anne all got in safe;" now the men could begin moving into the Kennedy farm.[15] John Jr. shipped fifteen crates containing arms to Chambersburg from Ohio via Pittsburgh and Harrisburg. Kagi sent orders from Chambersburg to various quarters for the men to report for duty.

By early August occupancy at the Kennedy farm had grown considerably. Besides the leader and the two teenage girls, there were Brown's sons Owen, Watson, and Oliver; William Thompson, another son-in-law; and two Quaker brothers from Springdale, Edwin and Barclay Coppoc, in addition to Jeremiah Anderson and Charles Plummer Tidd, soon to be joined by Albert Hazlett, William Leeman, and Steward Taylor. Aaron Stevens had taken up station in Hagerstown to assist in the forwarding of men and maintaining communications between Chambersburg and "headquarters." With matters progressing, Brown was distressed by the reluctance of some of the men to come forward. George Gill was one of these, prompting Brown to write Kagi, "I hope George G. will so far redeem himself as to try; & do his duty after all. I shall rejoice over 'one that repenteth.'"[16]

In his diary Brown recorded eight trips he made between the Kennedy farm and Chambersburg by mule or wagon, sometimes involving overnight lodging at the Union Hotel in Greencastle. These trips were accomplished mostly at night, and while in the Pennsylvania town he would stay for several days. In early August during one of these journeys Brown revealed to his son Owen, who was with him on the wagon, what only Stevens and Kagi knew—that the initial objective of the company would be the seizure of the government works at Harper's Ferry. Having frequented the town, Owen, easily apprehending the dangers, recoiled; he later recalled telling his father, "You are walking straight into the arms of the enemies as Napoleon did when he entered Moscow." When they returned to the farm and a meeting was held to acquaint the rest of the company with the new plan, there was immediate dissension. The younger Browns, Oliver and Watson, and Charles Plummer Tidd, in particular, opposed the action; bluntly put, it appeared to them that they would be committing suicide. Brown answered that even in the event of their deaths it would be a great gain: "We have only one life to live and once to die, and if we lose our lives, it will perhaps do more for the cause than any other way." This appeal was perhaps a startling one for young men to hear, but it was one in which the "old man" was in earnest. The quarrel was said to be so intense that it threatened to break up the camp. To calm dissension, Brown finally relented, saying if that was the way they felt he would resign as commander and follow another proposal if they had one. Tidd was so upset he went to stay for a few days with Cook at Harper's Ferry where Cook had been living since the Chatham Convention. Since they were an oath-bound company, all finally agreed to follow the elder man's leadership on the stipulation that both bridges in Harper's Ferry be fired. Owen drafted a note acknowledging their consent: "Dear Sir—We all agree to sustain your decisions until you have proved incompetent, and many of us will adhere to your decisions so long as you will."[17]

Toward the end of June Harriet Tubman again was in Boston, and on July 4 was introduced to a gathering in Framingham, Massachusetts, west of Boston, of the Massachusetts Anti-Slavery Society by its just-elected president, Thomas Wentworth Higginson. He presented "to the audience a conductor on the Underground Railroad, who having first transformed herself from a chattel into a human being, had since transformed sixty other chattels into other human beings, by her own personal efforts." Speaking briefly "in a style of quaint simplicity," Tubman aroused such interest in her hearers that in his *Cheerful Yesterdays*, Higginson wrote, "On the anti-slavery platform where I was reared, I cannot remember one real poor speaker; as Emerson said, 'eloquence was dog-cheap there'. . . . I know that my own teachers were the slave women who came shyly before the audience. . . . We learned to speak because their presence made silence impossible."

A meeting of the New England Colored Citizens convened on August 1, addressed by the Rev. J.W. Loguen and, according to the *Liberator*, by one "Harriet Garrison." The temporary bequeathal of the surname of its editor, no doubt, signaled acceptance into the anti-slavery family, but was also a precaution, insofar as Tubman was described as "one of the most successful conductors on the Underground Railroad." She made a brief speech denouncing the colonization movement by telling the story of a man who sowed onions and garlic on his land, hoping to increase dairy production. When he found his butter too strong and unable to bring a price, he concluded, she said, to sow clover instead. But the wind had blown the onions and garlic all over the field. "Just so," she stated, "the white people had got the Negroes here to do their drudgery, and now they were trying to root them out and ship them to Africa. But they can't do it, we're rooted here, and they can't pull us up." She was much applauded.

Shortly after this Tubman dropped out of sight and her whereabouts were unknown for many weeks. Given to bouts of illness brought on by years of exposure and frequent spells of unconsciousness from being hit in the head as a girl with a heavy object by an overseer, she had gone to convalesce at the home of a friend in New Bedford. Although few have looked beyond the simple assertion that there was a profound bond between Brown and Tubman, there has never been any doubt among those who have understood that bond about her determination to join his campaign in the Virginia mountains.

In Ohio, after arranging for the arms shipments to "headquarters," John Jr. awaited the order, contingent upon the state of readiness at the Kennedy farm, to begin his "Northern tour." The key to the full development of his Virginia campaign now lay, in Brown's estimation, with the Canadian recruits, and with Douglass and Tubman. Accordingly, knowing the details of the important work undertaken by his son, in its scope and bearing on that plan, and in its sequel, are indispensable to an understanding of that action and its outcome.

Shortly after the first week of August John Jr. arrived in Rochester. Finding Douglass away in Niagara Falls, John awaited his return. The next day Douglass arrived, and John Jr. informed Kagi in a letter dated August 11, "I spent remainder of day and evening with him and Mr. E. Morton, with whom friend Isaac is acquainted." Morton was then on an extended visit with Douglass and was undoubtedly engaged in more than social obligations. "He was much pleased to hear from you," the letter continued, "was anxious for a copy of that letter of instructions to show your friend at 'Pr.,' who, Mr. M. says, has his whole soul absorbed in this matter."[18] Said instructions, in part, were how to reach Brown by mail, namely by addressing an envelope to Mrs. Ritner in Chambersburg, Pennsylvania, and placing another inside marked "H.K." Referring broadly to his discussion with Douglass, John Jr. wrote, "The friend at Rochester will set out to make you a visit in a few days. He will be accompanied by that 'other young man,' and also, if it can be brought around, by the woman that the Syracuse friend could tell me of. The son will probably remain back for a while." The fact that Douglass's son Lewis was evidently being considered for active service with John Brown shows a level of commitment on Douglass's part beyond what is usually acknowledged. Douglass had also volunteered that "'the woman'. . . whose services might prove invaluable, had better be helped on." John Jr. added: "If alive and well, you will see him ere long. I found him in rather low spirits; left him in high."[19]

On August 11 John Jr., reporting from Syracuse where he had expected to meet with Loguen and Tubman, told Kagi that he and "also said women" had gone to Boston. Informed by Loguen's wife that he was expected to visit Canada soon, and "would contrive to go immediately," John resolved to go on to Boston. In his August 11 letter to Kagi, he added, "Morton says our particular friend Mr. Sanborn, in that city, is especially anxious to hear from you; has his heart and hand engaged in the cause. Shall try and find him. . . . I leave this evening on the 11:35 train from here; shall return as soon as possible to make my visit to Chatham."[20]

Arriving the next morning, a Friday, in Boston, John Jr. soon found the Reverend Loguen, who informed him that Tubman was not known to be in the city, nor was anything known of her present whereabouts. As for going to Canada, Loguen's engagements were such that he could not possibly leave till the end of the following week. It was not until the next Tuesday that the younger Brown posted a letter to Kagi informing him of this, also noting that he had decided in the meanwhile to make use of the time by "making acquaintance of those staunch friends of our friend Isaac."[21] First he called upon Dr. Howe, who although John Jr. had no letter of introduction, received him cordially. In his letter John Jr. wrote, "[Howe] gave me a letter to the friend who does business on Mills Street. Went with him to his home in Medford, and took dinner. The last word he said to me was, 'Tell friend Isaac that we have the fullest confidence in his endeavor, whatever may be the result.' I have met no man in whom I think more implicit reliance may be placed. He views matters from the standpoint of reason and principle, and I think his firmness is unshakable."[22]

One of the staunchest individuals John Jr. met with, and a figure who made a substantial contribution, was Lewis Hayden. At 33, after seeing all of his family separated and sold, and after seeing his mother descend into madness, Hayden fled Kentucky with his wife for Canada. Moving to Detroit, he became a prominent member of that city's growing Black community, building a church and a school. In the early 1850s Hayden moved to Boston, where he established a clothing store and played an outstanding role in the Beacon Hill African American community. He would be instrumental in locating the elusive Harriet Tubman, and also in raising money and recruits to be sent to the elder Brown in Virginia. Traveling to Concord, John Jr. found that Sanborn was away on a brief trip to Springfield. "The others here will, however, communicate with him," John Jr. wrote. "They are all, in short, very much gratified and have had their faith and hopes strengthened. Found a number of earnest and warm friends, whose sympathies and theories do not exactly harmonize; but in spite of them selves their hearts will lead their heads." On his return, Sanborn undertook a new round of fund-raising, guaranteeing that an additional $300 would reach Brown by the end of the month.

John Brown Sr. was back in Chambersburg on August 20 to arrange for the transport of the crated arms that had arrived from Ohio, and, just as crucially, to keep his appointment with Frederick Douglass. Joining Kagi at the boarding house of Mrs. Ritner, Brown was in touch as well with Henry Watson, confiding to him the details of his expected assignation—information likely disclosed to Joseph Winters, a known confidant of Brown and leader of Underground Railroad operations in Chambersburg, where he was a prominent person in that town's Black community. Selected for the site of the rendezvous was an old quarry on the south side of town near a bend in the Conococheague Creek before it meanders northward, only a short walk from central Chambersburg. At the scheduled hour, no doubt Brown and Kagi were near enough to hear a westbound train pulling into the depot among whose passengers would be the famed abolitionist and his companion, a vigorous young man with sharply drawn African features.

Although far from being the only anti-slavery action Douglass was prepared to embrace, in his view Brown's movement offered a more "zealous and laborious self-sacrificing spirit" that he saw as lacking in other quarters. Not only was Brown remarkable in his stewardship of his men; he also had heart enough to set his plan in motion while seeking to establish cooperation among abolitionists. In this spirit Douglass was prepared to answer John Brown's summons and do what he could in assuring the action's success. But despite his deep respect for the project, Douglass was never disposed, as some were, to subordinate himself entirely to it. He appears to have merely been prepared to offer his support, as he said, "in an individual way"; and while his commitment was considerable, he was also planning a trip for the fall and winter of 1859 to the British Isles and to France and was contracting for lectures to take place in Philadelphia, Boston, and Rhode Island before his departure—a departure unexpectedly hastened by what transpired. Brown however, it must be stipulated, evidenced a great deal of confidence in and respect for Douglass due to their past associations that could only have served as the basis for summoning him to Chambersburg.

While it was not entirely unexpected that Douglass should come to south-central Pennsylvania, passersby seeing and cordially welcoming him expressed surprise that he would appear unannounced. He explained that he was on personal business, and, offered the opportunity to speak that evening in Chambersburg, agreed to make an appearance. The duo made their way to the barbershop of Henry Watson, who, although busily engaged, pointed the way to where Brown and his lieutenant waited.

Knowing that Brown would be armed, and would be regarding strangers cautiously, Douglass was tentative on his approach. Soon, however, it became apparent that Brown recognized the pair, and as they came nearer greetings were cordial. "He had in his hand," Douglass wrote, "a fishing-tackle, with which he had apparently been fishing in a stream hard by, but I saw no fish, and did not suppose that he cared much for his 'fisherman's luck.'" Its wearer looked in every way like a farmer from the neighborhood, Douglass wrote, "[Brown's] hat was old and storm-beaten, . . . his clothing was about the color of the stone-quarry itself. . . . His face wore an anxious expression, and he was much worn by thought and exposure. I felt I was on a dangerous mission, and was as little desirous of discovery as himself."[23] Propriety perhaps dictated that Douglass first hand Brown a letter he had been asked to deliver. He and Green had stopped the previous night in Brooklyn where they had been the guests of the Gloucesters. Elizabeth had written expressing her best wishes for Brown's cause and for his welfare, enclosing a $10 contribution.

Now the quartet of John Brown, Frederick Douglass, John Henri Kagi, and Shields Green settled down among the detritus and castaways of the quarry, the wagon fully loaded with Brown's "mining tools" hard by, to discuss the impending enterprise.

Even as only the least hint of the exchange may be recoverable, a careful reading of Douglass's autobiography and other writings, and those of his contemporaries, may allow for a parsing of this interaction, which must be considered essential. While many of its elements can only be conjectured, it is known that Douglass, familiar with the earlier iteration of Brown's plan, was cognizant that Brown had something in mind concerning Harper's Ferry. Soon, however, Douglass was surprised to hear that Brown had renounced that previous plan in favor of a bold new strategy calling for the seizure of the federal arsenal at the outset.

The two principals would spend many hours of two days in debate and deliberation, while Green and Kagi remained, in Douglass's telling, "for the most part silent listeners throughout."[24] The idea behind the selection of Harper's Ferry for the initial salvo was twofold:

foremost that objective was meant to give "Southern firebrands" the justification they sought in carrying out their threat of secession. Once a complete schism had taken place, the predicate was, the North would be compelled to whip the seceded states back into the Union without slavery. This "far more than any other" was the propelling idea, Salmon Brown related to Oswald Garrison Villard's researcher Katherine Mayo, in remarks cited in Villard's *John Brown, 1800-1859: A Biography Fifty Years After,* published in 1911. "All writers," Brown's son said, had "failed heretofore to bring out this far-reaching idea to the extent it merits."[25] And as its corollary—not at all to be apprehended by Villard, but very much so by his exact contemporary W. E. B. Du Bois, as shown in his *John Brown* published in 1909—Brown's intention was to anticipate this rebellion by using Harper's Ferry as "a trumpet to rally the slaves," as Douglass phrased it—as a signal to be heard across the South that "friends" in the North were prepared to intervene on their behalf and to inspire them to rally to his standard.

The twelve-year alliance between the two men clearly had brought about an affiliation that was mutually more than friendship, and they argued from the fullness of their hearts, as of their minds—surely one of the more substantive get-togethers known to the American scene. At one blow, Brown reasoned, the political props upon which the country then precariously balanced would come crashing down— and a war would begin for the liberation of the slaves. Brown had "unsheathed his sword," as he said, to forestall for the nation the necessity of going through the war he had seen prefigured in the events of the day; a war issuing on the precedents of mass armies over a continental breadth; a war using the lightning communications links of telegraph and railroad, with the thunder and fire of massed muskets and repeating rifles and the immense explosive power unleashed by the cannon of the age.

As well as anyone, Douglass understood that the sectional contest was ultimately one for dominion. But for over a decade he had argued against abolitionists advocating the dissolution of the Union to disentangle the republic from slavery. He took the position espoused by Gerrit Smith and others—that the Congress had the right to legislate on slavery, and, as John Quincy Adams had argued, by its war powers under the Constitution could abolish it. Certainly, Douglass put in considerable effort along these lines trying to dissuade Brown, believing, contrary to Brown's expectation, that his gambit would only lead to a state of affairs the opposite of what he sought. The stroke was bound to misfire, said Douglass, and would sacrifice the lives of everyone engaged in it. The battle for freedom must be fought within the Union; it would only be the power of the federal government, after all, supported by its armed forces, that could deal with the issue on the scale proposed. Beginning with such a rousing blow would not help their cause and would do nothing to help the slave. Brown would be discredited and the South given the excuse it sought, not for secession, but for the complete suppression of all anti-slavery opinion throughout the northern states. Assuredly too, Douglass suggested, in attempting to mount such a scheme, however unlikely its success, an indiscriminate slaughter of male slaves would commence.

Clearly Brown felt none of Douglass's scruples, believing as he did that a resounding blow would be just the thing to wake the northern people out of their torpor on the subject of slavery. He expected, as Richard Realf later related before the Mason Committee, "that all the free negroes in the Northern states would immediately flock to his standard"; and as he called on the aroused strength of this Black Nation, that presumed unanimity would create among on-looking Whites the sympathy they would need to gain their support.[26] Any slaughter of the kind Douglass feared, once begun, Brown likely held, would cure itself. In the sight of the American people and of the world, slaveholders could proceed only to a limited extent in this shameless conduct. In Brown's view it was too late to destroy and erase the South's "peculiar institution"—Emerson's phrase—by means less harmful than the evil itself. The slaveholders not only lived in the South, to the exclusion of all others they were "the South" itself; they were the only active power there. They could not be "talked down" and would not consent to be hemmed in by political means alone. No one in the country better understood the nature of the business they were engaged in than these men themselves. They were broadcasting it in the powder they were buying and in the arms they were stealing. War was at that very moment being contemplated in the cabinet of President Buchanan. Out of his success at Harper's Ferry, Brown was convinced, would come freedom for the enslaved; and since slavery could only end in blood, there could be no better time to end it than now.

The strength of the Southern oligarchy was composed of three instrumentalities.[27] First came the omnipotence of money: with $2 billion invested in slaves, the South accrued the ability to draw into its reach the sympathy of all other large capital. A second strand maintaining this power came in the "three-fifths" clause in the Constitution, allowing three or four large planters of South Carolina "riding leisurely to the polls, and throwing in their visiting cards for ballots," to "blot out the entire influence of [a] New England town in the Federal government."[28] The third strand came in "the potent and baleful prejudice of color."

With no more than 50,000 of 300,000 slaveholders set up as planters, the ruling element of the South lived as an irresistible aristocracy in a population of five million Whites and four million Blacks. To these were added another 2,000 state officials, making a complete pro-slavery party that had gained ascendancy in the administrations of Pierce and Buchanan, exercising the immense powers of the federal government on behalf of slavery.

As a geographical entity, the "South" extended from the mid-Atlantic states down the seaboard through the "Old South," pushing westward through the tier of states known as the "Deep South"; touching on the Gulf of Mexico, the region ranged up the Mississippi River, claiming all land to the northern borders of Kentucky and Missouri, extending on the western bank of the Mississippi into the rich cotton country in Arkansas, and claiming the river valleys of eastern Texas. The "South" drew in fully fifteen states; with an extensive shoreline, that entity encompassed the broad middle region called the "border states," as well as a part of the "Southwest." Each of these regions was as different from the other as they were from any of the northern states—in geography and latitude, in the admixture of the emigrant European stock, in resources and in various pursuits of industry. What gave this expanse its cohesion was the recognition by law and custom of the ownership of black-skinned human chattel.

"The South . . . is neither a territory strictly detached from the North geographically, nor a moral unity," Karx Marx contended. "It is not a country at all, but a battle slogan."[29] Marx elaborated: "The soul of the whole secession movement is South Carolina. It has 402,542 slaves and 301,271 free men. Mississippi . . . comes second. It has 436,696 slaves and 354,699 free men. Alabama comes third, with 435,132 slaves and 529,164 free men." As Brown was continually reiterating, nowhere was the South more vulnerable than as indicated by this racial distribution and proportionality—nowhere more vulnerable than in its fear of servile insurrection. A successful assault at Harper's Ferry would recoil throughout the region, and the slaveholders would imagine the whole of the North and all of their slaves were down upon them pell-mell. "If I could conquer Virginia," Brown said, "the balance of the southern states would nearly conquer themselves, there being such a large number of slaves in them."[30] Brown and Kagi had devoted considerable effort to plotting out the "black belt" on a county-by-county basis in a series of large maps referenced earlier.

Douglass was familiar with those maps and would have been cognizant of their import, noting as they did such details as census figures, indicating many of the large plantations where the masses of slaves were held, as well as marking mountain ranges while also designating some of the places to be attacked as the campaign took hold and developed. That campaign, as mentioned, had been projected to extend down the mountainous line in Virginia into North and South Carolina and westward into Tennessee. Virginia held the largest number of slaves. Ranging through two principal areas of the South, starting at the head of the Blue Ridge, a continuous series of counties extended clear to Virginia's southern extremity, where Black outnumbered White. Together with the northern counties of North Carolina and the eastern counties of Maryland and its Eastern Shore—this comprised the first of slavery's great cantons. The other, from the Atlantic shore islands through South Carolina and mid-Georgia, taking in a large swath of north-central Florida to its panhandle, ranging through mid-Alabama down to the Gulf and embracing the whole of the southern Mississippi River Valley, found its western extent in the river valleys of east Texas. This was all justification enough for the inordinate importance Brown bestowed on his "Harper's Ferry" expedition.

The South's aim with secession, really, was not the dissolution of the national government, but its reorganization on the basis of slavery.[31] The motive of its political leaders in threatening secession was clear—by withdrawing from the authority of the Union and uniting the seceded states in a Confederacy, they sought to secure the border states and lay claim to the entire territory of the United States from the old line of the Missouri Compromise to the Pacific Ocean. They had set themselves on this course because their goals were no longer amenable under the Union. Since a large part of their claim was under control of that Union and would have to be wrested from it, this necessitated on their part "a war of conquest." If they did anything other than wage war on these terms, they would be relinquishing their capacity to continue with their dominion in the South, defeating the purpose of secession itself. Peaceable secession was impossible, Brown contended, because the divided sentiment of the border states made it so, as did an insatiable South. Once in possession of New Orleans and Charleston and Richmond, slaveholders would demand St. Louis and Baltimore. If they got these, they would insist on Washington. Once in Washington they would assume control of the army and navy and would force the North, while it would fight for the survival of the Union, to adopt on its banner the formal interment of slavery.

It was Brown's intention to anticipate this rebellion upon the soil where it originated, calling slaves into service to march as a liberating army into the South. Sanborn remarked, "In Kansas his bold policy had succeeded against the pro-slavery administration headed in its military department by Jefferson Davis. Now Brown hoped it might also succeed in the slave states."[32]

Douglass placed his various reminiscences within a curious template, which serve to obscure rather than reveal the true extent of his commitment prior to this last meeting with John Brown. Of his first meeting with Brown in 1847, Douglass related much later, "From 8 o-clock in the evening till 3 in the morning, Capt. Brown and I sat face to face, he arguing in favor of his plan, and I finding all the objections I could against it." And of the meeting in the quarry he wrote, "Our talk was long and earnest; we spent the most of Saturday and a part of Sunday in this debate . . . he for striking a blow which should instantly rouse the country, and I for the policy of gradually and unaccountable drawing off the slaves to the mountains, as at first suggested and proposed by him."

Of that earlier iteration of the plan, too, Douglass recalled Brown saying he "had been watching and waiting" for the heads of Black men such as he would need from among Douglass's race to "pop-up," as it were, above the surface of water.[33] In August 1859, at age 42, Frederick Douglass was a man of considerable bearing and at the height of his pre-civil war fame; he was a veritable Spartacus of his people, evidenced in his untiring oratorical and literary combat and commitment to all things pertaining to anti-slavery agitation.

By this time Frederick Douglass was a national presence, known in north, south, east, and west. His speeches were well-reported, he published his own newspaper and had three autobiographies in circulation; his image was well-known and ever proliferating. It would be said of him in the coming decades—he lived to be 88, dying in 1895—that he was the most photographed man of the 19th century. Douglass took special care on all of the occasions on which his portrait was being made to appear neatly and properly attired, with coat, collar, and tie, his mass of hair neatly brushed and parted, looking square-jawed and earnestly into the lens of the camera, and hence into the eye of the viewer. His practice in regard to the frequency and dissemination of his image was a deliberate one, meant to counterbalance, indeed to counteract, all of the negative and derisive images of Blacks, and in particular of Black men, which were being widely distributed throughout the country as well.

Given his prominence, Brown had summoned him not to elicit his further understanding prior to beginning "his work," but because he wanted Douglass to join in that effort as co-leader. He wanted Douglass to appear with him at Harper's Ferry; his success, Brown now believed, was contingent upon Douglass's participation. If Douglass be for him, who could be against him? This is the aspect of the drama passed over without remark by Douglass, concealed beneath the wavering conceit of a rhetorical device. Brown himself was possessed of complete composure and confidence, and this not just as is usually supposed because he had wrestled internally with his God, but more especially because he was thoroughly grounded in and responding to the American condition in relation to its racial division, of which he and Douglass were both profoundly aware. "There is no disguising the fact," Douglass wrote in *Life and Times*, "that the American people are much interested and mystified about the mere matter of color as connected with manhood." Brown himself had a three-quarters portrait taken; he is seen facing left in a suit of rough brown broadcloth, no doubt with his pocket watch resting in his vest pocket, looking directly into the lens, hands clasped behind, coat unbuttoned and opened at his waist; his gray hair is brushed back, his beard full, gray and "patriarchal"—this photograph was to be distributed as the war commenced, the portrait of the commander-in-chief of the Provisional Army for the United States.

Douglass wrote, "He described the place as to its means of defense, and how impossible it would be to dislodge him if once in possession. Of course I was no match for him in such matters, but I told him, and these were my words, that all his arguments, and all his descriptions of the place, convinced me that he was going into a perfect steel trap, and once in he would never get out alive.... He was not to be shaken by anything I could say, but treated my views respectfully, replying that even if surrounded he would find means for cutting his way out."[34]

Brown's plan called for a party to cross the Potomac Bridge at night, approaching Harper's Ferry from the west on the Maryland side of the river along the Chesapeake and Ohio Canal. The telegraph wire would be cut and the bridge seized, with Brown's men detaining the watchman as he was making his regular rounds. The telegraph on the Virginia side would also be cut. Crossing the Ferry Lot to the armory gate, the men would call out the watchman and compel him to open it or they would break it open. The two buildings fronting the government works overlooking the Ferry Lot were to be seized—the fire engine-house and the paymaster's office. On Shenandoah Street, across the Lot, the Arsenal would be invested—the watchman there also detained—and behind it, the bridge to Loudoun Heights. Finally, Hall's Rifle Works, a half-mile up on the Shenandoah River, would be seized and its watchman, along with the arsenal watchman—the facility's only guards—escorted to the engine-house in the Armory.

All the gaslights in the lower part of town would be extinguished; to assure unimpeded access and communication among the points held, sentries and a roving picket would be established. Trains arriving during the night would be stopped and prevented from passing, and the tracks torn up on each side of the river to ensure it. Incendiary devices in the form of pitch-soaked rope would be placed on the bridges so that they could be fired when that became advisable.

By beginning at night, the raiders would minimize the possibility of encountering many people, and the town would quickly be secured before alarm could be given. As people awakened and the day began, unaware of what was happening, they would find the government works and their streets under the control of armed men, who would have, as well, a monopoly on arms in the neighborhood. They would be dissuaded from opposing Brown and would hold to their houses or else flee the town; those who did not, and who sought to interfere, would, for their own safety, be held prisoner for a time in the engine-house. At the outset "without the snapping of a gun," said Brown, his company would have possession of the government property and of the rifle factory and the points of entrance and exit from the town, having severed all communication from the town with the outside.

With the ferry secure, before daybreak a second phase would commence. A party was to proceed up Bolivar Heights where selected slaveholding estates were to be visited. Slaves would be freed and brought to the ferry along with their masters and requisitioned property—horses, wagons, and selected valuables from the estates and farms. A similar process would be executed in Maryland, seizing selected slaveholders and their property and bringing them to the ferry to be held with the others. These prominent slaveholding citizens would be the very persons, said Brown, who could be expected to lead any resistance, and those who wished to oppose him would be restrained so as not to bring harm to these men. In the worst case, he would be able to dictate the terms of his withdrawal by trading on the influence and prominence of these individuals. His intention, moreover, was not to harm them, but to make a signal example of them by arranging with their "friends" to exchange them for able-bodied male slaves.

The dangers posed by Brown's radical inversion of priorities were palpable, and Douglass clearly recoiled at the suggestion of such a daring act. There were towns within a very short radius and the country was well settled, he would have pointed out; then, too, Harper's Ferry was serviced by two rail lines, one connecting to a major city—Baltimore, scarcely an hour away—and beyond that the nation's capital. On the first news of the uprising, troops were certain to be dispatched.

One of the difficulties Douglass foresaw was presented by the terrain itself; constrained by the natural setting and by the limited points of entrance and of egress, as by the large population, Brown, however securely in control, faced the obvious risk of being bottled up. One part of their party could become isolated from another, and any casualties could be catastrophic. If Brown and his men became isolated, Douglass predicted, those opposing them in the neighborhood would become an enraged mob and would attempt to seize the interlopers rather than let them escape, and lynch law would ensue.

For his part, Brown thought the local militia companies would not be eager to converge on Harper's Ferry until they had looked to their own neighborhoods. News that men were in possession of the armory and were freeing and arming slaves, would alarm and disconcert them. The militia companies weren't a serious military threat; they were poorly armed and poorly trained. Even if they did manage to converge on the town they would only come armed with outdated muskets and would quickly be dissuaded by the disproportion of force. Neither did Brown think federal troops would immediately be a factor. The governor of Virginia would have to call upon the president for them and would first want to see how the militia fared against the invaders. In any case, since he and his men didn't intend to remain at Harper's Ferry, a federal military response would be delayed, as all means of communication would have been severed—the telegraph wires cut, the rail lines torn up, the bridges burned. But even should they became surrounded, Brown assured Douglass, he would have ample means to cut his way out.

Despite all these assurances, Douglass warned that he could see Brown was thrusting himself and his men into dangers, and worse; he might find those dangers easy to get into, but impossible to get out of. He would be walking into a perfect cul-de-sac. Some observers have cited Harper's Ferry as evidence of Brown having lost his bearings in an "overlong contemplation" of the issue, and that his actions were a perfect demonstration of his military ineptitude. Many have pointed out that the locale Brown chose for his first sally had a relatively sparse slave population, and that in any case slavery in northern Virginia was comparatively benign, evidencing contacts and behaviors between the races of a more positive sort. It is often said slaves were neither ready or willing to take the arms and the freedom Brown was offering, with more than a few holding he was entirely deluded—or at least misinformed—gaining all of his information, so they suppose, from "abolitionist literature." But Brown did not imagine that men who had previously been peacefully at labor, other than the very brave or more desperate, would join a fight whose outcome was still in doubt. Nor would it have been prudent for him to expect it. He was only expecting enough men to man the freight in arms and equipment over the rough terrain, and to begin building the basis for the army he projected. These men would form a nucleus around which other slaves could later be drawn. With the success of the initial stroke, though, he expected a series of rapidly cascading events that would net him large numbers.

Accounts of John Brown's Harper's Ferry "expedition" have always been absent a crucial factor; a "missing element" meant by John Brown to have been actively present in the action, but was not. Namely of a body of men, led by Frederick Douglass, marching into Harper's Ferry once that town had been secured. He did not intend to thrust his friend into dangers, and worse, that he was scarcely prepared for, and was clearly projecting a company three or four times the size of the one that ultimately went with him—not nineteen, as it is generally accepted there were, but fifty to seventy-five men. With that number, he could have entirely thwarted the inundation by Virginia and Maryland militia companies that were to stymie his movements. The fact that Brown envisioned an exchange of his slaveholder hostages "for able-bodied male slaves" suggests a formal, even ceremonial setting in which he intended, after putting them into service while commanding his troops at Harper's Ferry, returning the weapons that once belonged to George Washington to the president's nephew and their current owner, Col. Lewis Washington, whom Brown had taken hostage. Brown had specified that these artifacts be surrendered into the hands of a Black man as Washington was being taken prisoner, and accordingly in the early morning hours of October 17, Stevens had ordered that Washington place the weapons in the hands of Osborne Anderson. All this highly symbolic theater was intended to be duly noted across the South, when, standing before a sizable assembly within the grounds of the United States Armory, Frederick Douglass would proclaim emancipation in Maryland and Virginia, to roll as a thunderclap through the nation. Then Brown had intended to have the bell in the cupola of the fire enginehouse rung, summoning slaves and others from the countryside: a culmination implicit in their movements on that day that has never appeared in accounts of the Harper's Ferry Raid!

It would not be wholly conjectural to propose that Brown also asked Douglass to prepare and publish a call upon the Negro in both North and South that would have sounded something like this: *There are men out there, Douglass, who only wait to be brought into this war. From Rochester and Auburn, from Syracuse and Ithaca, from Troy and Albany, could be drawn a hundred men. Your own son is one of these. Philadelphia alone has a hundred, as do New York and Boston. In the west—in Buffalo and Cleveland and Chicago—could be added five hundred to the cause. Add to these the hundreds in Canada West and the thousands of the South, and I have no hesitation in saying that ten thousand men might be raised in the next thirty days to march through and through the South.*

One Black regiment alone, in such a war, would be the full equal of two White ones. The very fact of color in this case would be more terrible than powder and balls.

Speaking at Storer College at Harper's Ferry, West Virginia, on May 30, 1881, Frederick Douglass addressed his relationship with

John Brown and the enduring significance of that "raid" of which Brown was commander. Casting a long view, Douglass said that " the bloody harvest of Harper's Ferry was ripened by the heat and moisture of merciless bondage of more than two hundred years. That startling cry of alarm on the banks of the Potomac was but the answering back of the avenging angel."[35] On "this simple altar of human virtue," said Douglas, which had been the sacrifice of Brown and of those who went with him, scholarship, eloquence, poetry, story, and song must needs retire dissatisfied with the paucity of their offerings, as he expected would be the case with his own. Then, indicating that judgment toward which all commentary must aspire, Douglass continued: "Though more than twenty years have rolled between us and the Harper's Ferry raid, though since then the armies of the nation have found it necessary to do on a large scale what John Brown attempted to do on a small one, and the captain who fought his way through slavery has filled with honor the Presidential chair, we yet stand too near the days of slavery, and the life and times of John Brown, to see clearly the true martyr and hero that he was and rightly to estimate the value of the man and his works."[36]

The perplexity that American historiography and scholarship have encountered in assessing Brown and the meaning of his actions results from the circumstance—and this was Douglass's contention—that the long shadow of slavery "yet falls broad and large over the face of the whole country." This is true even in our present age, and as its tendentious currents continually arise to pose an ongoing challenge to our clear perception, to our conceptions, and to our recurring assessments, we are continually overtaken as if by the uncanny, by all that remains undisclosed and mysterious in our American racial dilemma in black and white.

Salmon Brown remarked that his father and elder brother could sit and discuss the issues germane to slavery "by the hour." Certainly, his father did the same with his many other confidants, including Frederick Douglass. Douglass had observed in his last autobiography that after his initial meeting with Brown in 1847 his remarks on the lecturing circuit began to take on "a color more and more tinged" by his late friend's "strong impressions."[37] This is taken as a reference to Brown's influence on Douglass's position vis-a-vis "moral suasion" versus recourse to resistance, including insurrectionary means, in effect charting Douglass's evolution from a Garrisonian Abolitionist to a Radical Abolitionist in the late 1840s and early 1850s. But could it not be suggested more broadly still that it was after Harper's Ferry and Brown's death—in Douglass's speeches in the years 1859-1862—that there are also to be found traces of the words that passed between them in those August hours. Brown, as is well known, had a penchant for urging Blacks in the strongest terms to engage forcefully in a defense of their liberty; Douglass knew too well the proscriptions against that engagement facing his people in both sections of the nation.

In 1860, after the Republican Party had nominated a man of untried abilities, Abraham Lincoln, whose political history was "too meager to form a basis on which to judge of his future," the Democratic Party split, yielding the nomination of Breckinridge of Kentucky on one side and Stephen Douglas of Illinois on the other, thus preparing a coming victory for the Republican Party. Commenting in his *Monthly* that August, Douglass said the illusion of solidity and endurance that the Democratic Party had conveyed to the nation "is now dispelled. Babylon has fallen." With Douglass's pen sketching the ramifications of the momentous events of May and June in the great American contestation over slavery, from James Redpath came an invitation to attend a meeting of "friends" at John Brown's grave on the Fourth of July. Douglass replied that his heart was with them, but it would not be possible for him to break away from his duties on such short notice. Had the invitation reached his desk but a day or two earlier, he would have "very gladly" come "to do honor to the memory of one whom I regard as the man of the nineteenth century." It had been among his highest privileges, Douglass wrote, "to have been acquainted with John Brown, shared his counsels, enjoyed his confidence, and sympathized with the great objects of his life and death."[38]

Several days later in a letter to William Still, Douglass confided his deepest longing to the Underground Railroad leader "for the end of my people's bondage, and would give all I possess to witness the great jubilee." The signs on the road to the downfall of slavery were numerous, but, he recalled, twenty years before the beast had really seemed to be hastening to its death, only to become entrenched in a deeper abyss. Douglass remarked, "I will walk by faith, not by right, for all ground of hope founded on external appearance, have thus far signally failed and broken down under me."[39]

Douglass now began to place more emphasis than ever on the efficacy and necessity of revolutionary violence on the part of the slaves. He wrote Redpath, "The eight-and-forty hours of John Brown's school in Virginia, taught the slaves more than they could have otherwise learned in a half-century." Though Brown's effort seemed to have yielded little, Douglass affirmed that the action had "done more to upset the logic and shake the security of slavery, than all other efforts in that direction for twenty years." He repeatedly struck this theme canvassed by Brown in letters, in publications, and in speeches; in the August issue of the *Monthly*, "The Prospect of the Future," Douglass wrote, "Outside philanthropy never disenthralled any people. It required a Spartacus himself a Roman slave and gladiator, to arouse the servile population of Italy, and defeat some of the most powerful armies of Rome, at the head of an army of slaves; and the slaves of America await the advent of an African Spartacus." The following exchange has been culled from Douglass's own words, in composition with Brown's, expressions that may be regarded as bearing those qualities brought together by their convocation in an abandoned stone quarry outside Chambersburg:

Brown: The men I have with me, Douglass, stand ready to peril everything at the first opportunity for a fight. Neither I, nor my men, count our lives as anything outside this fight when weighted against the freedom of millions. There is a latent element in the national character, which, if fairly called into action, will sweep anything down in its course. The American people admire courage displayed in defense of liberty and will catch the flame of sympathy from the sparks of its heroic fire. This trait has been long manifest in the reception of the patriots who have been cast upon this country's shores from the wrecks of European revolutions. Call the servile population of the South to arms, and inspire them to fight a few battles for freedom, and the mere animal instincts and sympathies of this people will do more for them than has been accomplished by a quarter of a century of oratorical philanthropy.

Douglass: The Anglo-Saxon, Teutonic, and Celtic races have utterly failed in the magnanimity and philanthropy necessary to promote the rights of another and weaker race than themselves. As a nation America is bound as by a spell of enchantment to slavery. The attempt to reconcile slavery with freedom in this country has dethroned logic and converted statesmanship into stultified imbecility. For the non-slaveholding Whites of the South the highest ambition is to be able to own and flog a Negro. They are in the utmost dread of the slave. They furnish the overseers, the drivers, the patrols, the slave hunters, and are in their sphere, as completely the tools of slaveholders, as the slaves themselves. They are such because they can't be otherwise. The Whites of the North have no adequate idea of the power of these master spirits of the South; and yet the fact is they are under the same influence. The European races have drunk deep of the poisoned cup of slaveholding malignity, and only after they have been made to experience a little more of the savage barbarism of slavery will they be willing to make war upon it.

Brown: We can never cease to regret that an appeal to the higher and better elements of human nature is in this case, so barren of fitting response. But it is so, and until this people has passed through several generations of humanitarian culture, so it will be. Outside philanthropy never disenthralled any people. Heaven cannot help the Negro but by moving him to help himself. It required a Spartacus to arouse the servile population of Italy and defeat some of the most powerful armies of Rome.

Douglass: The Negro can do much, but he cannot hope to whip two sections of the country at once. I know well the proscriptions of each on the condition of the Negro in America. I long for the end of my people's bondage and would give all I possess to witness the great jubilee, but I cannot see that it will come out of this attack. Not even the allowance that the Whites of the North will wink at a John Brown movement could induce me to advocate it. I am sick of seeing mere isolated, extemporaneous insurrections, the only result of which is the shooting and hanging of a few brave men who take part in them—and not being willing to take the chances of such an insurrection myself I cannot advise anyone else to take part in them. The time is not right for such a war. The political uprising of the North against slavery has only risen to the level of being negatively anti-slavery; it now opposes the political power of slavery in the national government, and will one day arrest the spread of the system, humble its power and defeat its plans for giving any further guarantee of permanence. All this is desirable, but it still leaves the great work of abolishing slavery in the future.

Brown: If the Republican Party elects its candidate next year he will enter Washington upon his peril, the way a fugitive slave enters the North. But the result will show them merely to be the continuation of the Pierce and Buchanan administrations. They will bend a knee to slavery and be indebted to the South for their law and their gospel.

Douglass: Your attack will create a more active resistance by the party of slavery to the cause of freedom and its advocates. What is wanted is an anti-slavery government first—in harmony with anti-slavery speech. For this the ballot is needed, and if that is not to be heard ... then the bullet.

Brown: Whether the slaveholder is in South Carolina, in Virginia, in Missouri or in Kentucky—in the cotton states, the slave breeding states or in the border states—one is as bad as another. In every state where they hold the reins of government, they will take sides openly. They know that if the government is a miserable and contemptible failure—then that government must meet them in the field and put them down, or itself be put down. They are all traitors to the government and the constitution and are only waiting to spring up by the heat of surrounding treason. When Virginia is a free state, Maryland cannot be a slave state. This conspiracy must stand together or fall together. Strike it at either extreme—either on the head or at the heel, and it dies.

In the late afternoon of that day in Chambersburg, when Douglass and Green left the quarry, Douglass must have been overwhelmed by what he'd heard. But he might have also been a little buoyed—something new needed to be tried. The prospect of a nearing contestation on the very ground of slavery's existence in the United States would have made him somber, and his remarks that night in Chambersburg's Franklin Hall might have taken the form of an exposition of the hour and a denunciation of the Slave Power. That evening, after what he had heard, Douglass undoubtedly cast his thoughts onto the war John Brown was about to commence, mindful of his own relation to that war. On that night, as he surveyed the situation, it was evident that the previous twenty years had brought a marked change in the condition of the anti-slavery lecturer.

Once, he and his colleagues had been met by furious mobs with rotten eggs and brickbats, but now the country had been rocked end to end by the strength of the faithfulness of abolitionists to the freedom of the slave. Yet slaveholders were still coolly estimating the value of their victories and congratulating themselves upon their security. It was impossible to disguise the fact that slavery had made great progress and had riveted itself more firmly to the Southern mind and heart, and that the whole moral atmosphere of the South had undergone a decided change for the worse.[40] Douglass may not have acknowledged the man known as Isaac Smith in his coming and going at Franklin Hall that night; Brown would not have thought it prudent for his friend to do so—but he was there, perhaps coming and departing alone or sitting among and conversing with his confidants. After the meeting, as Douglass took his leave and walked to his lodgings, he could not have been cognizant that away in the night were dozens of names studded throughout the far-flung landscape of the American scene—names that in a few years would be lifted to immortality by a dignity only death could bestow, names that would be pronounced like anthems on the lips of those touched by what happened in or near them. On that night, the names of places that could have reached Douglass would have brought no special significance to his ear.

Returning the next morning to his conclave with John Brown in the quarry outside Chambersburg, he could have had no intimation that he would be called upon by President Abraham Lincoln in only three years to help raise ranks of Black recruits to fill regiments of the Union Army—troops who would march into the South carrying the banner of the Union and singing the "John Brown Song." Douglass sums up everything of his meeting with Brown in August 1859 in a succinct paragraph: "We spent the Saturday and succeeding Sunday in conference on the question, whether the desperate step should then be taken, or the old plan as already described should be carried out. He was for boldly striking Harper's Ferry at once and running the risk of getting into the mountains afterwards. I was for avoiding Harper's Ferry altogether. Shields Green and Mr. Kagi remained silent listeners throughout. It is needless to repeat here what was said, after what has happened. Suffice it, that after all I could say, I saw that my old friend had resolved on his course and that it was idle to parley."

Douglass indicates he was a full party to their talks; like those silent listeners, however, history itself has been mute. But this summons to a council of war, the details of which it is needless to repeat after what has happened, possesses an eloquence all its own. Through long hours Douglass tried to dissuade Brown from his course, seeking a return to an undertaking originally proposed by him, to which Douglass had pledged further aid. Some have suggested there were sharply bitter words exchanged between the two men. Brown is said by one account to have accused Douglass of cowardice, "of being afraid to face a gun." Although their differences may not have devolved in quite so acrimonious a fashion, one can see Brown rising to his feet, exasperated at not being able to win Douglass over; his friend was reluctant at the very moment decisive action was called for. One can hear Brown, as one writer has, bitterly accusing Douglass of becoming "soft"—he had already begun to develop a paunch—of enjoying overmuch "the limelight" that his position had brought him.

And when Douglass found he had exhausted himself trying to move Brown to renounce his new plan in favor of the old one, he too rose, announcing he could not countenance such an action. Expressing his "astonishment" that Brown "could rest on a reed so weak and broken," that he could think he would be able to guarantee his safety and that of his men by the fact he would retain hostages from among Virginia citizens, Douglass warned flatly "that Virginia would blow him and his hostages sky-high rather than that he should hold Harper's Ferry an hour."

Fully feeling he had justified himself, Douglass turned to Green.

"Now Shields, you have heard our discussion," he said. "If in view of it you do not wish to stay, you have but to say so, and you can go back with me."

As is known, Brown put his arms around Douglass in a most intimate way.

"Come with me, Douglass," he implored. "I will defend you with my life. . . ."

There is perhaps no ambiguity in his telling of the moment, when, tears glistening on his cheeks, Brown said poignantly, "I want you for a special purpose. When I strike, the bees shall begin to swarm and I shall want you to help me to hive them."

But Douglass only allowed: "Discretion or cowardice had made me proof against the dear old man's eloquence—perhaps it was something of both which determined my course. When about to leave I asked Green what he had decided to do, and was surprised by his coolly saying, in his broken way, 'I b'leve I'll go wid de ole man.' Here we separated—they to go to Harper's Ferry, I to Rochester."[41]

EPILOGUE

Miscellanies of a Movement

By way of a précis, the following fragments, drawn from prolonged research, are suggestive of a dimension to John Brown's Harper's Ferry enterprise that has received little, or at best attenuated attention from contemporary authors. Brown's efforts to have an important Black leader on hand also included attempts to enlist J.W. Loguen and a principal in the Oberlin-Wellington rescue trials, Charles Langston. In a letter dated May 17, 1859, Brown had written suggestively to Loguen, "I will just whisper in your private ear that I have no doubt you will soon have a call from God to minister at a different location. I trust you will obey the call." But John Jr. confided to Kagi that Loguen's "heart was only passively in the cause" and that he was "too fat" for the arduous undertaking. Charles Langston, of considerably slighter stature, had been ill, and moreover, John Jr. reported, he had become "discouraged about the mining business," believing there were too few hands. "Physical weakness is his fault," he concluded.

Hinton records a conversation between Anne Brown and Kagi about Douglass's failure to take a stake in the enterprise. Anne Brown related of that conversation: "I remember asking him what he thought of Fred Douglass' refusal to come down with us. He said he did not blame Douglass, for 'he is physically incapable of running';

that he had some disease in his feet and limbs that made him incapable of running';—Besides, if Douglass were caught it would be sure death for him, for he had been slave in Maryland." Evidently, in Kagi's observation, Douglass's condition was brought on by an over-rich diet, unlike that which he'd started out on. Assessing Douglass's justification in refusing to accompany Brown to Harper's Ferry and having to endure the rancor he was to encounter, Richard Hinton remarked, "Frederick Douglass's refusal to finally join the enterprise has never, to me, appeared to warrant adverse criticism. His position before the land justified, in 1859, a choice between both conditions, nor failed of endeavor. Certainly he was doing a large work, compelling, by his intellectual power and eloquence, a fast-growing recognition for the oppressed race, of which he was an able leader. He might well weigh, as he did, the question of casting this upon the 'hazard of a die.' The 'logic of events' at least has justified Frederick Douglass, and his faithful services must silence critics; those who also had the opportunity and did not follow John Brown."[1]

Cook asserted that Douglass had pledged to furnish additional men and had himself "promised to be present at Harper's Ferry." Douglass answered Cook's charges in a letter to the *Rochester Democrat and American* of October 31, 1859: "Mr. Cook may be perfectly right in denouncing me as a coward; I have always been more distinguished for running than fighting, and tried by the Harper's Ferry insurrection test, I am most miserably deficient in courage, even more so than Cook when he deserted his brave old captain and fled to the mountains."

With John Brown Jr. and J.W. Loguen on their way to Ontario by August 18, the prospects for organizing the recruits in Canada began to brighten. In the latter part of August and through the first week of September, the duo visited St. Catharines, Hamilton, London, Chatham, Buxton, and Windsor, and on the U.S. side of the border Detroit, Sandusky, and Cleveland. At each location, an auxiliary named the League of Liberty, taking the name of the Black organization already extant in the lake states, was formed to ensure a steady issue of recruits to John Brown's Virginia campaign. Thomas Cary became its chairman, its corresponding secretary was I.D. Shadd, its secretary James M. Bell, and William Lambert the treasurer. Kagi received an important letter from James M. Bell in Chatham regarding the Canadian recruits: "Dear Sir—Yours came to hand last night. One hand left here last night, and will be found an efficient hand.

Richardson is anxious to be at work as a missionary to bring sinners to repentance. He will start in a few days. Another will follow immediately after, if not with him. More laborers may be looked for shortly. 'Slow but sure.' Alexander has received yours, so you see all communications have come to hand, so far. Alexander is not coming up to the work as agreed. I fear he will be found unreliable in the end. Dull times affect missionary matters here more than anything else, however, a few laborers may be looked for as certain. I would like to hear your congregation numbering more than '15 and 2' to commence a good revival; still our few will be adding strength to the good work."[2]

The "hand" referred to was Osborne Anderson, who arrived in Chambersburg on the 11 o'clock train the morning of September 16. He had been sent under the auspices of the *Provincial Freeman*, whose editor, I.D. Shadd, felt it obligatory that his publication be represented. Lots had been drawn, the distinction falling to Anderson. Anderson was the only member of Brown's party to write a firsthand account—*A Voice from Harper's Ferry*, which he had undertaken with the assistance of Mary Shadd Cary—and remarked that on his arrival he was "surprised" to find that all but a small part of the arms had been removed from Chambersburg to the Kennedy farm. This would indicate that a date to begin operations had been selected. That date was October 25, which was subsequently advanced to October 16.

A letter posted in Boston from Lewis Hayden reached Kagi several days later: "My dear sir—I received your very kind letter, and would state that I have sent a note to Harriet [Tubman] requesting her to come to Boston, saying to her in the note that she must come right on, which I think she will do, and when she does come I think we will find some way to send her on. I have seen our friend at Concord; he is a true man. I have not yet said anything to any body except him. I do not think it is wise for me to do so. I shall, therefore, when Harriet comes send for our Concord friend, who will attend to the matter. Have you all the hands you wish? Write soon. / Yours, L.H."[3] Anderson wrote of the failure of the action that "Captain Brown was not seconded from another quarter as he expected at the time of the action, but could the fears of the neighbors have been allayed for a few days, the disappointment in that respect would not have had much weight." Hinton commented, "It is not of much moment to speculate as to the disappointment Anderson refers to, but it seems most probable in the reference is made both to the failure to make connection with the Canadian colored recruits, who had been expected, and to the disinclination to participate in the Harper's Ferry movement, as there is some evidence that other colored men made their possible activity contingent on that of their leading orator and statesman."[4]

William A. Boyle, a physician from Chambersburg, informed Virginia's governor Wise in a letter dated October 21, 1859, that "a portion of our Negroes knew of it and were expected to join in it."[5] Richard Hinton wrote that, in addition to these, other Black men who tilled small plots of land and worked "round" and could be depended upon knew about the plan. Osborne Anderson in conversation on meeting Hinton at Washington, D.C., in 1870, "estimated that there were at least one hundred and fifty actively informed slaves."[6]

On September 8, back in West Andover, John Jr. sent the following to Kagi: "I yesterday received yours of September 2, and I not only hasten to reply, but to lay its contents before those who are interested. . . . Through those associations which I formed in Canada, I am able to reach each individual member at the shortest notice by letter. . . . I hope we shall be able to get on in season some of those old miners of whom I wrote you. Shall strain every nerve to accomplish this." Hinton wrote: "John's letters are full of information, but all of them indicate delay on the part of the small number relied upon. He was in Detroit, conferring with DeBaptiste, and at Sandusky and Cleveland, urging others to work and assist."[7]

Quoting John Jr.'s enumeration in his letter to Kagi of the reasons for delay on the part of some of those expected, Hinton adds these details: Robinson Alexander "Thinks he can now close out by 1st November, and in the meantime to prove his devotion will furnish means to help on two or three himself." Richard Richardson was "away harvesting"; George J. Reynolds in Sandusky, Ohio, "had a job, which he cannot leave until finished."[8] On August 22, Kagi received the following from James H. Harris: "I wrote you immediately on receipt of your last letter; then went up to Oberlin to see Leary. I saw Smith, Davis, and Mitchell; they all promised, and that was all. Leary wants to provide for his family; Mitchell to lay his crops by; and all make such excuses, until I am disgusted with myself and the whole negro set. God dam em! . . . Charlie Langston says 'it is too bad,' but what he will do if anything, I don't know."[9]

In his correspondence with John Henri Kagi it is evident one of the persons John Jr. had sought out in Canada was William Parker, of the Christiana fugitive slave resistance. In a letter dated August 27,

1859, revealing his meeting with Parker, John Jr. wrote, "At 'B—n' I found the man, the leading spirit in that 'affair,' which you, Henrie, referred to. On Thursday night last, I went with him on foot 12 miles; much of the way through new paths, and sought out in 'the bush' some of the choicest. Had a meeting after 1 o'clock at night at his home. . . . After viewing him in all points which I am capable of, I have to say that I think him worth in our market as much as two or three hundred average men, and even at this rate I should rate him too low. For physical capacity, for practical judgment, for courage and moral tone, for energy and force of will, for experience that would not only enable him to meet difficulty, but give confidence to overcome it, I should have to go a long way to find his equal, and in my judgment, [he] would be a cheap acquisition at almost any price. I shall individually make a strenuous effort to raise the means to send him on."[10]

On September 14 Sanborn wrote to Thomas Wentworth Higginson that Tubman was "to be sent forward soon," but said later that she had still not been heard from. Lewis Hayden had been raising money and recruits, one of whom was to be on hand. In his article published in the *Atlantic Monthly* of December 1875, titled "The Virginia Campaign of John Brown," Franklin Sanborn wrote, "Mr. Hayden entered warmly into the work, and undertook to enlist a few colored men in Massachusetts. . . . According to his recollection he did enlist six such recruits."

Du Bois writes in his *John Brown* of Tubman having "wild, half-mystic ways with dreams, rhapsodies and trances."[11] She laid great stress on these nocturnal visitations, and just before meeting Brown in Canada had a recurring dream in which she saw the head of a snake rising among rocks and bushes in a rugged country. As the serpent's head rose it became the head of an old man with a long white beard gazing at her "wishful like," she related in Sarah Bradford's *Harriet, the Moses of Her People*, looking at her "jes as if he war gwine to speak to me." Then two younger heads rose up beside it, and as she stood wondering at the appearance a crowd of men rushed up to beat down the younger heads, and then the head of the old man who had continued looking at her. As the dream repeated over several nights, she could not guess at its meaning until Brown appeared in St. Catharines, and it was only when the news of the raid at Harper's Ferry broke that she knew that the two other heads she had seen were those of two of his sons Oliver and Watson.

With Harriet Tubman's whereabouts still unknown, and Douglass's refusal to take a direct hand, a crucial sector from which manpower was expected—New York and Pennsylvania—was unrepresented. To redress this, a meeting of select persons was arranged during the third week of September at an undisclosed location; a meeting which Anne Brown would refer to in Hinton's book as constituting the "missing link" in her father's movements. Although this meeting has escaped notice in the historical record, a likely site was a village about twelve miles east of Chambersburg called Mont Alto, on the western slope of South Mountain. This conjecture can be based upon Brown's connections there; he reportedly was a worshiper in Mont Alto at the Emmanuel Chapel, where he set up "Sunday school classes for Negro children," and is supposed to have contracted some work in an iron mill near there for the South Mountain Railroad. One or more buildings in or near the village may have been at his disposal, local historians have determined.

At a designated time, Osborne Anderson indicates, some unspecified "friend" was sent down to the Kennedy farm to accompany Shields Green to the mysterious location, "whereupon a meeting of Capt. Brown, Kagi and other distinguished persons, convened for consultation." Who were these men, and how many were attending? Anderson represents them as "distinguished," opening the likelihood that some were known leaders, possibly from Philadelphia, with others probably coming from Chambersburg, and it can be wondered, other locales in central Pennsylvania such as Mercersburg, where Brown is known to have had contacts in an African American community tracing back to the eighteenth century.

This meeting clearly was crucial to the maturation of Brown's plans, and although its impact on what ultimately transpired has never been weighted, it was undoubtedly great. That Green was attending led John Jr. and Hinton in later years to speculate that he was acting as a "representative" for Douglass. But there was no indication of this from Douglass. In the letter summoning Douglass to the meeting signed by a number of "colored men," he only mentioned it as an aside—"I never knew how they came to send it, but it now seems to have been prompted by Kagi who was with Brown when I told him I would not go to Harper's Ferry." That letter, addressed to Douglass and posted from Philadelphia, is found in Sanborn's *Life and Letters of John Brown* and in Douglass's *Life and Times*, while in both volumes the signatories have been omitted—Douglass only remarked that he received the summons "signed by a number of colored men." Two of the many visitors to Brown after his capture and confinement in Charlestown were Judge Russell and his wife, who came from Boston. Interviewing Mrs. Russell in later years, Katherine Mayo, a researcher for Oswald Garrison Villard, wrote that she said, "To my husband he [Brown] said but little of the raid, yet in that little it was evident that something had gone very wrong—that something had been done that he had expressly forbidden, or which was against his will. He had no fondness for Fred Douglass. Once I heard him say to my husband, of some defeated plan, some great opportunity lost, 'That we owe to the famous Mr. Frederick Douglass!' and he shut his mouth in a way he had when he thought no good."[12]

The last indication of Brown's attitude regarding Douglass came from Alexander Boteler, a member of Congress from the district that included Harper's Ferry, who was among those who interviewed Brown after his capture. Boteler had the opportunity to look at some of Brown's correspondence and papers and saw a page on which Brown had written two columns of names under the headings, "reliable" and "unreliable." Frederick Douglass headed the latter column.

With issues of importance remaining, Brown and Kagi journeyed to Philadelphia on October 6 where they would remain for three days. Du Bois remarked in *John Brown*, "[Thomas] Dorsey the caterer with whom he stayed, at 1221 Locust Street is said to have given him $300." When they returned to the Kennedy farm, a meeting of those present was called at which Brown acquainted all with what had transpired in Philadelphia. Anderson indicates the purposes touched upon, their significance, and the deep pathos felt by all as during his recital Brown wept. Anderson wrote: "How affected by, and affecting the main features of the enterprise, we at the farm knew well after their return, as the old Captain, in the fullness of his overflowing, saddened heart, detailed point after point of interest. God bless the old veteran, who could and did chase a thousand in life, and defied more than ten thousand by the moral solemnity of his death."[13]

Kagi expected to maintain correspondence so far as possible with three persons. One was John Brown Jr., as the organization's general agent in the North; the others were Charles A. Dana of the *Tribune* and William A. Phillips of Lawrence, Kansas. Earlier that week Lewis Sheridan Leary and his nephew John Copeland, whom Kagi had recruited during the Oberlin-Wellington rescue trials, received word to come forward. "Without tools" of their own, they were helped along by two Oberlin professors, brothers Ralph and Samuel Plumb. They were in Cleveland on October 10 at the home of the Sturtevants, supporters of John Brown, and while there met with Charles Langston and James H. Harris, who would not be coming with them, but did wish them Godspeed. Traveling via Pittsburgh and Harrisburg, Leary and Copeland arrived in Chambersburg on October 12 and stayed in the home of Henry Watson. Salmon Brown asserted "that the reason for his not joining the expedition was his belief that his father would hesitate and delay until he was trapped, precisely as happened, waiting for circumstances to be exactly as he wished them to be."[14] George Stearns had been in consultation with Lewis Hayden. Harriet Tubman had been convalescing at the home of a friend in New Bedford, Massachusetts, but now was feeling well enough to travel. Hayden had written Gerrit Smith requesting and receiving money for her expenses. By October 15 she was in New York City in the company of four recruits headed for Chambersburg.

That same day, Richard Hinton reached Hagerstown to be met with a letter and money instructing him to return to Chambersburg to hire a horse and wagon to carry a quantity of arms still in the town. Hinton arrived too late to effect this and lodged the night with Henry Watson. Later Hinton would speculate that his friend, Kagi, had sent him back to Chambersburg to save his life. Elsewhere men were on the road, George Gill among them. He wrote later, "I had been in correspondence with Kagi and knew the exact time to be on hand and was on my way to the cars when the thrilling news came that the blow had been struck. Of course, I went no further."[15]

Saturday, October 15, was a busy day for all hands at the Kennedy farm. Besides two hundred Sharps rifles and an equal number of revolvers and all the ammunition for these, there were 950 pikes, one small cannon mounted on a swivel, ten kegs of gunpowder, and sabers, bayonets, picks, shovels, axes, and torches. Further supplies included four large tents, blankets and clothing, field glasses, surgical equipment, and sundry other items. The next morning John Brown rose earlier than usual and called his men down for worship. Reading a passage from the Bible applicable to the condition of slaves and the duty of all to assist them, he offered up his prayer for the liberation of the bondsmen. Anderson wrote: "The services were impressive beyond expression. Every man there assembled seemed to respond from the depths of his soul, and throughout the entire day, a deep solemnity pervaded the place."[16]

After breakfast, a roll was called. With a sentinel posted outside the door, the men listened to preparatory remarks to a council, which was to assemble at 10 o'clock, chaired by Osborne Anderson. In the afternoon eleven orders were issued pursuant to the seizure of Harper's Ferry. In the evening Brown gave the men final instructions. "And now, gentlemen, let me impress this one thing upon your minds," Brown said in conclusion. "You all know how dear life is to you, and how dear life is to your friends; and remembering that, consider that the lives of others are as dear to them as yours are to you; do not, therefore, take the life of any one if you can possibly avoid it; but if it is necessary to take life in order to save your own, then make sure work of it."[17]

Biographers and historians of Brown and the war he heralded have written accounts and commentary on what occurred at Harper's Ferry, varying in details as well as in important phases of the action. Eighteen men made the march, thirteen White and five Black. Some had fought for the free-state cause in Kansas; some were carrying arms into battle for the first time; only one, Aaron Stevens, was a professional soldier. Among them, other than their leader, who was nearing sixty, only two had passed thirty years. Each man knew, however, the significance behind their march; a few felt with certainty that they were going to their deaths. But each equally knew they were about to strike a blow that would transform the politics of the nation and lead to ultimate victory that would mean the death of slavery.

On the cold, rainy evening of October 16 between 8 and 9 o'clock, John Brown gave the order for his men to get on their arms and proceed to the ferry. Each man tucked a bowie knife and a revolver in his belt, put on a cartridge belt with forty rounds, and pulled on a heavy woolen gray shawl for protection from the weather and to conceal his armaments. Finally, each man picked up a Sharps rifle. A horse and wagon were brought up loaded with a bundle of pikes, some extra Sharps rifles and ammunition, torches and incendiary devices, crowbars, and a sledgehammer. Brown climbed into the driver's seat. A procession formed with Cook and Tidd leading, while the others fell in at measured intervals two by two behind the wagon. Owen Brown, Barclay Coppoc, and Francis Merriam, the last recruit arriving sent by Lewis Hayden, delegated to guard the remaining arms and equipment until they were called for, stepped forward to take leave of the others.

At half past 10, without being seen by a single person, the cloaked invaders reached the abutment of the Potomac Bridge, where Cook climbed the telegraph pole and cut the wire. Kagi and Stevens proceeded onto the bridge, approaching the watchman at the opposite end, where they detained him. Brown entered the bridge in his wagon followed by the company in double file. Watson Brown and Stewart Taylor took positions assigned them, standing on opposite sides at the entrance to the bridge; the rest of the party proceeded across the nine-hundred-foot span.

BIBLIOGRAPHICAL ESSAY

Timepieces

A MECHANISM HAS CEASED ITS FUNCTIONING. In probability, the device at first needed only slight modification, then would no longer respond even to these promptings. Frustrated and tarnished by time—the thing became an object of aridity; a historical artifact, a representation—still bearing a signature and a date, and therefore becoming in time a passage. The timepiece from Gouldtown suggests the variety of historical pathways are nearly as vast as the world; everything we touch telling us something about our past. And some things even more than a contemporary manuscript or letters.[1]

Shut away for decades in a chest among remainders of a bygone era, the timepiece and its fate serve as a point of departure for a retrospective glance onto certain of our American Mysteries—the strange career of the color line and what that line signifies on a psychological and social plane, as indeed in historiography.

Perhaps there will be some readers, even a number of them, both incapable and unavailing of instruction; as for myself, this material has been a continual source of pleasure—a principle that underlies a historian's passion for stories, and doubtless for fairy tales. I have from the outset suggested that something has been lost to the historical record. A chronicler is therefore compelled to proceed by making prudent selections. My penchant has been to ignore well over one hundred years of commentary in favor of that original trio of journalist/writers publishing in the immediate aftermath of Harper's Ferry, and in the proximate decades following. These after all were the basis of all who were to follow—Redpath, Sanborn, and Hinton—followed by the curious coda of two biographies of John Brown at the beginning of the twentieth century by W. E. B. Du Bois and Oswald Garrison Villard.

After emigrating with his family from Scotland to Michigan in 1849, James Redpath by 19 had found employment with Horace Greeley's New York *Tribune*. Inspired by Frederick Law Olmsted's *The Cotton Kingdom*, appearing in letters published in the *New York Times* between 1856 and 1860, and subsequently in book format in 1861, Redpath's own *The Roving Editor, or Talks with Slaves in the Southern States*, was published in 1859 with a dedication to John Brown, and in support of his theory of a looming Southern-wide slave revolt. Starting in 1854, and extending to two more trips, the last in 1859, Redpath had toured the Southern states by rail, steamboat, and stagecoach, interviewing slaves and publishing his accounts in various abolitionist newspapers, while also publishing a recurring feature article in the *Tribune* called "The Facts of Slavery."[2]

By 1855 Redpath was in the Kansas Territory as a *Tribune* reporter, soon crossing the line between journalism and partisan engagement, becoming prominent in both the free-state political movement and in its paramilitary actions. He became at once a close associate of John Brown, and in 1858 in preparation for his campaign Brown persuaded Redpath to relocate to Boston to assist in recruitment for that campaign. Eluding arrest after Harper's Ferry, Redpath published within weeks of Brown's execution on December 2, 1859, his *Public Life of Captain John Brown*, displaying unabashed sympathy for his protagonist and forthrightly coming out in defense of his deployment of militant armed tactics. This was followed in 1860 by *Echoes of Harper's Ferry*, a compilation of speeches and writings of notables on John Brown and Harper's Ferry.

Franklin Sanborn first met John Brown in 1857 when Brown came to Boston for an interview with the members of the Massachusetts State Kansas Committee. Just two years since graduating from Harvard, Sanborn had established a school in Concord at the behest of Ralph Waldo Emerson. A key member of the so-called "secret six," he eluded arrest after Harper's Ferry and went into exile for a time in Canada. He published his first writing on John Brown, "John

Brown and His Friends," in April 1872 in the *Atlantic Monthly* and in 1885 a biography, *The Life and Letters of John Brown, Liberator of Kansas, and Martyr of Virginia*. *Recollections of Seventy Years* appeared in 1909; Sanborn also publishing biographies of his Concord friends Henry David Thoreau and A. Bronson Alcott.

Richard Hinton must be regarded as in many respects the most important witness among these to the John Brown movement, having displayed a commitment that went beyond Redpath's and insight into matters to which Sanborn was not privy. His contribution during the Civil War and its aftermath was likewise important, both for his activity and as a journalist and author. Serving in the Union Army for three years and four months, when he mustered out in November 1865 he bore the rank of brevet colonel, having commanded Black troops on the Kansas border, and afterward was acting inspector general of the Freedman's Bureau. In 1894, he published *John Brown and His Men; with some account of the roads they traveled to reach Harper's Ferry*. In 1898 there appeared a compilation of Richard Realf's poems edited by Hinton: *Poems of Richard Realf: Poet, Soldier, Workman. With a memoir by Richard J. Hinton*; as Realf remains along with John Henry Kagi, and Hinton himself, among the most cogent of those unusual adherents to Brown's movement.

The present author has also sought counsel in W. E. B. Du Bois's *John Brown*, published in 1909, and in Oswald Garrison Villard's *John Brown, a Biography Fifty Years After*, published in 1910.

Du Bois, as is well known, was from Great Barrington in western Massachusetts, and went on to become a graduate of Fisk University in Nashville, Tennessee, then earned his Ph.D. at Harvard; becoming a professor at Atlanta University, he achieved literary success in 1903 with the publication of *The Souls of Black Folk*. He'd written in the Forethought to his opus, "Herein lie buried many things, which if read with patience and interest may show the strange meaning of being Black. . . . The meaning is not without interest to you, Gentle Reader; for the problem of the Twentieth Century is the problem of the color line." Leaving academia, Du Bois was determined to take his critique into the world, as he together with other Black intellectuals and clergy founded what quickly began to be referred to as the Niagara Movement. Meetings convened originally in Buffalo, New York, but relocated, after accommodations could not be obtained across the border in Canada and the "Falls," where participants discussed the then current state of affairs of "Colored people" oppressed in the

United States with the consolidation of sharecropper tenancy and Jim Crow, with its concordant, the terror of lynch law, after the failure of Reconstruction in the decade following the Civil War.

The inaugural meeting for the movement had been in the summer of 1905, with the next meeting scheduled thirteen months later for a week in August 1906 on the campus of Storer College in Harper's Ferry, West Virginia. Du Bois and the other delegates felt that John Brown's movement represented the first battle of the yet to be concluded struggle, and that the fire-engine house where Brown made his last stand was an appropriate symbol and a shrine of importance to African Americans in their current travails, as the next year's gathering was slated for Boston's Faneuil Hall. With just over fifty delegates, a few of them women, and nearly one hundred participants, that gathering had as its highlight an early morning march around what is now designated John Brown's Fort. With a physician from Brooklyn leading the procession in a light rain who had removed his shoes and socks to walk barefoot as if on holy ground, the delegates formed a single line for their procession around the redbrick structure as they sang "The Battle Hymn of the Republic," intermingled with verses and phrases of the "John Brown Song."

In the afternoon, the Niagraites listened to an address by Henrietta Leary Evans, the sister of Brown's Cleveland recruit Lewis Sheridan Leary and the aunt of John A. Copeland. She was followed by Lewis Douglass, the son of Frederick Douglass, introduced as one who had known John Brown as a child, but who merely stood acknowledging the audience graciously. He was followed by Du Bois, who used the occasion to give a recitation of the history of slavery in America and John Brown's relation thereto. "So much of life must go, not to forward right, but to beat back wrong," he admonished his audience. Brown had made the ultimate sacrifice and so must he and they "sacrifice our work, our money, and our positions in order to beat back the evil of the world."[3] The last speech and most notable, designated "the most stirring single episode of the Niagara Movement," was by Rev. C. Ransom of the Charles Street African Methodist Episcopal Church in Boston. Ransom had pronounced "Thank God for John Brown!" as he'd recently, and in the clear memory of his audience, been subjected to the humiliation of being forcibly ejected from a Pullman car reserved for "whites only." Like the ghost of Hamlet's father, the minister declared, "the spirit of John Brown beckons us to arise and seek the recovery of our rights." The reporter for the

New York *Evening Post* wrote, "Mr. Ransom delivered an oration which one wished that Phillips and Parker and Beecher might have heard." Another of the participants, and a friend of Du Bois, was J. Max Barber, editor of Atlanta's militant newspaper *Voice of the Negro* who reported of that day the following October: "John Brown could not have imagined as he looked through the barred windows of his dungeon that some day such a remarkable tribute would be paid to him on the very ground where he made his gallant stand. But the old Puritan is not one of the vanishing figures of history."[4]

By 1907 Du Bois was planning to follow up his recent literary success with a study of the Nat Turner insurrection in Southampton County, Virginia, in 1831, a year that also notably had seen the inauguration of the modern anti-slavery movement in America and of the William Lloyd Garrison-published and -edited *Liberator*. But Du Bois's publisher would not countenance such, and they quickly mutually agreed that he write a biography of John Brown, as the interest in such by the author had so recently been stimulated. In his *John Brown*, published in 1909, Du Bois wrote in the preface, "this book is at once a record of and a tribute to the man who of all Americans has perhaps come nearest to touching the real souls of black folk." In 1908 in response to a deadly and devastating race riot in Springfield, Illinois, the journalist, labor leader, and neo-abolitionist William English Walling wrote an article published on September 3, 1908, in *The Independent* magazine titled "The Race War in the North," calling for an interracial movement to end the "white" violence directed against "blacks." Soon the National Association for the Advancement of Colored People was being proposed and planning for such ensued, for which Oswald Garrison Villard, editor and publisher of the New York *Evening Post* drafted a "Call."

That call aimed at securing the rights ostensibly established with the ending of the "Civil War," for those designated "colored," in a Du Bois-chosen appellation, of the 13th, 14th, and 15th amendments to the United States Constitution, and to ensure their political and educational equality and for the removal, through democratic processes, of all barriers enforcing racial discrimination. The Niagara Movement thus was seen to have laid the keel for a modern civil rights movement, as it debuted in 1909 with the founding of the "National Association," as the Niagara men and women transferred their allegiance to the new organization.

Villard was from a distinguished and wealthy family. His father Henry was a railroad magnate and the owner of the *Evening Post* and of *The Nation* magazine. His mother was the daughter and favorite child of William Lloyd Garrison. Upon the younger Villard's graduation from Harvard University in 1895, he began working at the *Post* and in time became a long-time publisher at both the paper and of *The Nation*. Villard and Du Bois crucially collaborated in the early years of the NAACP, Du Bois serving as executive director, a title soon changed to director of publicity and research, and editor of the organization's monthly journal *The Crisis*, with Villard sitting on the board and extending his largess to the organization, providing rooms at the *Post* for its offices and an interim salary for its staff while it got established. There would later be growing rancor between the men, leading to an inability to work together; tellingly, as Du Bois published the ongoing tally of "lynchings" against "Negroes" on the cover of *Crisis*, Villard suggested he also publish as their "counterpart" the monthly tally of Black-perpetrated crime. Villard's Brown biography came out a year after Du Bois's.

In a letter dated November 15, 1907, Du Bois answered Villard's query about his approach to the source material for Brown, saying he could offer little guidance as his work was "going to be an interpretation." Uncovering little that historians would regard as new material, Du Bois nevertheless wrote in his *Autobiography* that he regarded it as one of "the best written of my books . . . but one which aroused the unfortunate jealousy of Villard who was writing a biography of Brown." Scholars have long regarded Du Bois's effort as the merely tributary production of these competing biographies, some even calling his book tainted with "hero worship" and "sensationalism." The *Evening Post's* own reviewer found little in it to praise. Believing he had only nettled the "jealousy of Villard," Du Bois wrote a protest to him. Villard remarked to his research assistant, Katherine Mayo, "We have another nasty note from Du Bois in which he says I deliberately ran down his book unjustly to put it out of the way of the arrival of mine."[5]

Villard's own production was received as a landmark presentation of all the most reputable material, with a careful study of sources, while relying particularly on extended interviews with all those surviving who had known Brown—his sons Salmon, Jason, and John Jr., daughters Anne and Ruth, wife Mary, and others of his circle such as Mrs. Mary Stearns; all were interviewed in the field over a period of two years by Mayo. To Anne Brown Adams, Villard had written at the time he intended his writing to be that of an impartial historian, but one who felt a deep concert with abolitionist goals.

In the second chapter Villard asks, "When was it that John Brown . . . first conceived what he calls . . . 'his greatest or principal object' in life—the forcible overthrow of slavery." He hastens to add, "since the object adopted as the needle to guide his destiny eventually resulted in the raising of a nation to its smallest hamlet."[6] When did this first manifest itself in John Brown indeed? In a November 21, 1834, letter to his brother Frederick, then living in Randolph, Pennsylvania, Brown revealed his thinking on a matter that had gone so far as to consider how he could get a "negro boy or youth, and bring him up as we do our own." How could he obtain such, he asked as he revealed he'd also been thinking for years of "some way to get a school a-going here for blacks." "If the young blacks of our country could once become enlightened," he wrote, "it would most assuredly operate on slavery like firing powder confined in rock, and all slaveholders know it well." Villard reveals that Jason Brown recalled an oath-taking when the family resided in Franklin, Ohio, in 1839, when all the three adolescent Brown sons and their mother had vowed "to do all in their power to abolish slavery" before "a colored preacher" named Fayette. This event was also recalled in a detailed letter by John Jr. to Sanborn in December 1890; an event he said that was as perfect "in my memory as any other event in my life."[7] In 1839 the younger Brown was nineteen; his testimony at other times has placed the oath in 1836 and 1837; as Villard would write, "It can, therefore, best be stated as occurring before 1840." Du Bois accordingly underlines the incident in 1839 with "preacher" Fayette.

In 1840 Brown Sr. was contracted to survey lands in western Virginia for Oberlin College, and Villard writes that here the idea of using the Allegheny Mountains for an armed attack on slavery might have gained purchase in his mind. But so far as is known no "contemporary document" substantiates this.

The reader will recall that the pocket watch in the possession for decades of those descendants of the Gouldtown settlement contained along with the snippet of notebook paper bearing the signature *John Brown*, an identically scissored paper bearing the numerals *1839*. This author interprets this as a reference to the twenty-year span—1839-1859—with which the documentary evidence agrees, as does the testimony of John Brown and his family. Villard too agrees on the date, but the process he is tracing in John Brown's thought is not attributable to any extraneous force or cause, as I have done with the *Amistad* in the initial chapter of this work. Villard does bring his reader's attention to Brown's League of Gileadites, formed after the passage of the Fugitive Slave Law, and his residence in Springfield, Massachusetts, and rightly points out that Brown's turn to a more deeply radical critique of America under the baleful influences of slavery came with his deepening engagements personally with Blacks. But in his citation of the document Brown drafted for the Gileadites he omitted the crucial opening sentences—"Nothing so charms the American people as personal bravery. Witness the case of Cinques of everlasting memory...."—a witness Villard does not deem to hear.

In his *Autobiography,* Du Bois wrote, "To a white philanthropist like Villard a Negro was quite naturally expected to be humble and thankful or certainly not assertive and aggressive; this Villard resented." Du Bois also informs his readers that although Villard was reared in an abolitionist family, the woman he married was a Georgian who would never countenance the presence of a Black on equal social terms in their home, and thus Du Bois had never crossed its threshold. Nearly all biographers and historians excepting in this instance Du Bois, then, have been and remain tone-deaf to the whole man. They do not know John Brown; nay—they do not know the *time* of which they speak.

NOTES

A TESTAMENT
1. William Steward and Rev. Theophilus Gould Steward, *Gouldtown: A Very Remarkable Settlement of Ancient Date* (Philadelphia: J. B. Lippincott, 1913), "Fenwick; His Colony."
2. Ibid., 25
3. Ibid., "Gould Traditions," 49.
4. Ibid., 50.
5. Ibid., 54.
6. Ibid., 61.
7. Ibid., 53.
8. Ibid., 8.
9. Ibid., 62.
10. Theophilus Gould Steward—Wikipedia.
11. *Gouldtown*, 63-64.
12. Ibid., 113.
13. Ibid., 65.
14. Ibid., 121.
15. Ibid., 91-93.

CHAPTER 1: "O, THAT I WERE FREE"
1. Language used or partially suggested in Frederic Bancroft, *Slave Trading in the Old South* (New York: Frederick Ungar Publishing, 1967), 339.
2. Herbert Aptheker, *To Be Free: Studies in American Negro History* (New York: International Publishers, 1948), "Slave Guerrilla War."
3. W. E. B. Du Bois, *The Negro* (New York: Henry Holt and Company, 1915), 119.
4. Phrases taken from the narrative of Rev. James W.C. Pennington, *The Fugitive Blacksmith* (London: C. Gilpin, 1849).
5. Few are the records of Underground Railroad activity in any given locale, but there has been a proliferation in on-line sites dedicated to its vanishing traces, such as the Cumberland County Historical Society. The flavor and accuracy of the above comes from my interviews with Becky Lively, elsewhere cited in this text.
6. *The Century Magazine*, November 1881, 124-131.

7. Graham R. G. Hodges, *David Ruggles: A Radical Abolitionist and the Underground Railroad in New York City* (Chapel Hill: University of North Carolina Press, 2012).
8. Frederick Douglass, *The Life and Times of Frederick Douglass* (New York: Crowell-Collier, 1962), 205.
9. Frederick May Holland, *Frederick Douglass* (New York: Funk and Wagnalls, 1895), 363.
10. W. E. B. Du Bois, *John Brown* (Philadelphia: George W. Jacobs, 1909), 239.
11. Rowan University Libraries, African American Contributions to the History of New Jersey, on-line.
12. Merton L. Dillon, *The Abolitionists: The Growth of a Dissenting Minority* (New York: W. W. Norton & Co., 1979).
13. Du Bois, *John Brown*, 241.
14. Earl Conrad, *Harriet Tubman* (Washington, DC: Associated Publishers, 1943).
15. Horatio T. Strother, *The Underground Railroad in Connecticut* (Middletown, CT: Wesleyan University Press, 1970).
16. Cooper H. Wingert, *Slavery & the Underground Railroad in South Central Pennsylvania* (Cheltenham, UK: History Press, 2016).
17. Wilbur H. Siebert, *The Underground Railroad from Slavery to Freedom* (New York: Macmillan Company, 1898).
18. Figures cited by New Jersey City University, "The Underground Railroad in Jersey City."
19. Giles R. Wright, *Afro-Americans in New Jersey* (Trenton, NJ: Historical Commission, 1988), 29.
20. Ibid., 14.

CHAPTER TWO: "IN SOLEMN AND SECRET COMPACT"

1. Marker Quest on-line source, "Underground Railroad, Harrisburg, Dauphin County," see attachment, "Conductors and Stations on the Underground Railroad."
2. Du Bois, *John Brown*, 92.
3. James Redpath, *The Public Life of Captain John Brown* (London: Thickbroom and Stapleton, 1860), 46.
4. Letter to his brother, Frederick, of Hudson, Ohio, November 21, 1834; see Louis Ruchames, ed. *John Brown: The Making of a Revolutionary* (New York: Grosset & Dunlap, 1969), 51-52.
5. Richard J. Hinton in Redpath, *Public Life of Captain John Brown*, 199-206.
6. Du Bois, *John Brown*, 110.
7. *Life and Times of Frederick Douglass*, 274.
8. Philip S. Foner, ed., *The Life and Writings of Frederick Douglass* (New York: International Publishers, 1952), vol. 2, 86.
9. Ruchames, *John Brown*, Douglass's speech at Storer College, 278-299.
10. *Life and Times of Frederick Douglass*, 271-275.
11. Ruchames, *John Brown*, "Words of Advice," 84-86.

CHAPTER THREE: "I WANT MY PROPERTY, AND I WILL HAVE IT!"

1. Edward W. Emerson and Waldo E. Forbes, eds., *Journals of Ralph Waldo Emerson* (New York: Hougton Mifflin, 1911), vii, 206.
2. *Life and Times of Frederick Douglass*, 276.
3. James M. McPherson, *Battle Cry of Freedom: The Civil War Era* (New York: Oxford University Press, 1988), 66.

4. Frederick Douglass, *North Star*, "Weekly Reviews of Congress," March 15, 1850.
5. Charles M. Wiltse, *John C. Calhoun: Sectionalist, 1840-1850* (Indianapolis, IN: Bobbs-Merrill, 1951), 465.
6. Foner, ed., *The Life and Writings of Frederick Douglass*, vol. 2, 52, footnote 4.
7. Speech in Rev. J.W. Loguen, *As a Slave and as a Freeman: A Narrative of Real Life* (Syracuse, NY: J. G. K. Truair, 1859).
8. John Weiss, *Life and Correspondence of Theodore Parker* (London: Longman, Green, 1863), vol. 1, 102.
9. Dillon, *The Abolitionists*, 179.
10. Philip S. Foner, ed., *The Voice of Black America: Major Speeches by Negroes in the United States, 1797–1971* (New York: Simon & Schuster, 1972), vol. 1, 124-126.
11. *Douglass' Monthly*, February 26, 1852.
12. Stanley W. Campbell, *The Slave Catchers: Enforcement of the Fugitive Slave Law, 1850–1860* (Chapel Hill: University of North Carolina Press, 1970), Appendix.
13. Thomas Wentworth Higginson, *Cheerful Yesterdays* (Boston: Houghton Mifflin, 1898), 136.
14. Campbell, *The Slave Catchers*, 149.
15. Ibid.
16. Dillon, *The Abolitionists*, 182.
17. *Life and Times of Frederick Douglass*, 279.
18. Campbell, *The Slave Catchers*, 62.
19. Higginson, *Cheerful Yesterdays*, 139-140.
20. Campbell, *The Slave Catchers*, 99-100.
21. Fergus M. Bordewich, *Bound for Canaan: The Epic Story of the Underground Railroad, America's First Civil Rights Movement* (New York: HarperCollins/Amistad, 2005), 333.
22. Campbell, *The Slave Catchers*, Appendix.
23. Jonathan Katz, *Resistance at Christiana: The Fugitive Slave Rebellion, Christiana, Pennsylvania, September 11, 1851* (New York: Thomas Y. Crowell, 1974), "Prelude," 81-91.
24. William Parker, "The Freedman's Story," *Atlantic Monthly*, Feb. 1866.
25. Katz, *Resistance at Christiana*, 100.
26. Ibid., "Escape," 47-261.
27. *Life and Times of Frederick Douglass*, 281-282.
28. Katz, *Resistance at Christiana*, "Reaction," 120-123.
29. William Still, *Underground Rail Road Records* (Philadelphia: William Still, 1872), 349.
30. Katz, *Resistance at Christiana*, 125.
31. Ibid., 157.
32. Ibid.
33. Syracuse University Libraries, online exhibit.
34. Brown to Douglass, *Frederick Douglass' Paper*, August 18, 1853.
35. Samuel Ringgold Ward, *Autobiography of a Fugitive Negro* (London: John Snow, 1855), 116-117.
36. *Life and Times of Frederick Douglass*, 279.
37. Ruchames, ed., *John Brown*, 92-93.
38. Chuck Leddy, "The Fugitive Slave Case of Anthony Burns," *Civil War Times*, May 2007.
39. Herbert Aptheker, *A Documentary History of the Negro People* (New York: Citadel, 1973), vol. 1, 369.
40. Redpath, *Public Life of Captain John Brown*, 58.

41. Higginson, *Cheerful Yesterdays*, 149-150.
42. Speech reported in the *Liberator*, June 2, 1854.
43. Higginson, *Cheerful Yesterdays*, 158.
44. Campbell, *The Slave Catchers*, 129-130.
45. Quoted in USHistory.org—"The origins of the Republican Party."

CHAPTER FOUR: "WE NEED ARMS MORE THAN WE DO BREAD"

1. Franklin B. Sanborn, *The Life and Letters of John Brown: Liberator of Kansas, and Martyr of Virginia* (Boston: Roberts Brothers, 1891), 176.
2. Ruchames, ed., *John Brown*, 94.
3. Du Bois, *John Brown*, 110-111.
4. Sanborn, *Life and Letters of John Brown*, 97.
5. Statement of Ruth Brown, ibid., 100-101.
6. Ibid., 189.
7. Ruchames, ed., *John Brown*, 94-95.
8. *Frederick Douglass' Paper*, July 27, 1855.
9. Redpath, *Public Life of Captain John Brown*, 81.
10. Sanborn, *Life and Letters of John Brown*, 193-194.
11. Ibid., 165.
12. Jay Monaghan, *Civil War on the Western Border, 1854–1865* (New York: Bonanza, 1955), 204.
13. Sanborn, *Life and Letters of John Brown*, 204.
14. Ibid., 166.
15. Ibid., 217-221.
16. Richard J. Hinton, *John Brown and His Men With Some Account of the Roads They Traveled to Reach Harper's Ferry* (New York: Funk & Wagnalls, 1894), 45.
17. Sanborn, *Life and Letters of John Brown*, 220.
18. Redpath, *Public Life of Captain John Brown*, 90.
19. Ruchames, ed., *John Brown*, 100-101.
20. Hinton, *John Brown and His Men*, 71.
21. Monaghan, *Civil War on the Western Border*, 52-59
22. Hinton, *John Brown and His Men*, 88.
23. Ibid., 68.
24. Boyd B. Stutler Collection, West Virginia State Archives, on-line exhibit.
25. Sanborn, *Life and Letters of John Brown*, 260.
26. Monaghan, *Civil War on the Western Border*, 58.
27. Hinton, *John Brown and His Men*; account of James Hanway, 695.
28. August M. Bondi, *Transactions of the Kansas State Historical Society* (Kansas Historical Collections, 1904), vol. 8, 279.
29. Ruchames, ed., *John Brown*, Salmon Brown, 198-204.
30. Sanborn, *Life and Letters of John Brown*, 249.
31. Ibid., 273.
32. Ibid., 262.
33. Ibid., 248.
34. Bondi, *Transactions of the Kansas State Historical Society*, vol. 8, 285.
35. Ruchames, ed., *John Brown*, 102-105.
36. William Phillips, *The Conquest of Kansas by Missouri and Her Allies* (Boston: Phillips, Sampson and Company, 1856).
37. Sanborn, *Life and Letters of John Brown*, 236-241.

38. Jules Ables, *Man on Fire: John Brown and the Cause of Liberty* (New York: Macmillan, 1971), 92.
39. Redpath, *Public Life of Captain John Brown*, 139.
40. USHistory.org, Democratic National Convention in 1856, the nomination of James Buchanan.
41. Redpath, *Public Life of Captain John Brown*, 112-114.
42. Sanborn, *Life and Letters of John Brown*, 289.
43. Bondi, *Transactions of the Kansas State Historical Society*, vol. 8, 282-284.
44. Sanborn, *Life and Letters of John Brown*, 390.
45. Abels, *Man on Fire*, 94.
46. Ruchames, ed., *John Brown*, "Three interviews with John Brown," 216-226.
47. Monaghan, *Civil War on the Western Border*, 68.
48. Ibid.
49. Ibid.
50. Ibid.
51. *Frederick Douglass' Paper*, "The Republican Party—Our Position," Dec. 1855; "What is My Duty as an Anti-Slavery Voter?," April 1856.
52. Letter to Gerrit Smith, May 23, 1856, in Foner, ed., *The Life and Writings of Frederick Douglass*, vol. 2, 395-396.
53. *Frederick Douglass' Paper*, August 1856, " Frémont and Dayton."
54. Letter to Gerrit Smith, Sept. 6, 1856, in Foner, ed., *The Life and Writings of Frederick Douglass*, vol. 2, 395-396.
55. Higginson, *Cheerful Yesterdays*, 198.
56. Monaghan, *Civil War on the Western Border*, 69-70.
57. Hinton, *John Brown and His Men*, 203.
58. Monaghan, *Civil War on the Western Border*, 73.
59. Redpath, *Public Life of Captain Brown*, 145.
60. Hinton, *John Brown and His Men*, 55.
61. Ibid., 71.
62. Ibid., 53.
63. On-line source at Bleeding Kansas 1856-1857, latinamericanstudies.org.
64. Sanborn, *Life and Letters of John Brown*, 309.
65. Ibid., 311.
66. George W. Martin, ed., *Transactions of the Kansas State Historical Society* (Topeka, 1900), vol. 6, Samuel Walker.
67. J. W. Winkley, *John Brown the Hero: Personal Reminiscences* (Boston: James H. West Company, 1905), 79.
68. Monaghan, *Civil War on the Western Border*, 78.
69. Ibid., 79.
70. Ables, *Man on Fire*, 99.
71. Bridgman, *With John Brown in Kansas*, 7.
72. Martin, ed. *Transactions of the Kansas State Historical Society*, Governor Geary, 739.
73. Redpath, *Public Life of Captain John Brown*, 164-165.
74. Ibid.
75. Monaghan, *Civil War on the Western Border*, 88.
76. Ibid.
77. Ables, *Man on Fire*, 107.
78. Monaghan, *Civil War on the Western Border*, 88.

79. Ables, *Man on Fire*, 110.
80. Thomas Wentworth Higginson, *A Ride Through Kanzas* (n.p., 1856), 14.

CHAPTER FIVE: "'GIVE THEM JESSIE,' AND FRÉMONT BESIDES"

1. Sanborn, *Life and Letters of John Brown*, 342.
2. *Life and Times of Frederick Douglass*, 302; Foner, ed., *Life and Writings of Frederick Douglass*, vol. 2, 439.
3. Frank Preston Stearns, *The Life and Public Services of George Luther Stearns* (Philadelphia: J. B. Lippincott Company, 1907), 198.
4. Sanborn, *Life and Letters of John Brown*, 496.
5. Hinton, *John Brown and His Men*, reminiscences of Mrs. Mary Stearns, 719-727.
6. Stearns, *Life and Public Service of George Luther Stearns*, 137.
7. Frederick Douglass, speech before the American Anti-slavery Society, May 11, 1857, "The Dred Scott Decision," in Foner, ed., *Life and Writings of Frederick Douglass*, vol. 2, 407-424.
8. Ibid.
9. Sanborn, *Life and Letters of John Brown*, reminiscences of Dr. Wayland, 381.
10. Sanborn, *Life and Letters of John Brown*, letter dated April 15, 1857.
11. Ruchames, ed., *John Brown*, 111.
12. Sanborn, *Life and Letters of John Brown*, 508-511.
13. Ibid.
14. Stearns, *Life and Public Services of George Luther Stearns*, 137.
15. Brown's meeting with Thoreau is narrated in Franklin B. Sanborn, *Recollections of Seventy Years* (Boston: Gorham Press, 1909).
16. Hinton, *John Brown and His Men*, 123.
17. Stearns, *Life and Public Services of George Luther Stearns*, 136.
18. Ibid.
19. Sanborn, *Life and Letters of John Brown*, 114-115.
20. Hinton, *John Brown and His Men*, 125.
21. Sanborn, *Life and Letters of John Brown*, 390.
22. Ibid., 414.
23. Hinton, *John Brown and His Men*, 149-150.
24. Richard Watch and Jonathan Fanton, eds., *John Brown* (Englewood Cliffs, NJ: Prentice-Hall, 1973), 50.
25. N.Y. *Herald*, Oct. 29, 1859, letter of Forbes to Dr. Howe, May 14, 1858.
26. Hinton, *John Brown and His Men*, 147.
27. Ibid.
28. Ables, *Man on Fire*, 146-147.
29. Sanborn, *Life and Letters of John Brown*, letter to Augustus Wattles, 393.
30. Ables, *Man on Fire*, letter of Holmes, 149.
31. Monaghan, *Civil War on the Western Border*, chapter 8, "Buchanan Tries His Hand."
32. Ibid.
33. Ibid.
34. Stearns, *Life and Public Services of George Luther Stearns*, 160.
35. Ibid., 172.
36. Sanborn, *Life and Letters of John Brown*, 401-402, correspondence of Brown and Lane.
37. Ibid., 399.
38. Stearns, *Life and Public Services of George Luther Stearns*, 141.

39. Monaghan, *Civil War on the Western Border*, chapter 8, "Buchanan Tries His Hand."
40. Sanborn, *Life and Letters of John Brown*.
41. McPherson, *Battle Cry of Freedom*, 168.
42. Hinton, *John Brown and His Men*, "The Confession of John E. Cook."
43. Stearns, *Life and Public Services of George Luther Stearns*, 142.
44. Michael A. Ross, *Justice of Shattered Dreams: Samuel Freeman Miller and the Supreme Court during the Civil War Era* (Baton Rouge: Louisiana State University Press, 2003), 41.
45. Hinton, *John Brown and His Men*, "The Confession of John E. Cook."
46. Ibid.
47. Ables, *Man on Fire*, 162, the recollection of Owen Brown.
48. Irving B. Richman, *John Brown Among the Quakers, and Other Sketches* (Des Moines: Historical Department of Iowa, 1894), 58.
49. Monaghan, *Civil War on the Western Border*, 99.
50. Sanborn, *Life and Letters of John Brown*, 425.
51. Hinton, *John Brown and His Men*, 156.
52. Ibid., 499.
53. Helen Delay, "Richard Realf, Poet and Soldier," *Home Monthly*, May 1899.
54. Redpath, *Public Life of Captain John Brown*, 384.
55. *Life and Times of Frederick Douglass*, 317.

CHAPTER SIX: "THERE IS THE MOST ABUNDANT MATERIAL . . ."

1. Richman, *John Brown among the Quakers*, 17-18.
2. *Life and Times of Frederick Douglass*, 273-274.
3. Hinton, *John Brown and His Men*, 126.
4. *Life and Times of Frederick Douglass*, 315.
5. Du Bois, *John Brown*, 247.
6. Benjamin Quarles, *Frederick Douglass* (Washington, DC: Associated Publishers, 1948), 40.
7. Ibid., 39.
8. Sanborn, *Life and Letters of John Brown*, 434-435.
9. Watch and Fanton, eds., *John Brown*, 35.
10. Ibid., 36.
11. Sanborn, *Life and Letters of John Brown*, 434-435.
12. Ibid., 37.
13. Hinton, *John Brown and His Men*, 672-675.
14. Senate Select Committee Report on the Harper's Ferry Invasion, 1860, Testimony of Richard Realf.
15. *Life and Times of Frederick Douglass*, 316.
16. Ibid.
17. Ibid.
18. Sanborn, *Life and Letters of John Brown*, 437.
19. Ibid., 438-440.
20. Ibid.
21. Ibid.
22. Hinton, *John Brown and His Men*, 168.
23. Ables, *Man on Fire*, 176.
24. Sanborn, *Life and Letters of John Brown*, 444-445.
25. Ibid., 450.
26. Frederick Douglass, "The Meaning of the 4th of July to the Negro," July 5, 1852.

27. Frederick Douglass, "The Present Condition and Future Prospects of the Negro People."
28. Ibid., 416.
29. Sanborn, *Life and Letters of John Brown*, 443.
30. Ibid.
31. Sanborn, *Life and Letters of John Brown*, 448.
32. Ables, *Man on Fire*, 178.
33. Ibid., 146-147.
34. Du Bois, *John Brown*, 248.
35. Benjamin Quarles, *Allies for Freedom: Blacks and John Brown* (New York: Oxford University Press, 1974), 41.
36. Earl Ofari Hutchinson, *Let Your Motto Be Resistance: The Life and Thought of Henry Highland Garnet* (Boston; Beacon Press, 1972), 106
37. Hinton, *John Brown and His Men*, 170.
38. Ibid., 165.
39. Dorothy Sterling, *The Making of an Afro-American: Martin Robison Delany, 1812–1885* (New York: Doubleday, 1971), 226-227.
40. Testimony of Richard Realf, Reports of Senate Committees, 36th Congress, 1st Session, No. 278.
41. Ruchames, ed., *John Brown*, letter dated January 30, 1858.
42. Quarles, *Allies for Freedom*, 43.
43. Du Bois, *John Brown*, 244.
44. Sanborn, *Life and Letters of John Brown*, 452.
45. Conrad, *Harriet Tubman*, 113.
46. James Cleland Hamilton, *John Brown in Canada, a Monograph* (n.p. 1894), reminiscences of J.M. Jones, 14-15.
47. Frank A. Rollin, *Life and Public Services of Martin R. Delany* (Boston: Lea and Shepard, 1883), 85-90.
48. Richman, *John Brown Among the Quakers*.
49. Loguen, *As a Slave and as a Freeman*, see preface for letter.
50. Hamilton, *John Brown in Canada*, 14.
51. Ibid.
52. Reports of Senate Committees, 36th Congress, 1st Session, No. 278, Testimony of Richard Realf.
53. Quarles, *Allies for Freedom*, 46.
54. Hamilton, *John Brown in Canada*, 16.
55. Reports of Senate Committees, 36th Congress, 1st Session, No. 278, Testimony of Richard Realf.
56. Hinton, *John Brown and His Men*, 180.
57. Rollin, *Life and Public Services of Martin R. Delany*, 85-90.
58. Sanborn, *Life and Letters of John Brown*, 455.
59. Ibid., 448-461.
60. Ables, *Man on Fire*, 197.
61. Sanborn, *Life and Letters of John Brown*, 463-464.
62. Hinton, *John Brown and His Men*, reminiscences of George Gill, 732-733.
63. Ibid., 173.
64. James Redpath, *The Roving Editor: or, Talks with Slaves in the Southern States* (New York: A. B. Burdick, 1859), "A Southern Underground Telegraph," 284-287.
65. Ables, *Man on Fire*, 192.

CHAPTER SEVEN: "I CONSIDER IT MY DUTY TO DRAW THE SCENE ..."

1. Redpath, *Public Life of Captain John Brown*, 200.
2. Ables, *Man on Fire*, 203.
3. Redpath, *Public Life of Captain John Brown*, 199-206.
4. Ables, *Man on Fire*, 209-210.
5. Ibid.
6. Redpath, *Public Life of Captain John Brown*, 199-206.
7. Ibid., 203.
8. Hinton, *John Brown and His Men*, 672-675.
9. Ibid.
10. Richard Realf, *Poems by Richard Realf, with a Memoir by Richard J. Hinton* (New York: Funk & Wagnalls, 1898), xlii.
11. Hinton, *John Brown and His Men*, George B. Gill, 218.
12. Ables, *Man on Fire*, 222.
13. Ibid., 226.
14. Mortimer, "The Kansas War, the Disturbance in Southern Kansas—Brown and Montgomery—Facts of the Case," *New York Times*, January 28, 1859.
15. Ables, *Man on Fire*, 78.
16. For the interviews see appendix in Hinton, *John Brown and His Men*; also in Ruchames, ed., *John Brown*, "Three Interviews with Old Brown."
17. Ibid.
18. Hamilton, *John Brown in Canada*, 4-5.
19. Ables, *Man on Fire*, 228.
20. Ibid.
21. Sanborn, *Life and Letters of John Brown*, 491.
22. Quarles, *Allies for Freedom*, 76.
23. Abels, *Man on Fire*, 234-235.

CHAPTER EIGHT: "HARPER'S FERRY IS THE BEST NEWS ..."

1. Quarles, *Frederick Douglass*, 176.
2. *Life and Times of Frederick Douglass*, 317.
3. "A Plan of Anti-Slavery Action," *Frederick Douglass' Paper*, July 8, 1859, in Foner, ed., *The Life and Writings of Frederick Douglass*, vol. 5, 453-454.
4. Brown, letter dated June 1, 1859, in Conrad, *Harriet Tubman*, 122; also Sanborn, *Life and Letters of John Brown*.
5. Sanborn, *Life and Letters of John Brown*, diary of A. Brownson Alcott, 504-505.
6. Oswald G. Villard, *John Brown, 1800-1859, A Biography Fifty Years After* (Boston: Houghton Mifflin, 1910), 396.
7. Sanborn, *Life and Letters of John Brown*.
8. Ables, *Man on Fire*, 239-240.
9. Sanborn, *Life and Letters of John Brown*.
10. Mary Thaher Higginson, ed., *Letters and Journals of Thomas Wentworth Higginson, 1846-1906* (Boston: Houghton Mifflin, 1921).
11. Oscar Sherwin, *Prophet of Liberty: The Life and Times of Wendell Phillips* (Bookman Associates, 1958), 239-240.
12. This version of the story cited by the author is apocryphal; these words were spoken to James Redpath in a similar spirit by Brown in another setting.
13. Ables, *Man on Fire*, 240.

14. Sanborn, *Life and Letters of John Brown*, John Brown to "Wife and Children All," dated July 21, 1859.
15. Ables, *Man on Fire*, 255.
16. Ibid.
17. Sanborn, *Life and Letters of John Brown*, 450-451.
18. Sanborn, *Life and Letters of John Brown*, John Brown Jr. to Kagi, August 11, 1859, 452-453.
19. Ibid.
20. Ibid.
21. Ibid.
22. Ibid.
23. *Life and Times of Frederick Douglass*, 318.
24. Douglass, John Brown, in Ruchames, ed., *John Brown*, 296.
25. Villard, *John Brown*, Salmon Brown interview by Katherine Mayo.
26. Reports of Senate Committees, 36th Congress, 1st Session, No. 278, Testimony of Richard Realf.
27. Louis Filler, ed., *Wendell Phillips on Civil Rights and Freedom* (New York: Hill and Wang, 1965), "The Argument for Disunion."
28. Ibid.
29. Karl Marx and Friedrich Engels, "The Civil War in the United States," *Die Presse*, November 7, 1861.
30. Ables, *Man on Fire*, 242.
31. Ralph Waldo Emerson, "American Civilization," lecture delivered at the Smithsonian Institution, January 31, 1862.
32. Sanborn, *Life and Letters of John Brown*, 248.
33. Ruchames, ed., *John Brown*, 294; Douglass's speech at Storer College in 1881.
34. *Life and Times of Frederick Douglass*, 319.
35. Ruchames, ed. *John Brown*, 281; Douglass's speech at Storer College.
36. Ibid., 283.
37. *Life and Times of Frederick Douglass*, 275.
38. Letter to James Redpath, June 29, 1860, in Foner, ed., *Life and Writings of Frederick Douglass*, vol. 2, 487.
39. Letter to William Still, July 2, 1860, ibid., 488.
40. Frederick Douglass, "The Progress of Slavery," *Douglass Monthly*, August 1859, in Foner, ed., *Life and Writings of Frederick Douglass*, vol. 2.
41. *Life and Times of Frederick Douglass*, 320.

EPILOGUE: MISCELLANIES OF A MOVEMENT
1. Hinton, *John Brown and His Men*, 262-263.
2. Letter dated September 14, 1859, in Osborne P. Anderson, *A Voice from Harper's Ferry* (Boston: Printed for the Author, 1861), chapter V.
3. Conrad, *Harriet Tubman*, 124-125.
4. Ibid., 279.
5. Letter published in the *Evening Star*, November 9, 1859; cited in Quarles, *Allies for Freedom*, 105.
6. Hinton, *John Brown and his Men*, 272-273.
7. Ibid., 261.
8. Ibid., 262.
9. Sanborn, *Life and Letters of John Brown*, 541.

10. Katz, *Resistance at Christiana*, John Jr.'s letter cited, 281.
11. Du Bois, *John Brown*, 248.
12. Ruchames, ed., *John Brown*, 242-249; Katherine Mayo, "Brown in Hiding and in Jail": Interview with Mrs. Russell, October 23, 1909.
13. Anderson, *A Voice from Harper's Ferry*, chapter III.
14. Hinton, *John Brown and His Men*, 424.
15. Ables, *Man on Fire*, 257.
16. Anderson, *A Voice from Harper's Ferry*, chapter VIII.
17. Ibid., also cited with slightly different wording in Hinton, *John Brown and His Men*, John Cook's Confession.

BIBLIOGRAPHICAL ESSAY

1. Marc Bloch, *The Historian's Craft* (New York: Alfred A. Knopf, 1953), 67.
2. John R. McKivigan, *Forgotten Firebrand: James Redpath and the Making of the Nineteenth Century* (Ithaca, NY: Cornell University Press, 2008).
3. Benjamin Quarles, *Allies for Freedom*, "John Brown Day (August 17, 1906)," 7.
4. Ibid., 3.
5. W. E. B. Du Bois, *The Autobiography of W. E. B. Du Bois* (New York: International Publishers, 1968), 259.
6. Villard, *John Brown*, 42.
7. Ibid., 45.

ACKNOWLEDGMENTS

In addition to having done my research, principally in the New York Public Library at 42nd Street, I have amassed a considerable reading library of my own—on the antebellum period, on the abolition movement, on the Civil War, the Underground Railroad with a number of the fugitive slave narratives, and of historiographical commentary. This has furnished me with material for three studies, all published with Westholme Publishing; but the books I own now bear the wear and tear evidencing the passage of time.

W.E.B. Du Bois's *John Brown* was the first to enter this collection. Its covers are worn and repaired in various tapings. I must have turned through its pages numberless times over a span nearing fifty years. Douglass's *Life and Times* leaves a similar impression. Its binding has split, its pages detaching. Another of these, one of my favorites, Oscar Sherman's *Prophet of Liberty, The Life and Times of Wendell Phillips*, has shed its spinal cover, as it too bears the taping of fruitless repairs. All these I had thought might one day go to a younger scholar, or perhaps a club or association—long after I had finished with them. But in the condition they are in, that is no longer possible, and in any case the reality of a ready recipient can scarcely exist today.

As I indicated in the text, my attention was brought to the "timepiece from Gouldtown" by a man also living in Ocala, Florida. This is Joe Eber, also a transplant to the state, who brought with him a forty-year engagement with Tai Chi. I had joined him in the classes he was conducting, and he had read two of my books, one of them *To Raise Up a Nation*, on the Brown/Douglass relationship and the Civil War, as we had embarked on a mutual friendship. One day he mentioned that a cousin of his wife was in possession of John Brown's pocket watch, whereupon I requested to see it. Soon I was meeting with Becky Lively. The items she brought out are displayed on the dust-jacket of the book and as variously located in the text, as photographed by Joe, and artfully arranged in design by Trudi Gershenov.

I at once sensed this might serve as occasion for a further elaboration of the pertinent issue of John Brown and related topics, which I had been aware were still advancing in my thought. Soon I had embarked on the writing with the departure point being that "timepiece." Drafting my initial chapter, I sent it to publisher Bruce H. Franklin at Westholme Publishing. Soon he had consented to publish the book, saying in effect he would be "in the boat" for the effort.

Having completed three-quarters of the projected manuscript, I encountered deep-seated medical issues, resulting in open heart surgery with a prolonged convalescence in the hospital. Acknowledgment is due to the doctors and nurses and the staff who assured my recovery. Within days of being discharged I returned to the writing, in weakened state and with a memory such that, standing in the kitchen with my back to the sink, I did not know where the sink was.

When I had finished, the manuscript may have lacked the polish and completeness of my previous efforts; nevertheless, I sent it off to Bruce who proceeded with the work of preparing the manuscript for publication and assigning an editor. This was Michael Dolan, whom he knew would know how to wrangle the text and author, and we proceeded rapidly through at least three iterations. By the time we finished, the text appeared to write itself.

To my publisher and editor, as to my recovered self, as to all others involved is owed the completed book, demonstrating that book-making is a collaborative affair, and an art in itself.

INDEX

Acorn, 46
Adair, Samuel, 71, 103, 148, 175, 181
Adams, Anne, 20
Adams, Anne Brown, 245
Adams, Charles Francis, 41
Adams, Edmund Quincy, 43
Adams, Elizabeth, x, 20
Adams, John, x
Adams, John Quincy, 27, 212
Adirondack Mountains, 23, 67-68, 97, 117
The Adventures of Huckleberry Finn (Twain), 11
African Civilization Society, 191-192
African Free School, 4
African Methodist Episcopal Church, xiii, xv, 15, 19, 56, 161, 242
Alcott, A. Bronson, 62, 111, 199, 241
Alcott, Louisa May, 110
Allen, Henry, 54
Allen, Richard, 15
America House, 144-145, 150
American Anti-Slavery Society, 25, 43, 147
American Colonization Society, 8, 37
American Missionary Association, 27
Amistad mutineers, 24-29, 33, 246
Anderson, Jeremiah, 199, 202-203, 206
Anderson, Osborne, 23, 157-166, 221, 231-237
Andrew, John, 15, 113, 201

Anglo-African Magazine, 168, 195
Anthony, Susan B., 102
Anthony, "Win", 102
Army of the Potomac, 103
Articles of Confederation, 184
Astor House, 109, 120
Asylum for the Blind, 112
Atchison, David Rice, 57, 64, 71, 80-81, 90-91, 98-101, 105, 107, 121
Atlanta University, 241
Atlantic Monthly, 48, 92, 111, 183, 233, 241
Atlantic Slave Trade, 26-27, 184
Autobiography of a Fugitive Negro (Ward), 4

Baltimore & Ohio Railroad, 7
Baltimore and Erie Canal, 128
Band, Lawrence Cornet, 133
Banks, Nathaniel, 78
Barber, J. Max, 243
Barber, John W., 26
Beecher, Henry Ward, 71, 96, 149
Bell, James Madison, 159, 161-162, 165, 230
Benton, Thomas Hart, 90, 146
Bethel African Methodist Episcopal Church, 15
Bird Club, 200
Bissell, William H., 96
Black Jack, 84-88, 97, 114
Blair, Charles, 114, 202-203

Blue Ridge Mountains, 23, 123, 142, 170, 215
Blunt, J.G., 181
Bolding, John, 47
Bondi, August, 89-90, 101
Border Star, 77, 80
Boston and Worcester Railroad, 130
Boston Artillery, 62
Boston Courier, 46
Boteler, Alexander, 235
Boyle, William A., 232
Bradford, Sarah, 233
Brent, William, 58
Bridgman, Edward, 102-103
Brown, Anne, 22-23, 199, 205, 229, 234, 244-245
Brooks, Preston, 82-83, 151
Brown, Frederick, 68, 82, 102-103, 120
Brown, G.W., 75
Brown, Jason, 68, 72, 74, 83-84, 88, 99, 103, 107, 110, 132, 244-245
Brown, John
  arrival at Adair farm and, 72
  arrival in Kansas and, 72-73
  Chatham convention and, 154-162, 168, 176, 191-192, 196, 201, 205-206
  convocation in abandoned stone quarry and, 224-226
  educating slaves and, 29
  effective consequences of Wakarusa war and, 76
  giving the order to proceed to Harper's Ferry and, 237
  hiring Forbes as drill instructor and, 117, 122-123
  League of Gileadites and, 33, 246
  Lovejoy's murder and, 27-28
  Mary Stearns description of, 113-114
  meeting and correspondence with Frederick Douglass and, 30-33, 36, 68, 110-111, 140-143, 149, 151, 190, 197-201, 210-213, 216-228, 235
  obtaining aid from state legislature and, 110
  Old Brown's Parallels and, 182
  Osawatomie, 71, 74, 77, 81, 84-87, 98, 101-103, 108-109, 116, 134, 161, 175, 178, 181
  passage of Fugitive Slave Law and, 42
  Phillips description of, 183-187, 201
  plan of action and, 139
  pursued by John Reid and, 102
  pursued by posse and, 84-85
  rescue of Anthony Burns and, 59
  riding back into Kansas and, 98
  studying the military arts and, 78
  Syracuse convention and, 54
  timepiece of, 20-22
  Virginia campaign and, 171
  W. E. B. Du Bois and, 28
Brown, Jr., John, 67-73, 79-84, 99, 102, 105, 107, 110, 116-120, 132, 141, 143, 151, 174, 196, 203-205, 208-209, 229-234, 244-245
Brown, Mary, 68, 244
Brown, Oliver, 70, 74, 82, 117, 203-206, 233
Brown, Owen, 68, 82, 97, 99, 107-108, 111, 117, 120, 133, 136, 166-167, 203-206, 237
Brown, Ruth, 29, 68-69, 99, 120, 154-155, 244
Brown, Salmon, 68, 79, 82-83, 88, 97, 128, 212, 222, 236, 244
Brown, Watson, 70, 82, 117, 205-206, 233, 238
Brown, William Wells, 112, 155
Buchanan, James, 88, 114, 121, 133, 174, 181, 187-188, 193-194, 213-214, 225
Buena Vista, battle of, 36, 96
Buford, Jefferson, 71, 77, 80
Burleigh, C.M., 51
Burlington & Mount Holly Railroad, 7
Burlington and Missouri Railroad, 96
Burns, Anthony, 58-63, 95, 108
Bushnell, Simeon, 193, 195
Bustill, Joseph, 24
Butler, Andrew, 82-83

Cabot, Samuel, 111, 113
Calhoun, John, 37-39, 56
Campbell, Alexander, 101
Canadian Magazine, 160

Cary, Mary Shadd, 157, 231
Cary, Thomas, 157, 230
Cass, Lewis, 36, 76, 82
Cato, Sterling, 79-80
Central America, 129
Charles II, ix
Charleston's Slave Mart, 46-47
Charleston Navy Yard, 62
Chase, Salmon P., 194
Cheerful Yesterdays (Higginson), 44, 46, 60, 108, 200, 207
Cherokee Nation, 160
Chicago Tribune, 93, 100
Christian Register, 52
Christiana Resisters, 49
Cinque (Sengbe Pieh), 24-29, 33, 246
Clarke, George Washington, 80, 101, 105, 173-174
Clarke, James Freeman, 151
Clay, Henry, 8, 37-39, 45, 56, 77, 80, 84, 105
Cleveland Leader, 110, 194-195
Cline, James B., 101
Coates, Elizabeth, 49
Coffin, Levi, 12
Cohansey River, xi-xii, xvi, 4
Coleman, E.A., 75, 80
Coleman, John, 16
Coleman, Lucy, 198
Columbia Artillery, 62
Columbus State Journal, 195
Committee of Vigilance, 5-6, 8, 14-15
Compromise of 1850, 13, 38-39, 57, 110, 116, 148
The Condition, Elevation, Emigration and Destiny of the Colored People in the United States (Delany), 154
Conococheague Creek, 210
Constitution
　anti-slavery and, 40
　Article IV and, 2-3
　founders not using the word slavery and, 184
　Frederick Douglass study of, 40, 212
　Garrison calling it a "covenant with death" and, 9
　removal of all barriers enforcing racial discrimination and, 243
　rights of slaveholders and, 115

"three-fifths clause" and, 214
war powers and, 212
Constitutional Convention, 122, 125, 184
Conway, Martin, 129
Cook, John E., 128-129, 132, 134, 160, 165, 167, 170, 206, 230, 237-238
Cooke, Philip St. George, 91, 104-105, 108
Cooper, Ezekiel, 157
Copeland, John, 193-195, 235-236, 242
Coppoc, Barclay, 134, 205-206, 237
Coppoc, Edwin, 134, 205-206, 237
Cornell, Cornelius, 16
The Cotton Kingdom (Olmsted), 240
Covey, James, 26-27
Cox, Isaac, xvii
Crimean War, 130
The Crisis, 244
Crittenden, John, 53
Cromwell, Oliver, 93, 113
Cuba, 24-27, 147, 202
Cuff, Cuffee, xv
Curry, John Stewart, 148-149

Daily Commonwealth, 112-113
Dana, Charles A., 235
Dana, Richard H., 44-45, 59
Daniels, Jim, 180-181
Daniels, John Brown, 181
Darwin, Charles, 132
Davis, Daniel, 47
Davis, Jefferson, 37, 62, 86, 91, 216
Day, William Howard, 155, 159, 192
DeBaptiste, George, 13, 191, 232
Deitzler, G.W., 71, 133
Delany, Martin, 141, 153-166, 192-193
Delaware River, ix-x, 4, 10, 15-16
Denver, James W., 133
Des Moines Register, 189
Detroit Free Press, 191
Dickinson, Emily, 112
Disciples of Christ, 101
Donaldson, Israel, 80-81, 93, 105
Dorsey, Thomas, 235
Douglas, Stephen A., 39-41, 76, 82, 121, 125, 127, 223
Douglass, Frederick
　American and Foreign Anti-Slavery Society speech, 147-148

Century Magazine article and, 5
Constitution as pro-slavery and, 40
convocation in abandoned stone quarry and, 224-226
Corinthian Hall speech and, 146
Dred Scott decision and, 114-116, 120, 129
evolution away from Garrisonian orthodoxy and, 36
first months in New Bedford and, 7
Fugitive Slave Law and, 44-45
Harriet Tubman and, 156
implicated in the insurrection at Harper's Ferry and, 23
lecturing circuit and, 191-193
letter from John Brown, Jr. and, 78, 208
Letter to Louis Kossuth and, 43
The Life and Times of Frederick Douglass and, 6, 30, 32, 45, 51, 56, 122, 139, 217, 222, 234
marriage to Anna Murray and, 5
meeting and correspondence with John Brown and, 30-33, 36, 68, 110-111, 140-143, 149, 151, 190, 197-201, 210-213, 216-228, 235
My Bondage and My Freedom and, 6
North Star and, 13, 36, 40-41, 154
Radical Abolition Party and, 70, 93-95
refusing to participate in Harper's Ferry raid, 228-230, 234
Storer College speech and, 221-222
Douglass, H. Ford, 190-191
Douglass, Lewis, 242
Downing, George T., 43, 141
Doyle, James, 83
Dred Scott decision, 114-116, 120, 129
Du Bois, W. E. B., 10, 28, 31, 67, 140, 151, 156, 212, 233, 235, 240-246
Duke of York, x

Ebony, 18-19
Echoes of Harper's Ferry (Redpath), 240
Ellis, Charles Mayo, 59
Ellsworth, A.M., 166
Emancipation Proclamation, 19, 101
Emerson, Ralph Waldo, 35, 110, 112, 199, 207, 213, 240

Emigrant Aid Company, 64, 71, 75-76, 81, 95, 113
Emmanuel Chapel, 234
Engels, Frederick, 130-131
Evans, Henrietta Leary, 242
Evans, Robert, 16
Everett, John, 17

Faneuil Hall, 41, 59-62, 242
54th Massachusetts Infantry Regiment, 15
Finley, Robert, 8
Fenwick, Elizabeth, xiii, 19-20
Fenwick, John, ix-xiii, 19-20
Fillmore, Millard, 39, 43, 45, 47, 51, 53, 57
First Religious Society of Newburyport, 112
The First Settlement of Salem (Johnson), 20
Fisk University, 241
Fitzhugh, George, 147
Fond du Lac Railroad, 130
Forbes, Hugh, 116-117, 122-126, 132, 134, 136, 138-139, 166-167, 171
Forbes, John Murray, 200-201
Forsyth, John, 26-27
Fort Independence, 62
Fort Leavenworth, 73, 91
Fort Saunders, 99
Fort Scott, 98, 173, 177-179
Foster, Stephen S., 40
Franklin, Carolina, 47
Frederick the GReat, 129
Free Haven, 8
Free-Soil Party, 36, 57
Free Labor MOvement, 150
Free State Hotel, 74, 80-81
Freedman's Bureau, 241
Freeman, Watson, 58
Fremont, John C., 90, 93-94, 191
French and Indian War, xv
Fugitive Slave Law, 13, 33, 37-47, 52-56, 110, 150, 155, 166, 195, 246
Fuller, Abram, 187-188

Garibaldi, Giuseppe, 116-117, 132
Garnet, Henry Highland, 13, 30, 56, 141, 150, 152, 192

INDEX

Garrett, Thomas, 9, 13, 156
Garrison, William Lloyd, 6-7, 9, 13, 31, 36, 40, 43, 95, 103-104, 110, 114, 159, 222, 243-244
Geary, John W., 103-107, 121
Genesee River, 51
Gibbs, Josiah, 25
Giddings, Joshua, 110, 194-195
Gill, George, 99, 134-135, 162, 166, 168, 170, 178-182, 187-189, 206, 236
Gloucester, James N., 141, 149, 152, 192, 211
Goodell, William, 40, 95
Goodwin, Abigail, 15-16
Gorsuch, Edward, 47-55
Gould, Anthony, xi-xii, xiv-xv
Gould, Benjamin, xi-xii, xvi, 20
Gould, Henry, xvi-xvii
Gould, John, xvi-xvii
Governor Livingston, xvi
Grant, Ulysses, 47
Greeley, Horace, 65, 124, 135, 182, 240
Green, Shields, 198, 211, 226-228, 234
Griffin, ix
Griffiths, Julia, 41, 51
Grimke, Angelina, 28
Grinnell, Josiah Bushnell, 189

Hall, William S., 16
Hambelton, Charles A., 173
Hamilton, James Cleland, 160
Hamilton, Thomas, 168, 170
Hammond, C.G., 190
Hammond, James, 145
Hampton, Wade, 202
Hanway, Castner, 51, 53
Hardin, J.J., 96
Harper, Samuel, 188
Harper's Weekly, 129
Harriet, the Moses of Her People (Bradford), 233
Harris, James H., 232, 236
Harvard, 63, 111, 240-241, 244
Harvey, James, 96, 104-105
Hawkins, Daniel, 47
Hayden, Lewis, 13, 46, 60-61, 209, 231, 233, 236-237
Hazlett, Albert, 206

Hegel, G.F.W., 131
Hemmings, Sally, 20
Henry, William "Jerry", 53-55, 59
Henson, Josiah, 11
Herald of Freedom, 74, 81
Higginson, Thomas Wentworth, 29, 44, 59-62, 91, 95-96, 106, 108, 111-113, 140-144, 151-152, 155, 167, 170-171, 200-201, 207, 233
Hinton, Richard J., 29, 77, 97-99, 120-124, 128, 132-136, 140, 152, 164, 168-180, 199, 229-236, 240-241
An Historical Sketch of the Greek Revolution (Howe), 112
History of Salem (Sickler), 20
Holden, David, 16
Holden, Isaac, 161-162, 192
Holmes, James H., 101, 107, 124-125
Howe, Julia Ward, 110, 112
Howe, Samuel Gridley, 60, 95, 98, 111-113, 122, 140, 167, 200, 202, 209
Hoyt, Hiram, 54
Hungarian Revolution, 42
Hurd, Harvey B., 120, 140
Hyatt, Thaddeus, 95, 98, 101

The Independent, 243
Ingalls, John J., 102
Ingraham, Edward, 51
Isabella II, 26

Jackson, Andrew, 27
Jackson, Claiborne, 77
Jackson, John J., 162
Jackson, Patrick T., 111
Jacksonville Floridian and Journal, 52
Jefferson, Thomas, 20, 184
Jim Crow, 242
Jocelyn, Simeon, 25
John Brown 1800-1859 (Villard), 103
John Brown and His Men (Hinton), v, 77, 136, 172, 180, 241
John Brown's Fort, 242
Johnson, Robert Gibbon, 20
Johnston, Joseph E., 107
Jones, James Munroe, 192
Jones, James M., 161
Jones, John, 13, 99, 141, 157-162, 165, 190-191

Jones, Samuel, 72-73, 79-81

Kagi, John Henry, 132-135, 162-165, 170, 175-178, 182-183, 187-189, 192-195, 201, 203, 205-211, 215, 227-238, 241
Kaiser, Charles, 89
Kansas-Nebraska bill, 57, 64, 80, 88, 113, 116
Kansas Free State, 81
Kansas State Committee, 167
Kaw River, 99, 104
Keitt, Lawrence, 83
Kinnard, Thomas, 162-165
Kline, William, 51, 53
Knox, John, 104
Kossuth, Louis, 42-43

Lafayette, Marquis de, 129
Lambert, William, 13, 162, 191, 230
Lane, James H., 73-76, 96-101, 104-107, 122, 125-126, 133, 135, 175
Langston, Charles H., 193, 195, 229, 232, 236
Langston, John Mercer, 193
Lawrence, Amos, 71, 75, 120, 200
Lawrence, William R., 111
League of Gileadites, 246
Leary, Lewis Sheriand, 194-195, 232, 235-236, 242
Leaves of Grass (Whitman), 29
Leavitt, Joshua, 25
Lecompte, Samuel D., 71, 78, 84, 105
Lecompton Constitution, 125, 127, 133, 145, 148, 173-174
Leeman, William, 132, 206
Lenhart, Charles, 79, 85
Lennox, Francis, 51
Letters on American Slavery (Rankin), 11
Liberator (Garrison), 9, 13, 46, 64, 95, 106, 155, 207, 243
Liberty Party, 4-5, 36, 53-55, 69-70
Life and Letters of John Brown (Sanborn), 67, 234, 241
The Life and Times of Frederick Douglass, 6, 30, 32, 45, 51, 56, 122, 139, 217, 222, 234
Lincoln, Abraham, 14, 19, 38, 64, 87, 101, 127, 223, 227

Lively, Becky, 21-22, 34
Loguen, Jermain Wesley, 13, 30, 41, 54-55, 141, 152-156, 159, 162, 165, 192, 207-209, 229-230
Long, Henry, 43-44
Lord Byron, 112
Loring, Edward, 59, 63
Louisiana Purchase, 184
Lovejoy, Elijah, 24, 27

A Manual for the Patriotic Volunteer, 117, 138-139
Marais des Cygnes Massacre, 173
Marcy, William, 103
Mars, John, 34
Marx, Karl, xvii, 130-132, 214
Mason, James, 38-39
Mason Committee, 125, 213
Massachusetts Anti-Slavery Society, 9, 207
Massachusetts Arms Company, 119
Massachusetts State Kansas Committee, 95, 106, 110-113, 240
Maxton, William, 133-134, 158
May, Samuel J., 13, 40, 54-55, 95
Mayo, Katherine, 212, 235, 244-245
Mazzini, Giuseppe, 117
McGuire, Horace, 197
McKim, James Miller, 15
McReynolds, John, 53
Melville, Herman, 28-29
Memaha River, 188
Mende, 24-27
Merriam, Francis, 237
Mexican War, 39, 99, 101, 104, 116
Middleton, Enoch, 16
Minkins, Frederick, 44, 47
Mississippi, 42
Mississippi River, 11, 36, 214-215
Missouri Compromise, 12, 37, 57, 184, 215
Missouri River, 12, 68, 77, 87, 97, 107, 188
Moby Dick (Melville), 28-29
Moffat, Charles, 132, 134
Montgomery Advertiser, 71
Montgomery, James, 170-182
Morse, Samuel, 7
Morton, Edwin, 142-144, 199, 208

INDEX

Mosely, Clifton, 22-23
Mott, Lucretia, 15
Mount Oread, 80, 92, 107
Mt. Pisgah Church, 15
Munroe, William C., 162, 191-192
Murray, Othniel, xv
Murry, Nathaniel, 16

Nation, 113, 244
National Anti-Slavery Standard, 52
National Association for the Advancement of Colored People, 243-244
National Committee, 95-96, 109, 120, 124
National Era, 135
National Hotel, 116
National Kansas Committee, 95, 97, 109, 111, 140
New American Cyclopedia, 130
New England Anti-Slavery Society, 9
New England Colored Citizens, 207
New York Daily Tribune, 135
New York Evening Post, 135, 243-244
New York Herald, 121
New York Sun, 26
New York Times, 87, 182, 240
New York Tribune, 52, 86, 91-92, 106, 114, 117, 124, 130-132, 182, 240
New York University, 117
Northwest Ordinance, 64, 184

Oberlin College, 155, 245
Oberlin-Wellington fugitive slave trial, 193-195, 229, 235
Ohio Anti-Slavery Society, 193
Ohio River, 11, 203
Oliver, Thomas Clement, 16
Olmsted, Frederick Law, 71, 145-146, 240
Ordinance of 1787, 64, 184
Osage River, 102-103
Osawatomie, 71, 74, 77, 81, 84-87, 98, 101-103, 108-109, 116, 134, 161, 175, 178, 181

Panic of 1857, 145
Parker, Theodore, 41, 59-61, 95, 109-114, 117-119, 140-141, 144, 150, 202, 243

Parker, William, 47-51, 157, 167, 232-233
Parsons, Luke, 128, 132, 183
Pate, Henry Clay, 77, 80, 84-88, 105, 114
Payne, Daniel A., 56
Penn, William, ix-x, xii
Pennington, James, 5, 7, 27
Peunell, James W., 161
Philadelphia Vigilance Committee, 24
Phillips, Wendell, 41, 60-62, 114, 120, 201-202
Phillips, William Addison, 85-86, 91-93, 124, 183-187, 235, 243
Pierce, Franklin, 57, 62-63, 75-78, 86, 88, 91, 93, 100, 104, 214, 225
Pierce, J.J., 170
Plain Dealer, 194
Platte County Rifles, 73
Plumb, Ralph, 236
Plumb, Samuel, 236
Poems of Richard Realf, 241
Polk, James, 88, 121
Potomac River, 128, 203-204, 218, 222, 238
Pottawatomie Creek, 82-83, 87-88, 181
Pottawatomie Rifles, 79, 81
Preston, Ann, 49
Price, John, 193, 195
Princeton Theological Seminary, 150
Provincial Freeman, 156-159, 161, 231
Public Life of Captain John Brown (Redpath), 240

Quakers, ix, xii, 3-4, 6, 8-10, 12-13, 15-17, 48, 50-51, 134, 189, 205
Quantrill, Charles, 101

Radical Abolition Party, 70, 93-95
Rankin, John, 11
Ransom, C., 242-243
Raritan River, 16
Reading Railroad, 130
Realf, Richard, v, 99, 128, 132-136, 142, 160-167, 170, 179, 213, 241
Recollections of Seventy Years, 241
Redpath, James, 29, 64, 77, 84, 88-90, 93, 98-99, 106, 136, 151, 169-172, 223, 240-241

Reeder, Andrew, 64, 66, 79, 87, 95, 100
Reid, John W., 98, 101-102, 105
Remond, Charles Lenox, 159
Revere House, 62, 170-171
Richardson, Richard, 133, 231-232
Reminiscences of Mrs. Mary Stearns (Stearns), 113, 118
Reminiscences of Old Brown (Brown), 75
Republic, 52
Reynolds, George J., v, 162, 164, 168, 170, 232
Ricketson, Joseph, 6
Ritner, Mary, 203, 205, 208, 210
Robinson, Charles, 71, 74-81, 87, 91, 105, 107, 174-175
Robinson, Sara, 91
Rochester Democrat and American, 230
Rock, John S., 15, 193
Ross, A.M., 157
The Roving Editor, 169, 240
Ruggles, David, 5-7
Russell, Thomas, 111, 117-121, 235

Sabine, Joseph, 53
San Francisco Mint, 129
Sanborn, Franklin, 27, 67, 73, 77, 80, 84, 89, 95, 99, 106, 111, 113, 118, 126, 133, 136, 138, 142-144, 167, 173, 199-202, 208-209, 216, 233-234, 240-241, 245
Sanford Street Church, 34
Sanitary Commission, 112
Seward, William H., 14, 39, 76, 125, 167, 201
Shadd, Abraham, 157
Shadd, I.D., 157, 159, 161-162, 230-231
Shannon, Wilson, 66, 73-75, 79, 91, 100, 104
Shenandoah River, 128, 135, 204, 218
Sheppard, J.R., 16
Sheppard, Thomas R., 16
Sherman, John, 78, 80
Sherman, William, 83
Shiloh Presbyterian Church, 150
Shore, Samuel, 81, 84-85
Sickler, Joseph S., 20
Siebert, Wilbur H., 16

Siloam Presbyterian Church, 149
Sims, Thomas, 46-47, 61
Smedley, R.C., 49
Smith, Adam, 131
Smith, Charles Gonzales, xvi
Smith, Gerrit, 40, 54-55, 67-70, 85, 93-95, 110-111, 119-120, 124, 140-144, 156, 182, 199-200, 212, 236
Smith, Isaac, 203, 226
Smith, James McCune, 70, 141, 166
Smith, Persifor, 86, 91, 100
Smith, Ralph, 8
Smith, Stephen, 13, 141, 152
Smith, William, 47
Smithsonian Institution, 22
Society of Friends, ix
Sociology of the South (Fitzhugh), 147
The Souls of Black Folk (Du Bois), 241
South Mountain Railroad, 234
"Squatter Sovereign" bill, 57, 66, 76, 80
St. Catharines, 11, 155-156, 162, 198-199, 230, 233
St. Domingo, 2, 184
Stamford, Alges, 16
Stanton, Elizabeth Cady, 110
Stamford, Julia, 16
Stearns, Frank Preston, 113-114, 125-127
Stearns, George Luther, 95-96, 110-114, 118-120, 129, 140, 142, 144, 167, 171, 200, 202, 236
Stearns, Mary, 118, 244
Steel, Levin, 7-8
Stephens, Alexander, 127
Stevens, Aaron Dwight, 98, 108, 165, 167, 170, 177-180, 187, 206, 221, 237-238
Stevens, Samuel, 16
Stevens, Thaddeus, 53
Stevens, Whipple, 105, 132, 134
Steward, Theophilus Gould, xii-xvi, 19
Steward, William, xii
Stewart, Charles, 143-144
Stewart, Frank H., 20
Stewart, John, 148
Still, William, 8, 13, 15, 24, 48, 141, 152, 156, 223
Storer College, 221-222

INDEX

Stowe, Harriet Beecher, 11, 29-30
Stowell, Martin, 59-61, 95, 97
Stringer, Thomas, 157, 161-162
Stringfellow, J.H., 66, 71, 76, 80, 91, 98, 100, 105
Stuart, J.E.B., 86
Summit Beacon, 76
Sumner, Charles, 15, 57, 73, 82-83, 86-87, 91, 93, 112, 114, 136, 151
Sumner, Edwin, 73
Supreme Court, 15, 27, 61, 79, 114, 129, 165, 173
Suttle, Charles, 58-59, 63

Taber, William C., 6
Taney, Roger, 115-116
Tappan, Lewis, 25
Taylor, James H., 49
Taylor, Steward, 134, 206
Taylor, Stewart, 238
Taylor, Zachary, 36-39, 42
Thayer, Eli, 75, 95, 113, 116-117
Thompson, Henry, 69-70, 79, 82, 97, 120, 155, 205
Thompson, Martha, 22
Thompson, William, 97, 205
Thoreau, Henry David, 241
Tidd, C.P., 132, 177, 189, 195, 206, 237
Titus, Harry, 77, 80, 99-100
Toombs, Robert, 71
Tragic Prelude (Curry), 148
Transcendental Club, 110
True Bands, 156
Truth, Sojourner, 6-7, 33
Tubman, Harriet, 9-10, 14, 155-156, 159, 162, 192-193, 199-201, 205, 207-209, 231-236
Turner, Nat, 2, 168-169, 177, 243
Twain, Mark, 11
28th Congregational Society of Boston, 110

Uncle Tom's Cabin (Stowe), 11, 29
Underground Railroad, v, 5, 7-8, 10-13, 16-17, 24, 27-28, 31, 34, 45, 49, 112, 121, 139, 149, 152, 156, 162, 193, 205, 207, 210, 223

The Underground Railroad from Slavery to Freedom (Siebert), 16
Union Hotel, 206
Union Safety Committee, 45
United Presbyterian Church of Scotland, 150
University of Heidelberg, 5

Vail, Alfred, 7
Van Buren, Martin, 26, 36
Vigilance Committees, 5-6, 8, 14-15, 24, 45-46, 59-60, 110, 152, 162, 191
Villa Mansion, 158-159
Villard, Oswald Garrison, 103, 212, 235, 240-246
A Voice from Harper's Ferry (Anderson), 162, 231
Voice of the Negro, 243

Wagner, Henry O., 141, 190
Wakarusa War, 76, 81, 91, 97
Walker, George, 111
Walker, Robert J., 121
Walker, Samuel, 97-100, 104-105, 121, 125, 127, 133
Walling, William English, 243
Ward, Samuel Ringgold, 4-7, 41, 45, 55-56
Washington, George, 129, 204, 221
Washington, Lewis, 129, 221
Watson, Henry, 236
Wattles, Augustus, 99, 107, 124, 175, 181-183
Webb, William, 191-192
Webster, Daniel, 37-39, 45, 47, 53, 55-56, 82
Weekly Anglo African, 157
Weld, Theodore, 28
West India Committee, 150
West Point, 181
Weston Argus, 101
Wheaton, C.A., 54-55
Whigs, 36, 39, 57, 64-65, 76
Whipper, Alfred, 162
Whipper, Francis Rollin, 158, 160
Whipper, William, 13
Whitfield, J.W., 64, 105
Whitman, Edmund, 124, 127-128
Whitman, Walt, 29

Whitney Hotel, 183
Whittier, John Greenleaf, 26, 56
Williams, Elizabeth, 47
Williams, Isaac, 159
Wilmot Proviso, 35-39
Wilson, Henry, 124, 167, 200
Winkely, Jonathan, 100, 103
With John Brown in Kansas (Anthony), 103
Woodson, Daniel, 100
Woolman, John, 12
Worcester Spy, 75
World Anti-Slavery Convention, 150
Wright, Theodore, 150
Wright, William, 11